Focus on Ethnicity and Religion

ISBN 1-4039-9328-9

CORRECTION

Page 152

Appendix Table A5.4

The first row:

White British   72   64   92   93   80   83   83   84

is incorrect and has been included in error. The correct data for 'White British' are shown in the second row. The remaining data in Appendix Table A5.4 are correct.

Page 153

Appendix Table A5.5

Row one heading should read 'White British' not 'British'.
Row two heading should read 'White Irish' not 'Irish'.

The pdf on the ONS website www.statistics.gov.uk shows the correct information.

Office for National Statistics
October 2006
Basingstoke: Palgrave Macmillan

FOCUS ON Ethnicity and Religion

2006 edition

Editors: Joy Dobbs, Hazel Green and Linda Zealey

First published 2006 by
PALGRAVE MACMILLAN
Houndmills, Basingstoke, Hampshire RG21 6XS and
175 Fifth Avenue, New York, NY 10010
Companies and representatives throughout the world.

PALGRAVE MACMILLAN is the global academic imprint of the Palgrave Macmillan division of St. Martin's Press, LLC and of Palgrave Macmillan Ltd. Macmillan® is a registered trademark in the United States, United Kingdom and other countries. Palgrave is a registered trademark in the European Union and other countries.

ISBN 1-4039-9328-9

This book is printed on paper suitable for recycling and made from fully managed and sustained forest sources.

A catalogue record for this book is available from the British Library.

10   9   8   7   6   5   4   3   2   1
15   14   13   12   11   10   09   08   07   06

Printed and bound in Great Britain by
Hobbs the Printers Ltd, Totton, Hampshire.

A National Statistics publication

National Statistics are produced to high professional standards as set out in the National Statistics Code of Practice. They are produced free from political influence.

About the Office for National Statistics

The Office for National Statistics (ONS) is the government agency responsible for compiling, analysing and disseminating economic, social and demographic statistics about the United Kingdom. It also administers the statutory registration of births, marriages and deaths in England and Wales.

The Director of ONS is also the National Statistician and the Registrar General for England and Wales.

For enquiries about this publication, contact:
E-mail: Ethnicity&Identity@ons.gsi.gov.uk
Tel: 020 7533 5741

For general enquiries, contact the National Statistics Customer Contact Centre.
Tel: 0845 601 3034 (minicom: 01633 812399)
E-mail: info@statistics.gsi.gov.uk
Fax: 01633 652747
Post: Room 1015, Government Buildings,
          Cardiff Road, Newport NP10 8XG

You can also find National Statistics on the internet at www.statistics.gov.uk

Contents

Page

List of tables, figures and maps

3: Geographic diversity

5:   Employment and labour market participation

Page

List of contributors

Authors:	Karin Bosveld
	Ben Bradford
	Helen Connolly
	Frances Forsyth
	David Gardener
	Camellia Raha
Typesetting:	ONS Desktop Publishing Unit
Production Manager:	Sini Dominy
Production Team:	Sharon Adhikari
	Alistair Dent
	Steve Wyman

Acknowledgements

The editors wish to thank all authors who have helped in the production of *Focus On Ethnicity and Religion*. Special thanks go to our colleagues in the Office for National Statistics for their invaluable support and advice in the preparation of this report.

We are grateful for the advice, comments and suggestions from independent reviewers: Angela Dale (University of Manchester); Anthony Heath (University of Oxford); Ceri Peach (University of Oxford); Lucinda Platt (University of Essex); and Ludi Simpson (University of Manchester).

We would also like to thank our reviewers from the following departments and devolved administrations: Department for Communities and Local Government; Home Office; Department for Work and Pensions; Department for Environment, Food and Rural Affairs; General Register Office for Scotland; Northern Ireland Statistics and Research Agency.

Introduction

The UK is an area of increasing ethnic and religious diversity. Modest migration has always been a feature of the UK, but large scale migration since the middle of the 20th century has produced a substantial ethnic minority population. In 2001, the majority of people in the UK were White British and Christian but the ethnic minority population accounted for 8 per cent of the population.[1] The ethnic minority population includes many distinct ethnic and religious groups. The original migrants came from different regions including the West Indies, Indian subcontinent and Africa. Their religious, socio-economic and educational backgrounds differed, as well as their economic resources. These differences were reflected in their experiences in the UK, often, but not always, resulting in disadvantages in employment, housing and education.

Growing recognition of the differences between ethnic groups led to an increasing need for data on the size and characteristics of ethnic groups, so that it would be possible to identify any inequalities and monitor progress to address them.

The 1991 Census in England and Wales, and in Scotland, provided the first opportunity to accurately measure the size and characteristics of ethnic minority populations in Great Britain. The data confirmed widespread variations between ethnic groups with regard to housing conditions and labour market and employment patterns. Ten years later, the 2001 Census gave the opportunity to confirm whether those differences still existed, whether they were greater or whether they had declined as ethnic populations became established. The 2001 Census also included a question on religion for the first time in a British Census, although not for the first time in Northern Ireland. This presented an opportunity to clarify whether the differences between ethnic groups also existed between religious groups, and to examine the relationship between these two important aspects of identity.

These central concerns form the basis of the chapters in this report. All chapters present data for ethnic and religious groups and include further analysis of particular ethno-religious groups where this helps to clarify the relationship between these two identities. Where possible, comparisons are made between the positions of ethnic groups in 1991 and 2001.

Contents and structure of the report

This report is organised into five chapters.

Chapter 1, Measurement and classification considers issues surrounding the classification of individuals and households to ethnic and religious groups. The ethnic and religious groups discussed in this report are those identified by the standard classifications used by the Office for National Statistics (ONS) in all surveys and censuses.[2] The groups arise out of a complex and sometimes contentious process of classification. Classifications are not fixed and have changed over time. The 2001 Census adopted a different classification of ethnic groups from the 1991 Census. These methodological variations have important implications for analysis of ethnic groups between 1991 and 2001. There were also differences in the classifications of ethnic group and religious group adopted in the censuses of the countries of the UK in 2001. These complicate the production of statistics for Great Britain and the UK. The chapter explains how these problems were addressed for the analyses presented in this report.

While classification of individual ethnic and religious identity is complex, the classification of households is further complicated as they may contain people belonging to more than one ethnic or religious group. High levels of heterogeneity (where households contain people from different ethnic or religious groups) mean that it could be misleading to describe households as, for example, 'White British' or 'Muslim'. The chapter demonstrates that the majority of households contain people from the same ethnic or religious groups.

Chapter 2, Population describes the ethnic and religious diversity within the population as a whole, identifying the main ethnic, religious and ethno-religious groups. Classification into ethno-religious groups takes account of both the ethnic and religious composition of populations. Because ethnic identity is often associated with religious identity the majority of people in a given ethnic group often identify with one particular religion and, conversely, the majority of people in a given religious group often belong to one ethnic group. For example, in 2001 the majority of White British people identified as Christian and the majority of Hindus were Indian. Awareness of the ethno-religious composition of groups contributes to increased understanding of each of the ethnic and religious populations.

The chapter concludes with profiles of each of the main ethnic groups: White British, Indian, Pakistani, Bangladeshi, Black Caribbean, Black African and Chinese. We describe and contrast the countries of birth, religious affiliation, age structure and socio-economic characteristics of each group. These characteristics are related to labour market and household variations described in the other chapters of the report. For example, the younger age structure of some ethnic minority populations is associated with larger households (Chapter 4, Households and families) and higher rates of unemployment and economic inactivity (Chapter 5, Employment and labour market participation).

Chapter 3, Geographic diversity shows how different ethnic and religious groups are spread throughout Great Britain. It illustrates which areas were the most and the least diverse, and which ethnic and religious groups tended to live in diverse areas.

People from ethnic minority groups tended to be concentrated in specific geographical areas, particularly in London, the Midlands and North West of England. Concentrations of specific ethnic groups were more apparent at small area (MSOA) level than at local authority or regional level. While the White British ethnic group and Christian religious group formed a majority in almost all parts of Britain, there were a few MSOAs where ethnic minority groups formed the majority of the local population.

Indians formed a majority in some parts of Leicester, as did Pakistanis in some areas within Bradford, Birmingham and Rochdale, and Bangladeshis in some areas within Tower Hamlets and Oldham. In contrast, people from the Chinese and Mixed groups were the most spread out, making up no more than one in ten of the population of any small area.

People from religious minorities also tended to be clustered in relatively small areas: Muslims made up a majority of the population in parts of Birmingham; Hindus formed the majority in some areas of Leicester; Jews made up almost half the population in one part of Salford; and Sikhs made up more than a third of the local population in parts of Ealing and Birmingham.

The tendency of different ethnic and religious groups to concentrate in particular geographic areas has prompted much public debate about the integration of the diverse communities in Great Britain. Research has found that residential concentration can occur for reasons of both positive choice and negative constraint. However, the areas where groups settled have implications for their labour market and housing circumstances.

Chapter 4, Households and families describes differences between ethnic and religious groups at the household level. Variations in the age structure of populations (discussed in Chapter 2, Population) are important in explaining many differences between groups. White British, White Irish, Christian and Jewish populations have an older age structure and a correspondingly larger number of pensioner households and one-person households. By comparison, the younger age structure of Bangladeshi, Pakistani and Muslim populations is associated with larger households and a greater proportion of households with dependent children. However, age variations do not always explain differences between households. Mixed, Black African, Chinese and Indian populations have similar age profiles to Bangladeshi and Pakistani groups but their households are less likely to contain dependent children. Religion may play some part in the differences – in all ethnic groups, Muslims tended to have larger average household sizes and a greater number of dependent children – but others factors are also important.

Larger household size is associated with overcrowding in some groups but not in others. Pakistani and Bangladeshi households have similar household sizes but Bangladeshi households are more likely than Pakistani households to be overcrowded. This could reflect differences in tenure and the areas where populations lived. For example, Bangladeshi households were far more likely than Pakistani counterparts to live in socially-rented accommodation and to live in London, and both of these factors were associated with overcrowding.

Results from the 1991 and 2001 Censuses are used to examine changes in households over the ten year period. For example, average household size fell in all groups between 1991 and 2001, with the greatest change among Indian, Pakistani and Bangladeshi households. However, the direction of change was not always the same for all ethnic groups. Lone parent households with dependent children decreased among Black groups between 1991 and 2001 but increased among White and Asian groups. Over the same period home ownership increased among White households but fell among Indian, Pakistani and Bangladeshi households.

Chapter 5, Employment and labour market participation illustrates the position of people from different ethnic and religious groups in the labour market and describes changes between 1991 and 2001. It examines differences in employment, unemployment and economic inactivity rates by ethnic and religious group, and the main reasons for being outside the labour market. It looks in detail at labour market activity among different ethnic and religious groups. Unemployment, a key measure of labour market disadvantage, is also examined in depth, and attention is drawn to those groups with disproportionately high rates of unemployment. Ethnic and religious differences in areas such as occupational status, self-employment and part-time working are also compared.

The chapter analyses labour market differences between ethnic and religious groups by sex, age, country of birth and educational attainment; all are key influences on labour market position. The presence of dependent children is also considered in the discussion on economic activity.

The analysis indicates that many ethnic and religious minorities tended to do less well in the labour market than the majority White British and Christian population, although some ethnic and religious groups were exceptions to this pattern. The investigation into the effects of age, qualifications and country of birth show that members of ethnic and religious minority groups were more likely to be outside the labour market, and those within it had greater risk of unemployment, even when born in the UK and with equivalent age and educational characteristics to the White British and Christian populations. Muslims, those ethnic groups comprised mainly of Muslims, and Black Africans and Black Caribbean men appeared to experience the greatest disadvantage in the labour market.

Data sources, presentation and discussion of groups in tables, figures and text

The analyses in this report predominantly use data from the 2001 Census, complemented, where possible, with data from the 1991 Census. Although more recent data is available from survey sources, for example the ONS Labour Force Survey (LFS), small numbers for ethnic and religious minorities present some problems. For example, data on small ethnic groups cannot be broken down by other variables, including religion, age and sex, and region. Census data provides the opportunity to explore in detail the smaller ethnic and ethno-religious groups, which forms the basis of this report.[3]

The ordering of groups in data presentations throughout the report sometimes differs for tables and figures. In all tables, the presentation of ethnic and religious groups corresponds with the presentation of categories in the ethnic and religious classifications for Great Britain (Chapter 1, Measurement and classification). Data in figures is usually sorted to show the groups with the highest and lowest proportion on the measure being discussed.

Tables and figures by ethnic and religious group show data for all groups contained in the classifications but in general only the main ethnic and religious groups are discussed in the text of the report. This is because of the highly heterogeneous composition of the non-specific 'other' groups.

The non-specific 'other' ethnic groups are formed from many different ethnic groups. For example, the 'Other ethnic' group includes people from the Far East, Middle East, Africa and South Asia. The people in the 'other' groups may have little in common apart from the consensus that they do not fit into any of the main ethnic groups within the classification. All findings for them must be considered in this context, being averages for the whole group that almost certainly do not describe the diverse experiences of the individual groups contained within. Findings for the Other Black group are more often discussed. This group predominantly comprised young, UK-born Black people, many of whom selected the Other Black category and wrote in their ethnic description as 'Black British'. Results for the Other Black group often reflect both their young age structure and their Black Caribbean origins and it is therefore more meaningful to discuss findings for them, within this context. Detailed analysis of the four 'other' ethnic groups has been published separately and is available from ONS.[4]

Where data is presented for Great Britain, results for the combined Mixed group are shown in figures and tables but generally not discussed in the text. This is because the Mixed

population is highly heterogeneous. Previously published analysis of the four specific Mixed groups in England and Wales has identified very different characteristics for the Mixed White and Black Caribbean, Mixed White and Black African and Mixed White and Asian groups. Results for the combined Mixed group in Great Britain obscure these differences. The four Mixed groups are however discussed in Chapter 5, Employment and labour market participation as these analyses present data for England and Wales rather than Great Britain. Detailed analysis of the four Mixed groups has been published separately and is available from ONS.[5] The combined Mixed group are also discussed in Chapter 3, Geographic diversity.

Data, definitions and classifications

Chapter 1, Measurement and Classification describes the ethnic and religious classifications, and data, used in the report. More information on methodologies and classifications adopted in individual chapters is provided within the chapters or in the chapter appendices. The glossary provides useful explanations of the terminology used.

Notes and references

1. The ethnic minority population for the UK is calculated as the percentage of the population from a non-White group. This is because the 2001 Census in Northern Ireland did not distinguish between White British, White Irish and Other White. In analyses for Great Britain the ethnic minority population can be calculated in two ways - either as the percentage of the population belonging to a non-White group or as the percentage belonging to any group other than White British. The latter definition counts White Irish and Other White as ethnic minorities and produces a larger ethnic minority population (12 per cent).

2. Office for National Statistics (2003) *Ethnic group statistics: A guide for the collection and colassification of ethnicity data*, TSO: London.

3. ONS regularly provide updated information in two web publications, *Focus on Ethnicity & Identity Overview* and *Focus on Religion Overview*. These present the most recent survey data on labour market, employment, education, and other survey-based information. Available at: www.statistics.gov.uk/focuson/default.asp#ethnicity

4. Gardener D and Connolly H (2005) *Who are the 'Other' ethnic groups?* Available at: www.statistics.gov.uk/cci/article.asp?id=1291

5. Bradford B (2006) *Who are the 'Mixed' ethnic groups?* Available at: www.statistics.gov.uk/cci/article.asp?id=1580

Measurement and classification

Karin Bosveld, Helen Connolly and Camellia Raha

Chapter 1

Introduction

This chapter describes some of the main issues surrounding the collection and measurement of ethnic and religious identity. This contextual information is important for interpreting the findings reported throughout the report.

The first part of the chapter covers the different measures of ethnicity and religion that have been used at various points in time and the different measures adopted in the countries of the UK for the 2001 Census. This includes some discussion of the differences in the census classifications adopted in 1991 and 2001 which have important implications for the interpretation of findings from the two censuses.

The second part of the chapter covers the classification of households to an ethnic or religious group. Whilst classification of each individual's ethnic and religious identity is complex, the classification of households is further complicated as households may contain people belonging to more than one ethnic or religious group.

Measurement and classification of individuals

Ethnicity is a multi-faceted concept covering many different aspects of identity, including racial group, skin colour, country of birth and parental country of birth, language spoken at home, religion and nationality.[1] These complicate the matter of defining a person's ethnic group. Also, however defined, ethnic groups change over time, reflecting social developments. As a result, ethnic group questions and classifications in surveys and censuses have undergone changes since measurement began and they will continue to do so.

The introduction of four new Mixed ethnic group categories on the 2001 Census in England and Wales illustrates the changing nature of ethnicity. The new ethnic group categories of Mixed White and Black Caribbean, Mixed White and Black African, Mixed White and Asian and Other Mixed were developed in response to evidence from the 1991 Census that many people of mixed heritage did not feel that their ethnicity was captured by any of the unmixed ethnic groups. The new Mixed categories allowed many people who had identified as White, Black Caribbean, Black African or Other ethnic group in the 1991 Census to identify with the new Mixed groups that better reflected their ethnicity.[2] In 2001, the new Mixed groups accounted for 677,000 people, or 1 per cent of the UK population.

Because of the subjective nature of ethnic identity, the Office for National Statistics (ONS) produces a self-identification measure of ethnic group. In censuses and surveys, respondents are invited to select the ethnic group that they consider they belong to, from a list of categories. The ethnic group that each person chooses reflects their self-identity, rather than being defined by anyone else.[3]

Religion is also a self-identification measure in censuses and surveys, reflecting the subjective nature of religious identity. The measurement of religion is complicated by the distinction between religious background, belief and practice. The way that people answer questions on religion is sensitive to the wording of the question, particularly for people who have a loose religious affiliation. Religious practice is particularly difficult to measure, as what constitutes 'practising' a religion may vary from one religion to another and from one person to another. The approach adopted for the 2001 Census was a deliberate decision to use a measure based on identity rather than practice.

ONS produces standard classifications for ethnic and religious groups. These classifications allow the identification of groups of people who share common characteristics. These characteristics, in turn, differentiate them from other people. There is always diversity within each of these groups but there is also commonality of experience. The ONS harmonised ethnic group classification in England and Wales distinguishes 16 categories of ethnic group and 8 categories of religious group. These groups by no means capture all of the ethnic and religious diversity within the UK. Many of the classified groups include smaller populations that may regard themselves as belonging to different ethnic or religious groups. For example, the Other White category includes people born in Australia, Bosnia, Poland and Turkey, to name just a few, each of whom may regard themselves as belonging to different ethnic groups. Similarly, the Muslim population includes Sunnis and Shias, some of whom may differentiate themselves in religious terms. While more detailed classifications of ethnic and religious identity may have the advantage of providing greater information, measurement of ethnic and religious identity must take account of practical issues surrounding data collection and presentation. A classification with 50 categories might allow researchers to identify many smaller ethnic and religious groups. However, numbers in many groups would be too small for reliable analysis, particularly those produced by sample surveys. In practice, organisations would respond to the difficulties of small numbers by combining categories. In effect respondents would have been asked to assign themselves to one of a large number of categories, only to be unable to find their specific group represented in any data outputs. Classifications of ethnic and religious group must therefore find the best solution, providing information of sufficient differentiation to identify, and reliably analyse the main groups, while having regard for the burden on respondents and data collectors.

Measurement of ethnicity

Before an ethnic group question was included in surveys and censuses, estimates of the size and characteristics of ethnic minority groups relied on proxy measures, including country of birth, parents' country/countries of birth, language spoken and nationality. The first ethnic group question was asked in the National Dwelling and Household Survey carried out for the Department of the Environment in 1976. Three years later, an ethnic group question appeared for the first time in a continuous social survey, when it was included in the 1979 Labour Force Survey (LFS).

The terminology used in ethnic group questions and the ethnic group categories have changed over time. LFS respondents in 1979 were asked to select the groups from which they were 'descended', but from 1981 onwards respondents were asked to identify the group that they considered they 'belonged' to. The Black Caribbean group was referred to as 'West Indian' in early ethnic group classifications, the term 'Black' then being regarded as derogatory. By 1991 the term 'Black Caribbean' was preferred.

Some groups have ceased to be identified in the more recent period. The categories Arab, Italian, Other European, Polish and Turkish were collected variously until 1992 but not afterwards.[4] Early surveys included just one 'White' group but this has been disaggregated in recent years into White British, White Irish, Other White, and in Scotland, White Scottish. A category for White Welsh was not included on the 2001 Census in England and Wales to the disappointment of some people in Wales.[5] Following the 2001 Census, a question on national identity was introduced in all ONS surveys so that people could record their Welsh identity, as well as British, English, Irish, Scottish or any other national identities. ONS recommend that organisations collecting ethnic group data include the national identity question alongside the ethnic group question wherever possible.[6] Some ethnic group categories have remained constant over time, for example, the Indian, Pakistani, Bangladeshi and Chinese groups.

Measurement of religion

Questions on religious group have also undergone changes. The 2001 Census was the first time that a religion question had been asked in England, Scotland and Wales, although Northern Ireland had included a religion question in their censuses for some time. Estimates of the religious populations of Great Britain relied on survey estimates before the 2001 Census. The most reliable of these were produced by the LFS. With a sample size of over 300,000 people, the LFS is one of the few surveys with enough respondents from ethnic minority groups for reliable analysis. The LFS religion question asks respondents, *What is your religion, even if you are not currently practising?* The question encompasses religious background and current affiliation or practice. It produces a religious distribution very similar to the 2001 Census question in England and Wales, *What is your religion?* In both sources, around eight in ten people were classified as Christian. The proportion reporting that they had no religion was also similar, as were the proportions identifying as Buddhist, Hindu, Jewish, Muslim or Sikh (Table 1.1).

Other surveys have also collected data on religion in recent years. The Home Office's Citizenship Survey (HOCS) has an ethnic boost sample sufficiently large to enable reliable analysis of ethnic and religious minorities. A number of social surveys, including the ONS General Household Survey (GHS) and British Social Attitudes survey (BSA) have also included questions on religion. However, in the absence of an ethnic boost, few surveys will produce sufficiently large samples of people from ethnic minority groups for detailed analysis of the non-Christian religious groups.

Table 1.1

Census and Labour Force Survey measurement of religion

England and Wales		Percentages
	Census[1]	Labour Force Survey[2]
Christian	77.7	79.9
Buddhist	0.3	0.3
Hindu	1.2	1.1
Jewish	0.5	0.5
Muslim	3.2	3.0
Sikh	0.7	0.6
Any other religion	0.3	0.8
No religion	16.1	13.8
Total[3] (=100%) (Numbers)	48,031,258	148,540

1 2001 Census in England and Wales asked 'What is your religion?'
2 2003/4 Labour Force Survey asked 'What is your religion even if you are not currently practising?'
3 Total excludes 'religion not stated'.

Sources: Census 2001, Office for National Statistics; Labour Force Survey 2003/2004, Office for National Statistics

The BSA question demonstrates the effect of question terminology upon estimates of religious affiliation. The 2001 BSA question asked respondents, *Do you regard yourself as belonging to any particular religion?* The question produced a much smaller proportion of Christians and a much larger proportion of people with no religion compared with the 2001 Census question, *What is your religion?* In response to the BSA question, 54 per cent of people in England and Wales reported that they were Christian and 40 per cent reported that they had no religion, compared with 72 per cent and 15 per cent respectively in response to the 2001 Census question in England and Wales.[7] A very small part of the difference is due to the different populations. The BSA is a sample survey and excludes children, while the Census includes the total population. However, responses to the Census question among the population aged 16 and over showed the same pattern. Almost three-quarters (73 per cent) of adults in England and Wales identified as Christian in the 2001 Census while 14 per cent stated that they had no religion. The differences between the Census and the BSA data partly reflect differences in question wording. The phrasing of the Census question, *What is your religion?*, may have suggested an expectation that people would have a religion, thereby increasing the number identifying as such. The BSA question, *Do you regard yourself as belonging to any particular religion?,* introduced the possibility that people might not have a religion.[8] In addition, the term 'belonging' may have been interpreted by respondents as requiring membership of a church or other practising faith group, reducing the number identifying as such. It is also possible that the position of the religion question on the census form, following the question on ethnic group, encouraged some people to answer the question in terms of cultural identification.

While estimates of Christians and those with no religion are vulnerable to question wording, estimates of other religions are more stable. The proportion of people identifying with a non-Christian religion was similar for BSA respondents (5 per cent) and Census respondents (6 per cent). This corresponds with evidence from the 2001 HOCS, which suggested that religious identity is stronger among Muslims, Hindus and Sikhs compared with Christians. The survey presented respondents with a list of characteristics related to identity including age, work, education, ethnicity, religion and family. Respondents were asked to indicate which characteristics said something important about them. Religion was of much greater importance to people from non-Christian groups. Around seven in ten Muslims (67 per cent), six in ten Sikhs (61 per cent) and five in ten Hindus (51 per cent) said that their religion said something important about them, compared with two in ten Christians (21 per cent).[9]

Census classification of ethnic group in 1991 and 2001

The 1991 Census in England and Wales, and in Scotland, included an ethnic group question for the first time in a British census. All three countries asked their populations the same ethnic group question (Figure 1.2). Northern Ireland did not include a question on ethnic group at this time.

In 2001, all four countries of the UK, including Northern Ireland, included an ethnic group question in their Censuses. England, Wales and Scotland revised their ethnic group questions. The four countries did not ask the same question in 2001: England and Wales both asked the same revised ethnic group question in 2001; Scotland asked a different revised question; the Northern Ireland question was similar to the 1991 Census question for Great Britain but included new categories for 'Irish Traveller' and 'Mixed ethnic group' (Appendix Figures A1.1–A1.3).

Because of the different ethnic group categories in 1991 and 2001 it is not possible to compare the 1991 and 2001 populations in all ethnic groups.[10] Statistics for the Mixed group cannot be produced for 1991 as the Mixed category was not included in the 1991 Census. The inclusion of the new Mixed categories in 2001 also has implications for the residual categories: Other Black, Other Asian and Other ethnic group. Although the Other Black and Other ethnic group categories were present in both censuses, many people who identified as Other Black and Other ethnic group in 1991 identified with one of the new Mixed groups in 2001. This means that the 1991 and 2001 populations for these groups are not comparable. The 'Other Asian' category in 1991 also cannot be compared with the same category in 2001. Other Asian was not included on the 1991 Census form but was created afterwards from answers provided in the 'Black-other' and 'Any other ethnic group' write-in boxes.[11] In 2001, the Other Asian category was included on the Census form. The 1991 and 2001 Other Asian groups have very different characteristics. For example, 40 per cent of the 1991 Other Asian population were born in the Far East compared with 2 per cent of the 2001 Other Asian population. This report only presents data on the main ethnic groups for comparison between 1991 and 2001. The groups compared are White, Black Caribbean, Black African, Indian, Pakistani, Bangladeshi and Chinese.

Figure **1.2**

1991 Census ethnic group question asked in England, Scotland and Wales

Ethnic group	
Please tick the appropriate box	White ☐
	Black-Caribbean ☐
	Black-African ☐
	Black-Other ☐ *please describe*
	Indian ☐
If the person is descended from more than one ethnic or racial group, please tick the group to which the person considers he/she belongs, or tick the 'Any other ethnic group' box and describe the person's ancestry in the space provided.	Pakistani ☐
	Bangladeshi ☐
	Chinese ☐
	Any other ethnic group ☐ *please describe*

Source: Office for National Statistics

There are other important differences between the 1991 and 2001 Censuses which affect comparisons between 1991 and 2001. In both censuses, population data was adjusted to take account of under-enumeration (undercounting) but the treatment differed. In 1991 adjustment factors were calculated that could be applied to previously published census counts. In 2001 the One Number Census (ONC) project was designed from the beginning to enable the integration of census counts with the estimated level of under-enumeration. Households and persons estimated to have been missed by the census were imputed to produce a fully adjusted census database at the time of publication.[12] The project was largely successful although some estimates were subsequently revised to account for a minority of people missed by the ONC.

Because of the differences between 1991 and 2001, estimates of growth in the ethnic minority population are particularly difficult to measure. Some allowance must be made for the undercount of ethnic minority populations in 1991 as this may have the effect of over-estimating growth in these populations between 1991 and 2001. A number of different estimates of population change can be produced according to whether allowances are made for changes to the ethnic classification between 1991 and 2001 and for the undercount of ethnic minority populations in 1991.[13]

Allowing for these factors it is clear that the ethnic minority population increased between 1991 and 2001, while the White population remained stable, although growth varied by ethnic group. The Black Caribbean population experienced the smallest growth among ethnic minority groups, increasing by around 7 per cent to 19 per cent depending on whether allowances are made for changes in the ethnic group classifications and the undercount of the Black Caribbean population in the 1991 Census.[14] The Indian population increased by around 20 per cent over the same period while the Chinese population increased by around 40 per cent. The Pakistani and Bangladeshi populations experienced greater growth of around 50 per cent and 60 per cent respectively. The Black African population experienced the greatest growth, more than doubling over this period. The growth in the ethnic minority populations can be attributed to a combination of natural growth and migration. Much of the growth of the Black African population in particular is likely to reflect migration rather than births in the population.

Because of the growth in ethnic minority populations between 1991 and 2001 some caution is recommended when comparing how the position of any particular group has changed over the decade, as the group's characteristics may also have changed in other ways. For example, changes in birth and migration rates since 1991 may have affected both the age profile of each group and the ratio of migrants to the UK-born. Differences between the characteristics of recent migrants compared with earlier migrants may also have an impact.

The position of a group recorded in the 2001 Census does not provide information about what has happened to the people in the 1991 population over the previous 10 years. This would require longitudinal analysis that follows individuals over time, for example the Longitudinal Study in England and Wales.[15] However, a comparison of the experiences of an ethnic group in 2001 with that ethnic group in 1991 is still important in helping to identify whether a population as a whole is experiencing more or less disadvantage. This information can be used to direct resources and services at the groups with greatest need.

2001 Census ethnic group classification across the United Kingdom

Figure 1.3 shows the ethnic groups covered in the 2001 Census classifications across the UK. The question in England and Wales included 16 groups: three White groups; four Mixed groups; four Asian groups; three Black groups; a Chinese group; and an 'Other ethnic' group. Scotland's 2001 Census ethnic group question included 14 groups: four White groups, including White Scottish; four Asian groups; three Black groups; a Chinese group; a Mixed group; and an 'other ethnic' group. The 2001 Census question in Northern Ireland covered 11 groups: one White group; three Asian groups; three Black groups; a Chinese group; a Mixed group; and a new category for 'Irish Traveller', which was not included elsewhere in the UK.

Figure **1.3**

Overview of 2001 Census ethnic group classifications in the United Kingdom

United Kingdom

	England and Wales	Scotland	Northern Ireland
White	White British White Irish Other White	White Scottish White Irish Other White British Other White	White
Mixed	Mixed White and Black Caribbean Mixed White and Black African Mixed White and Asian Other Mixed	Mixed	Mixed
Asian	Indian Pakistani Bangladeshi Other Asian	Indian Pakistani Bangladeshi Other Asian	Indian Pakistani Bangladeshi
Black	Black Caribbean Black African Other Black	Black Caribbean Black African Other Black	Black Caribbean Black African Other Black
Chinese and Other	Chinese Other ethnic group	Chinese Other ethnic group	Chinese Other ethnic group Irish Traveller

Source: Office for National Statistics

The presentation of ethnic groups also differed. The Chinese category was grouped under the sub-heading 'Chinese and Other ethnic group' in England and Wales, under the 'Asian' sub-heading in Scotland and was listed after the White category in Northern Ireland. Appendix Figures A1.1–A1.3 show the ethnic group questions as they appeared in the 2001 Census in England and Wales (Appendix Figure A1.1), in Scotland (Appendix Figure A1.2) and in Northern Ireland (Appendix Figure A1.3).

2001 Census religious group classification across the United Kingdom

A religion question was included for the first time in a British census in 2001 although Northern Ireland had been collecting religion data in their censuses for many years. There were differences in the religion questions asked across the UK in 2001. England and Wales asked only one question, *What is your religion?* making no distinction between practice, belief or background. Tick-boxes were provided for six of the main world religions. A write-in box was provided for any non-specified religion and respondents could also tick that they had no religion (Appendix Figure A1.4).

Scotland asked two questions in their 2001 Census. The first aimed to capture current belief or practice, asking, *What religion, religious denomination or body do you belong to?* The second question captured religious background and asked, *What religion, religious denomination or body were you brought up in?* In both questions, the answer categories divided the Christian group into Church of Scotland, Catholic and Other Christian. In all other respects the categories were the same as for England and Wales (Appendix Figure A1.5).

In Northern Ireland, more than in the other countries of the UK, the distinction between Catholics and Protestants has long been important and for this reason a question on religion has been asked for some time. The 2001 Census religion question in Northern Ireland reflected the importance of producing accurate estimates for Catholic and Protestant groups; the answer categories included four Christian groups and one 'Other' group. Respondents were presented with three questions, asking, first, whether they regarded themselves as 'belonging to any particular religion', and then, depending on their answer, directing them to tick either a religious denomination that they belonged to or a denomination that they had been brought up in (Appendix Figure A1.6).

The different ethnic group and religion questions asked in the countries of the UK largely reflect variations in their populations. The ethnic minority and religious minority populations in England and Wales are larger than those in Scotland and Northern Ireland. Different questions, although necessary, complicate the process of producing estimates for the UK and GB population. The next section looks at how data can be combined to provide estimates at these geographical levels.

Producing statistics for Great Britain

Differences in the ethnic group and religion questions asked in the countries of the UK mean that it is necessary to combine some groups to present statistics for the UK or Great Britain. However, it is not possible to combine data from England, Wales, Scotland and Northern Ireland because of the very different ethnic and religious group questions asked in Northern Ireland.

Ethnic group statistics

Northern Ireland contained only one White category in the 2001 census so it is necessary to merge the White groups in England, Wales and Scotland to present ethnic group statistics for the UK. The White British, White Irish and Other White groups cannot then be separately analysed. For the purpose of many analyses, including those within this report, the distinction between the White groups is too important to lose. In these instances it is practical to produce ethnic group statistics for Great Britain rather than the UK.[16]

To produce ethnic group statistics for Great Britain, 'White Scottish' and 'White Other British' respondents in Scotland are combined with 'White British' respondents in England and Wales to produce a single 'White British' group. Three White groups can then be analysed: White British, Other White and White Irish. Scotland's single Mixed category is combined with England and Wales' four separate Mixed ethnic groups – White and Black Caribbean, White and Black African, White and Asian and Other Mixed. Data is presented for the combined Mixed group only. This reclassification produces a 13-category ethnic group classification for Great Britain, which is used for many analyses in this report (Figure 1.4 overleaf).

Religious group statistics

Variations in the religion questions asked across the UK also complicate the production of religion statistics for the UK and Great Britain. Religion data from Northern Ireland cannot be combined with data from the other countries of the UK because of the different questions and answer categories. Smaller religious groups such as Muslims were not provided with a tick-box on the census form in Northern Ireland as they constitute a much smaller proportion of their population. Statistics for the UK as a whole cannot be compiled therefore without losing information about non-Christian groups.

Figure **1.4**

Ethnic group classification for Great Britain[1]

Great Britain	England and Wales	Scotland
White British	White British	White Scottish
		Other White British
White Irish	White Irish	White Irish
Other White	Other White	Other White
Mixed	Mixed White and Black Caribbean	Mixed
	Mixed White and Black African	
	Mixed White and Asian	
	Other Mixed	
Indian	Indian	Indian
Pakistani	Pakistani	Pakistani
Bangladeshi	Bangladeshi	Bangladeshi
Other Asian	Other Asian	Other Asian
Black Caribbean	Black Caribbean	Black Caribbean
Black African	Black African	Black African
Other Black	Other Black	Other Black
Chinese	Chinese	Chinese
Other ethnic group	Other ethnic group	Other ethnic group

1 Based on the 2001 Census questions.

Sources: Census 2001, Office for National Statistics; Census 2001, General Register Office for Scotland

As with ethnic group statistics, it is possible to produce religion statistics for Great Britain by combining data for England, Wales and Scotland. However, this is not without problems. While England and Wales asked only one religion question in their census, Scotland included two questions; asking, first, which religion people 'belong to' and, second, which religion people were 'brought up' in. Some consideration must be given to deciding which of the two Scottish questions is suitable for merging with data from England and Wales' single religion question. The main difference in estimates produced from the two Scotland questions is in the proportion who described themselves as either Christian or as having no religion. Many respondents in Scotland said that they did not *belong* to any religion but that they were *brought up* in the Christian religion. When Scotland's question on 'religion people belonged to' is compared with the England and Wales question, Scotland appears to have a greater proportion of people than England and Wales with no religion (29 per cent and 16 per cent respectively), and a smaller proportion of Christians (69 per cent and 78 per cent respectively). However, Scotland's question on the religion that people were brought

up in produces very similar results to the England and Wales question; 79 per cent of people in Scotland identified as Christian when asked, *What religion were you brought up in?*, as did 78 per cent of people in England and Wales when asked, *What is your religion?* (Table 1.5).

The proportions with no religion were also similar when the England and Wales question was compared with Scotland's religious upbringing question (16 per cent and 19 per cent respectively). The results suggest that Scotland's question on religious upbringing is most suitable for combining with the question asked in England and Wales.

There are further grounds for combining these two questions. The sheer number of people identifying as Christian in the 2001 Census in England and Wales suggests that the majority of people answered the question in terms of their religious upbringing rather than current practice. Data from the 1999 British Social Attitudes survey showed that, among adults who had or were brought up in a religion, more than half (54 per cent) 'never or practically never' attended church.[17] Data on weekly church attendance or membership of the main Christian

Table **1.5**

Religious identification in the Census in England and Wales, and in Scotland, April 2001

England and Wales, Scotland   Percentages

	England and Wales	Scotland	
	Religion[1]	Religion of upbringing[2]	Current religion[3]
Christian	77.7	79.2	68.9
Buddhist	0.3	0.1	0.1
Hindu	1.2	0.1	0.1
Jewish	0.5	0.2	0.1
Muslim	3.2	0.9	0.9
Sikh	0.7	0.1	0.1
Any other religion	0.3	0.2	0.6
No religion	16.1	19.1	29.1
Total[4] (= 100%) (Numbers)	48,031,258	4,639,149	4,783,950

1 *2001 Census question in England and Wales asked 'What is your religion?'*
2 *2001 Census question in Scotland asked 'What religion, religious denomination or body were you brought up in?'*
3 *2001 Census question in Scotland asked 'What religion, religious denomination or body do you belong to?'*
4 *Excludes 'Religion not stated'.*

Sources: Census 2001, Office for National Statistics; Census 2001, General Register Office for Scotland

churches in 2004 produces a rough estimate of fewer than 5 million practising Christians in the UK.[18] Although this does not include membership of the smaller Christian churches, the total number of regularly practising Christians is considerably fewer than the 37 million that identified as Christian in the 2001 Census in England and Wales.

In conclusion, Scotland's question on religious upbringing is most suitable for combining with the question asked in England and Wales to produce religion statistics for Great Britain. However, it is important to recognise that the Christian group represents people that have a Christian background as well as those who would regard themselves as practising Christians.

The first column of Figure 1.6 shows the resulting religious group classification for Great Britain. This measure is used in all analyses of religious group presented in this report.

Ethnic and religious classification of households

As discussed ethnicity and religion are self-identification measures in the Census and are recorded separately for every member of the household. Ideally, the information recorded on the census form will have been entered by each person in the household, rather than being completed by one person on

Figure **1.6**

Religious group classification for Great Britain

Great Britain	England and Wales[1]	Scotland[2]
Christian	Christian (including Church of England, Church in Wales, Catholic, Protestant and all other Christian denominations)	Church of Scotland Roman Catholic Other Christian
Buddhist	Buddhist	Buddhist
Hindu	Hindu	Hindu
Jewish	Jewish	Jewish
Muslim	Muslim	Muslim
Sikh	Sikh	Sikh
Any other religion	Any other religion	Any other religion
No religion	No religion	No religion

1 *2001 Census in England and Wales asked respondents 'What is your religion?'*
2 *2001 Census in Scotland asked respondents 'What religion, religious denomination or body were you brought up in?'*

Sources: Census 2001, Office for National Statistics; Census 2001, General Register Office for Scotland

behalf of all others as this will be an accurate reflection of the ethnic or religious group to which each person feels that they, individually, belong. In practice, the ethnic and religious group of all members of the household is sometimes entered on the census form by one person. However, in most cases the group selected by the form-filler will correspond with the group that each individual member of the household would have selected, if they had completed the form themselves.

It follows that households may contain people from more than one ethnic or religious group. The ethnic or religious group of the household reference person, upon which most household analyses are based, may therefore not reflect the ethnic group of the other household members. The growth of the Mixed population, for example, suggests that the proportion of households where parent and child may be classified to different ethnic groups will increase with time. Religious diversity within households is also likely to increase over time. In particular the increasingly secular nature of the UK creates the potential for households to contain people with no religion as well as people of faith.

These issues have important implications for analysis. Extensive heterogeneity (diversity) within households could undermine the value of undertaking ethnic and religious analyses at the household level. The next section considers the evidence for ethnic and religious homogeneity within households (that is all people belonging to the same ethnic and religious group).

Homogeneity within households

A homogeneous household is one in which all members of the household share the same ethnic or religious group category as the household reference person (HRP). Households can have complete ethnic homogeneity or broad ethnic homogeneity. Households with complete ethnic homogeneity are ones in which all members of the household are classified to exactly the same 'specific' ethnic group category. For example, every member of the household being classified as White British. Households with broad ethnic homogeneity are ones in which all members of the household are classified to the same 'major' ethnic group category. For example all members of the household are classified as White.

Heterogeneity within households

Heterogeneous households are ones in which members of the household are classified to a different ethnic or religious group from the household reference person (HRP).

Ethnic classification of households

Households are classified according to the ethnic group of the household reference person (HRP).[19] In ethnically homogeneous households, all members of the household share the same ethnic group category as the HRP. A narrow definition of homogeneity requires that all members of the household are classified to the exact same 'specific' ethnic group category. For example, every member of the household being classified as Black Caribbean. A broader definition of homogeneity requires that all members of the household are classified to the same 'major' ethnic group category, for example all people being classified as Black. Table 1.7 shows the variation in the proportion of households which can be classified as homogeneous using these two definitions.

The second definition produces a higher proportion of homogeneous households for all ethnic groups but the difference between the two measures is greater among some groups. Households headed by a White British, Indian,

Table **1.7**

Ethnic homogeneity in households: by ethnic group,[1] April 2001

England and Wales — Percentages

	Households with complete homogeneity[2]	Households with broad homogeneity[3]	All households (Numbers)
White British	97	99	19,336,648
White Irish	53	97	357,289
Other White	57	93	556,180
Mixed	..	45	146,309
Indian	85	90	314,952
Pakistani	85	91	172,510
Bangladeshi	85	91	61,939
Other Asian	60	74	80,748
Black Caribbean	76	83	275,628
Black African	81	86	176,436
Other Black	58	72	31,218
Chinese	81	..	77,384
Other ethnic group	60	..	73,234

1 Of household reference person.
2 Households in which all members share the ethnic group of the HRP. Includes one person households. The measure of complete homogeneity is not applicable for the combined Mixed group as this group contains people classified to the four Mixed groups in England and Wales.
3 Households in which all members are classified within the same major ethnic group category: all being White; all being Black; all being Asian; all being Mixed. The measure of broad homogeneity is not applicable for the Chinese or Other ethnic group as these categories were not grouped with any other similar categories in the classification.

Source: Census 2001, Office for National Statistics

Pakistani, Bangladeshi, Black Caribbean or Black African person were highly homogeneous with both definitions. Chinese households were also highly homogenous, the majority of households being composed wholly of Chinese people. The measure of broad homogeneity is not applicable for the Chinese group as this ethnic category was not grouped with any other similar categories in the classification.

White British people make up the majority of Britain's population and households headed by someone from the White British group were the most homogeneous, 97 per cent of households containing exclusively White British people and 99 per cent containing people from a White ethnic group. Among households headed by an Indian, Pakistani or Bangladeshi person, nine in ten households contained only people from an Asian group and 85 per cent contained members classified to the same specific ethnic group as the HRP. Households headed by a Black African or Black Caribbean person were only slightly less homogeneous, with 86 per cent and 83 per cent of households respectively containing exclusively Black people and a slightly smaller proportion containing only people classified to the same specific Black group as the HRP.

Some household homogeneity results from one-person households, which are automatically homogeneous as they can only contain one ethnic group. In 2001, one-person households formed a larger proportion of Black Caribbean (38 per cent), White British (31 per cent) and Black African (30 per cent) households than Indian (16 per cent), Pakistani (12 per cent) and Bangladeshi (9 per cent) households (Chapter 4).

Households headed by someone classified to the Other White, Other Black or Other Asian groups were less likely to contain people classified exclusively to the same specific category but the majority of people within the household shared the same major ethnic group, majorities being classified to a White, Black or Asian group respectively. The measure of broad homogeneity is not applicable for the Other ethnic group as this category was not grouped with any other similar categories in the classification.

It is not meaningful to calculate complete homogeneity for households headed by someone from a Mixed group in this data presentation. The four separate Mixed groups identified in the 2001 Census in England and Wales are combined to produce an overall 'Mixed' category, which is used in all household analyses in this report. Just over four in ten (46 per cent) households headed by someone classified to a Mixed group contained only Mixed people. The majority were one-person households; 30 per cent of households headed by someone from a Mixed group in Great Britain in 2001 were

one-person households (see Chapter 4, Households and Families). Where people from a Mixed ethnic group did not live alone, they generally lived with people from a different ethnic group to themselves. This corresponds with high rates of inter-ethnic marriage among people from a Mixed group; in 2001, more than three-quarters (78 per cent) of married people from a Mixed group in England and Wales were married to someone from a different ethnic group.[20]

Almost all White Irish households (97 per cent) contained only White people but a smaller proportion (53 per cent) contained exclusively White Irish people. This partly reflects partnerships between White Irish and White British people. It also reflects changes between generations, that is, whether the children of White Irish parents identify as White Irish or White British. The next section examines the sources of ethnic diversity within households.

Sources of ethnic diversity in households

Table 1.8 overleaf shows the sources of ethnic heterogeneity (diversity) within households in which all household members were classified to the same broad ethnic group – for example all were classified to a White, Asian or Black group – but not all were classified to the same specific ethnic groups. Heterogeneity within households may arise from inter-ethnic couples, ethnic differences between parents and children and/ or from unrelated people living together. Most households contain a family[21] and therefore most heterogeneity arises out of different ethnicity between partnerships or between generations.

For example, in White Irish households in which all members were classified to a White group but not all were classified to the White Irish group, most heterogeneity arose from different identities being recorded both between generations and within partnerships within the household (64 per cent). This might arise from an inter-ethnic partnership of a White Irish and White British couple and their children, classified as White British. In a further 25 per cent of cases, the heterogeneity arises from different identities being recorded between the generations only, between parents and children. For the White, British-born, children of White Irish parents, the White British category may seem a better description of their ethnicity than White Irish. Among Black Caribbean households most heterogeneity arose from differences between the generations (67 per cent). An example might be a parent classified as Black Caribbean and their son or daughter classified as Other Black. In the 2001 Census in England and Wales, many young, Black, British born people chose the Other Black category and wrote in the description 'Black British'.[22]

Table 1.8

Sources of ethnic diversity in households with broad homogeneity:[1] by ethnic group,[2] April 2001

England and Wales

Percentages

	Different ethnicity between generations only	Different ethnicity between generations and within partnerships	Others[3]	Base (=100%) (Numbers)
White British	8	72	20	351,581
White Irish	25	64	11	157,205
Other White	21	64	15	199,695
Indian	48	28	23	13,461
Pakistani	44	29	27	9,971
Bangladeshi	54	22	24	3,826
Other Asian	28	49	23	11,250
Black Caribbean	67	19	15	17,537
Black African	54	28	18	10,182
Other Black	37	36	27	4,323

1 Households in which all people share the major ethnic group but not the specific ethnic group category of the household reference person.
2 Of household reference person.
3 Any other combination (including different ethnic identities between partnerships and between unrelated people).

Source: Census 2001, Office for National Statistics

Religious classification of households

Households are classified according to the religious group of the Household Reference Person (HRP). A household is classified as being religiously homogeneous where all members of the household have the same religion as the HRP. This includes one-person households (which are automatically homogeneous), households where all members have no religion and households where all members are classified as 'religion not stated'. The majority of households in England and Wales are religiously homogeneous, all members of the household being classified to the same religious category.

Figure 1.9 shows the extent of religious homogeneity within households. The first category represents households in which all members were classified to the same religious category, all members having the same religion or all having no religion or all being classified 'religion not stated'. These households accounted for the majority of households in all religious groups and 85 per cent of households in England and Wales overall. A further one in seven households (14 per cent) contained people classified to one of the main religions, plus one or more people who had no religion or who chose not to state their religion. The third category represents households that contained people from different faiths, for example Christians and Muslims. These heterogeneous households accounted for 2 per cent of households in England and Wales.

Figure 1.9

Percentage of homogeneous and heterogeneous households: by religion,[1] April 2001

England and Wales

Percentages

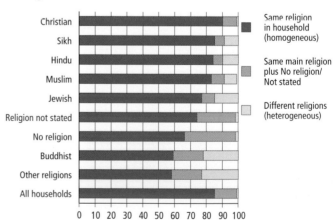

Households headed by a Christian are the most religiously homogeneous, nine in ten containing exclusively Christian people. This corresponds to the high level of ethnic homogeneity in White British households. In both cases, these groups form the majority of the population and around three in ten households headed by these groups are one-person households which are, automatically, homogeneous (Chapter 4). Where households headed by a Christian were not homogeneous it usually resulted from someone in the household having no religion and/or someone choosing not to state their religion (9 per cent). Only 1 per cent of Christian households contained someone classified to another religion (Table 1.10).

Sikh, Hindu and Muslim households were also highly homogeneous, around 84 per cent of households containing people classified to the same religious group as the HRP. These households were less likely than Christian households to be one-person households; no more than one in seven Sikh, Hindu and Muslim households were one-person households in 2001. Sikh, Hindu and Muslim households were more religiously diverse than Christian households; about one in ten contained someone who belonged to a different religion to the HRP, compared with 1 per cent of Christian households. A further 6 to 8 per cent of Muslim, Sikh and Hindu households contained someone classified as having no religion or someone who did not state their religion. The majority of these probably contained someone who chose not to state their religion, rather than someone of no religion – 6 per cent of people from South Asian groups chose not to state their religion in the 2001 Census compared with 1 per cent who identified as having no religion.[23]

Jewish households had high levels of homogeneity (77 per cent) and, similar to Christian households, a relatively high proportion were one-person households (36 per cent). However, more than one in seven (16 per cent) Jewish households was religiously diverse, containing both a Jewish person and someone who belonged to another religion.

Buddhist households also had high levels of religious diversity; 22 per cent of households headed by a Buddhist contained a person who belonged to a different religion to the HRP. Six in ten Buddhist households (59 per cent) contained exclusively Buddhist people but, as with Christian and Jewish households, many of these were one-person households; 36 per cent of Buddhist households contained one person in 2001 (Chapter 4).

Three-quarters (74 per cent) of households headed by someone classified as 'religion not stated' were homogeneous,[24] as were two-thirds (66 per cent) of households headed by someone with no religion. Many of these were one-person households; 38 per cent of households headed by someone classified as 'religion not stated' and 29 per cent of households headed by someone with no religion (Chapter 4). Where these households were not homogeneous, they generally contained people classified to both the 'no religion' and 'not stated' categories; only 2 per cent of households headed by someone from either of these groups contained a person who identified with any religion.

Table **1.10**

Religious homogeneity in households: by religion,[1] April 2001

England and Wales   Percentages

	All people in household classified to same religious group[2]	Household includes one religious group plus no religion and/or religion not stated	Household includes different religious groups	All households (=100%) (Numbers)
Christian	90	9	1	15,995,596
Buddhist	59	19	22	64,360
Hindu	84	6	11	172,379
Jewish	77	8	16	116,330
Muslim	83	8	8	411,415
Sikh	85	6	10	93,188
Any other religion	58	19	23	76,190
No religion	66	32	2	3,140,413
Religion not stated	74	24	2	1,590,604
All households	85	14	2	21,660,475

1   Of household reference person.
2   Includes one person households.

Source: Census 2001, Office for National Statistics

It is not possible to establish the extent of religious diversity in households classified as belonging to an 'other religion'. Six in ten (58 per cent) households headed by someone classified to an 'other religion' contained only people classified to the 'other religion' category but this category contains many different religious groups and the classification does not clarify which religious group they belonged to. However, these households were at least as diverse as Buddhist households; 23 per cent of households headed by someone belonging to an 'other religion' contained a person that was classified to a main religion, either Christian, Hindu, Jewish, Muslim or Sikh.

The examination of ethnic and religious diversity in households suggests that the majority of households in Great Britain contain people who share ethnic and religious characteristics. It is likely that they also share experiences related to the ethnic and religious identity of the household. Chapter 4 describes some of the key differences between households when they are analysed by ethnic and religious group.

Notes and references

1.   Office for National Statistics (2003) *Ethnic group statistics: A guide for the collection and classification of ethnicity data*, TSO: London, pp 12–14.

2.   Bradford B (2006) *Who are the 'Mixed' ethnic groups*? Available at www.statistics.gov.uk/cci/article.asp?id=1580

3.   Office for National Statistics (2003) *Ethnic group statistics: A guide for the collection and classification of ethnicity data*, TSO: London, p 11.

4.   Bulmer M (1996) 'The ethnic group question in the 1991 Census of population', in Coleman D and Salt J (eds.) *Ethnicity in the 1991 Census: Volume One: Demographic characteristics of the ethnic minority populations*: London: HMSO: London, pp 44–46.

5.   For further information see www.statistics.gov.uk/CCI/nugget. asp?ID=449

6.   Office for National Statistics (2003) *Ethnic group statistics: A guide for the collection and classification of ethnicity data*, TSO: London, p31.

7.   Voas D and Bruce S (2004) The 2001 Census and Christian identification in Britain. *Journal Of Contemporary Religion* **19(1)**, 26.

8.   Voas D and Bruce S (2004) The 2001 Census and Christian identification in Britain. *Journal Of Contemporary Religion* **19(1)**, 23–28.

9.   Office for National Statistics (2005) 'Country of birth & national identity', in *Focus on Religion Overview Report*. Available at: www. statistics.gov.uk/cci/nugget.asp?id=958

10. For full discussion see Office for National Statistics (2005) *A guide to comparing 1991 and 2001 Census ethnic group data*, p 33. Available at: www.statistics.gov.uk/CCI/article.asp?ID=1471

11. For full discussion see Office for National Statistics (2005) *A guide to comparing 1991 and 2001 Census ethnic group data*, p 14. Available at: www.statistics.gov.uk/CCI/article.asp?ID=1471

12. Office for National Statistics (2005) *A guide to comparing 1991 and 2001 Census ethnic group data*, pp 16–21. Available at: www. statistics.gov.uk/CCI/article.asp?ID=1471

13. Office for National Statistics (2005) *A guide to comparing 1991 and 2001 Census ethnic group data*, pp 41–48, Table 18. Available at: www.statistics.gov.uk/CCI/article.asp?ID=1471

14. Office for National Statistics (2005) *A guide to comparing 1991 and 2001 Census ethnic group data*, Table 18. Available at: www. statistics.gov.uk/CCI/article.asp?ID=1471

15. The ONS Longitudinal Study (LS) of England and Wales is available at: www.statistics.gov.uk/ls

16. Data on ethnicity and religion in Northern Ireland is available on the NICA website at www.nicensus2001.gov.uk

17. Nan Dirk De Graaf and Arianna Need (2000) *Losing faith: is Britain alone?* British Social Attitudes (17th Report), Sage Publications, London, p 124, Table 6.3.

18. Office for National Statistics (2004) *UK 2004: The Official Yearbook of the United Kingdom of Great Britain and Northern Ireland*, TSO: London, pp 212–214. Also available at: www.statistics.gov.uk/StatBase/Product.asp?vlnk=5703

19. See Glossary for definition of HRP.

20. Office for National Statistics (2004) 'Inter-ethnic marriage', in *Focus on Ethnicity & Identity Overview Report*. Available at: www. statistics.gov.uk/cci/nugget.asp?id=1090

21. See Glossary for definition of a family.

22. Gardener D and Connolly H (2005) Who *are the 'Other' ethnic groups*? Available at: www.statistics.gov.uk/cci/article.asp?id=1291

23. Office for National Statistics (2005) 'Religious Populations', in *Focus on Religion Overview Report*. Available at: www.statistics.gov.uk/cci/nugget.asp?id=954

24. Households in which the religion of all household members was not stated were homogeneous only in the sense that religion was unknown for all.

Appendix Figure A1.1

The 2001 Census ethnic group question asked in England and Wales

8	**What is your ethnic group?**
	Choose ONE section from A to E, then tick the appropriate box to indicate your cultural background.

A   White

☐ British   ☐ Irish

☐ Any other White background, *please write in*

[   ]

B   Mixed

☐ White and Black Caribbean

☐ White and Black African

☐ White and Asian

☐ Any other Mixed background, *please write in*

[   ]

C   Asian or Asian British

☐ Indian   ☐ Pakistani

☐ Bangladeshi

☐ Any other Asian background, *please write in*

[   ]

D   Black or Black British

☐ Caribbean   ☐ African

☐ Any other Black background, *please write in*

[   ]

E   Chinese or other ethnic group

Chinese

Any other, *please write in*

[   ]

Source: Office for National Statistics

Appendix Figure A1.2

The 2001 Census ethnic group question asked in Scotland

15	**What is your ethnic group?**
	Choose ONE section from A to E, then tick the appropriate box to indicate your cultural background.

A   White

☐ Scottish

☐ Other British

☐ Irish

☐ Any other White background, *please write in*

[   ]

B   Mixed

☐ Any Mixed background, *please write in*

[   ]

C   Asian, Asian Scottish or Asian British

☐ Indian

☐ Pakistani

☐ Bangladeshi

☐ Chinese

☐ Any other Asian background, *please write in*

[   ]

D   Black, Black Scottish or Black British

☐ Caribbean   ☐ African

☐ Any other Black background, *please write in*

[   ]

E   Other ethnic background,

Any other background, *please write in*

[   ]

Source: General Register Office for Scotland

Appendix Figure A1.3

The 2001 Census ethnic group question asked in Northern Ireland

10	To which of these ethnic groups do you consider you belong?

tick one box only

☐ White

☐ Chinese

☐ Irish Traveller

☐ Indian

☐ Pakistani

☐ Bangladeshi

☐ Black Caribbean

☐ Black African

☐ Black Other

☐ Mixed ethnic group, *write in*

☐ Any other ethnic group, *write in*

Source: Northern Ireland Statistics and Research Agency

Appendix Figure A1.4

The 2001 Census religion question asked in England and Wales

10	What is your religion?

This question is voluntary
tick one box only

☐ None

☐ Christian (including Church of England, Catholic, Protestant and all other Christian denominations)

☐ Buddhist

☐ Hindu

☐ Jewish

☐ Muslim

☐ Sikh

☐ Any other religion, *please write in*

Source: Office for National Statistics

Appendix Figure A1.5a

The 2001 Census religion questions asked in Scotland

13

What religion, religious denomination or body do you belong to?

☐ None

☐ Church of Scotland

☐ Roman Catholic

☐ Other Christian, *please write in*

[   ]

☐ Buddhist

☐ Hindu   ☐ Jewish

☐ Muslim   ☐ Sikh

☐ Another Religion, *please write in*

[   ]

Source: General Register Office for Scotland

Appendix Figure A1.5b

14

What religion, religious denomination or body were you brought up in?

☐ None

☐ Church of Scotland

☐ Roman Catholic

☐ Other Christian, *please write in*

[   ]

☐ Buddhist

☐ Hindu   ☐ Jewish

☐ Muslim   ☐ Sikh

☐ Another Religion, *please write in*

[   ]

Source: General Register Office for Scotland

Appendix Figure A1.6a

The 2001 Census religion questions asked in Northern Ireland

8

Do you regard yourself as belonging to any particular religion?

☐ Yes   ➔   Go to   8a

☐ No   ➔   Go to   8b

Source: Northern Ireland Statistics and Research Agency

Appendix Figure A1.6b

8a

What religion, religious denomination or body do you belong to?

☐ Roman Catholic

☐ Presbyterian Church in Ireland

☐ Church of Ireland

☐ Methodist Church in Ireland

☐ Other, *please write in*

[   ]

Source: Northern Ireland Statistics and Research Agency

Appendix Figure A1.6c

8b

What religion, religious denomination or body were you brought up in?

☐ Roman Catholic

☐ Presbyterian Church in Ireland

☐ Church of Ireland

☐ Methodist Church in Ireland

☐ Other, *please write in*

[   ]

☐ None

Source: Northern Ireland Statistics and Research Agency

Population

Karin Bosveld and Helen Connolly

Chapter 2

Introduction

The population of Great Britain includes many different ethnic groups. The majority of people belong to the White British ethnic group, but there are established populations of White Irish, Indian, Pakistani, Bangladeshi, Black Caribbean, Black African and Chinese people, as well as numerous smaller ethnic groups. The population of Great Britain also includes many different religious groups. Most people are Christian, but the population includes Muslims, Hindus, Sikhs, Jews, Buddhists and many other smaller religious groups. Ethnic and religious groups are often closely related. For example, the majority of White British and Black Caribbean people are Christian and the majority of Pakistani and Bangladeshi people are Muslim. Some ethnic groups have greater religious diversity; the Indian population, for example, includes Hindus, Sikhs, Muslims and Christians.

Aside from religious diversity, ethnic populations differ on a number of important factors including their migration histories (when and from where they came), the age structure of their populations and their occupational distribution. These factors are associated with labour market and household variations discussed in Chapters 4 and 5.

Modest migration has always been a feature of Great Britain, but much of the ethnic and religious diversity of the current population is a result of large scale migration from the 1950s onwards. Early immigration waves included economic migrants from Ireland, the Caribbean and India, followed by migrants from Pakistan and Bangladesh, their wives and dependants. Since the 1980s migration from Africa and China has increased and has included students and asylum-seekers, as well as economic migrants.

The timing of the various immigrant waves is reflected in the age structure of the different populations with ethnic minority populations generally having younger age structures than the White British population. Migration patterns, including the countries of origin, the timing of migrant's arrival and the skills that they brought with them, are also related to present-day socio-economic variations between ethnic groups. Some groups have a socio-economic profile similar to the White British majority but other groups are very different. For example, in 2001 a third (34 per cent) of Indian and White British men of working age were in a managerial or professional occupation compared with less than one in five Pakistani (18 per cent) and Bangladeshi (14 per cent) men.

This chapter begins by presenting information on the size and distribution of the ethnic and religious populations measured in the 2001 Census in England and Wales, and in Scotland. Data

for ethnic and religious populations are followed by data on the main ethno-religious groups (which take account of both the religious and ethnic composition of groups). These groups are considered in respect of their size in the general population and their size within the ethnic and religious groups from which they are derived. For example, although Indian Hindus constitute less than 1 per cent of the general population, they account for almost half (45 per cent) of Great Britain's Indian population and the vast majority (84 per cent) of Great Britain's Hindu population.

The chapter concludes by profiling and comparing the 8 main ethnic groups in Great Britain: White British; White Irish; Indian; Pakistani; Bangladeshi; Black Caribbean; Black African; and Chinese.[1] The profiles demonstrate important demographic differences between groups, including variations in population size and differences in the age structure of the populations. They also demonstrate the diversity of geographic origins and socio-economic backgrounds, within ethnic groups as well as between them.

The size and distribution of ethnic and religious groups in Great Britain

The majority of the population of Great Britain are White British. In 2001 they accounted for over 50 million people, 88 per cent of the population. The Indian population formed the largest non-White ethnic group, accounting for around 2 per cent of the population, followed by the Pakistani, Mixed, Black Caribbean and Black African populations (each 1 per cent). The other non-White groups each accounted for less than 1 per cent of the population in 2001 (Table 2.1).

Christians formed the largest religious group, accounting for almost three in four people (72 per cent) in Great Britain in 2001. Muslims (3 per cent) formed the second largest religious group, followed by Hindus (1 per cent). The other religious groups each represented less than 1 per cent of the population. Around one in seven people (15 per cent) reported having no religious affiliation (Table 2.2).

These two aspects of identity – ethnicity and religion – are often closely related but there is not complete homogeneity (that is all people in a particular ethnic group belonging to the same religion). Most ethnic groups include people of different religions and most religions encompass people from different ethnic groups. Within a particular ethnic group, people of different religions may have very different characteristics. For example, in 2001 Indian Muslim women were considerably less likely than Sikh, Hindu and Christian counterparts to be in work or seeking work; 39 per cent of Indian Muslim women were economically active compared with 65 to 71 per cent of Sikh,

Table 2.1

Population: by ethnic group, April 2001

Great Britain		Numbers and percentages
White British	50,366,497	88.2
White Irish	691,232	1.2
Other White	1,423,471	2.5
Mixed	673,798	1.2
Indian	1,051,844	1.8
Pakistani	746,619	1.3
Bangladeshi	282,811	0.5
Other Asian	247,470	0.4
Black Caribbean	565,621	1.0
Black African	484,783	0.8
Other Black	97,198	0.2
Chinese	243,258	0.4
Any other ethnic group	229,325	0.4
All ethnic groups	**57,103,927**	**100.0**

Source: Census 2001, Office for National Statistics; Census 2001, General Register Office for Scotland

Table 2.2

Population: by religious group, April 2001

Great Britain		Numbers and percentages
Christian	41,014,811	71.8
Buddhist	149,157	0.3
Hindu	558,342	1.0
Jewish	267,373	0.5
Muslim	1,588,890	2.8
Sikh	336,179	0.6
Any other religion	159,167	0.3
No religion	8,596,488	15.1
Religion not stated	4,433,520	7.8
All religious groups	**57,103,927**	**100.0**

Source: Census 2001, Office for National Statistics; Census 2001, General Register Office for Scotland

Hindu and Christian Indian women. Similarly, Black Caribbean and White British people may share a Christian religious identity but in 2001 the unemployment rate among Black Caribbean Christians (11 per cent) was twice the rate among

White British Christians (5 per cent) (Chapter 5). Hence, while looking at groups only in terms of their ethnicity or religion provides useful information, it can obscure differences within each religious or ethnic group.

Further differentiation, into composite ethno-religious categories produces groups that may have more in common. Table 2.3 overleaf shows the main ethno-religious groups in Great Britain in 2001.

Two-thirds (67 per cent) of the population described themselves as White British and Christian in 2001. Accounting for 38.1 million people, they are by far the largest ethno-religious group in Great Britain. The size of this group reflects Great Britain's history of Christianity but an affiliation to the Christian faith does not necessarily indicate religious practice (Chapter 1). White British people with no religion were the second largest ethno-religious group in 2001, accounting for 7.9 million people or 14 per cent of Great Britain's population.

Pakistani Muslims formed the largest non-White ethno-religious group in Great Britain, with a population of 686,000 people in 2001 – 1.2 per cent of the population. The Pakistani population has a greater religious homogeneity than most ethnic groups; nine in ten Pakistanis (92 per cent) were classified as Muslim in the 2001 Census and most of the remainder were classified as Religion not stated (6 per cent). It is possible that those who did not state their religion shared a Muslim background, as less than 1 per cent were affiliated to another religion or recorded as having no religion. Pakistani Muslims were the largest ethnic group represented in the Muslim population, accounting for 43 per cent of Great Britain's Muslims. Bangladeshis have a similar religious profile with 92 per cent being classified as Muslim and 6 per cent as Religion not stated in 2001. Bangladeshi Muslims were fewer in number than Pakistani Muslims and accounted for 16 per cent of Great Britain's Muslims in 2001.

Both the Black Caribbean and Black African populations in Great Britain are predominantly Christian. Almost three-quarters (74 per cent) of the Black Caribbean population were recorded as Christian in the 2001 Census while about one in ten (11 per cent) were classified as having no religion. This gave them a religious distribution very similar to the White British population. Among Black Africans, Christians formed a slightly smaller proportion (69 per cent) and one in five was Muslim. Although most Black Africans were Christian, they made up a smaller proportion of Great Britain's Christians (1 per cent) than Great Britain's Muslims (6 per cent).

Table **2.3**

Largest ethno-religious groups,[1,2] April 2001

Great Britain

Percentages and numbers

	Proportion of total population	Proportion of ethnic group	Proportion of religious group	Total population (Numbers)
White British Christian	66.8	75.7	93.0	38,137,157
White British No religion	13.8	15.7	91.7	7,886,968
White British Jewish	0.4	0.4	84.0	224,467
White British Muslim	0.1	0.1	4.0	63,891
White British Buddhist	0.1	0.1	34.2	51,006
White Irish Christian	1.0	85.7	1.4	592,218
White Irish No religion	0.1	6.2	0.5	42,569
Other White Christian	1.6	62.9	2.2	895,729
Other White No religion	0.4	16.1	2.7	228,646
Other White Muslim	0.2	8.3	7.4	117,713
Other White Jewish	0.1	2.3	12.4	33,126
Mixed Christian	0.6	52.3	0.9	352,616
Mixed No religion	0.3	23.3	1.8	157,271
Mixed Muslim	0.1	9.7	4.1	65,592
Indian Hindu	0.8	44.8	84.4	471,480
Indian Sikh	0.5	29.2	91.3	307,096
Indian Muslim	0.2	12.6	8.3	132,566
Indian Christian	0.1	5.0	0.1	52,128
Pakistani Muslim	1.2	91.9	43.2	686,179
Bangladeshi Muslim	0.5	92.4	16.5	261,380
Other Asian Muslim	0.2	37.5	5.8	92,761
Other Asian Hindu	0.1	26.3	11.7	65,175
Other Asian Christian	0.1	13.5	0.1	33,319
Black Caribbean Christian	0.7	73.7	1.0	417,053
Black Caribbean No religion	0.1	11.3	0.7	63,645
Black African Christian	0.6	68.8	0.8	333,530
Black African Muslim	0.2	20.0	6.1	97,109
Chinese No religion	0.2	53.0	1.5	128,935
Chinese Christian	0.1	21.1	0.1	51,387
Chinese Buddhist	0.1	15.1	24.7	36,809
Other ethnic group Christian	0.1	32.8	0.2	75,233
Other ethnic group No religion	0.1	14.0	0.4	32,162
Other ethnic group Muslim	0.1	26.0	3.8	59,675
Other ethnic group Buddhist	0.1	15.3	23.6	35,140
Largest ethno-religious groups[1,3]	**91.6**	.	.	**52,281,731**

1 Excludes ethno-religious groups with populations of less than 30,000 people.
2 Eight per cent of respondents chose not to state their religion. The percentage classified as religion not stated was greater in Black and Mixed groups.
3 '.' not applicable.

Source: Census 2001, Office for National Statistics; Census 2001, General Register Office for Scotland

As discussed previously, the Indian population is religiously diverse and includes Hindus, Sikhs, Muslims and Christians. Indians comprise the majority of Great Britain's Sikhs (91 per cent) and Hindus (84 per cent) but they make up a smaller proportion of Great Britain's Muslims (8 per cent) and only 0.1 per cent of Great Britain's Christians.

Profiling ethnic populations: demographic and socio-economic characteristics of the main ethnic groups

There are many important differences between ethnic groups, aside from religious affiliation. Ethnic minority populations generally have a younger age profile than White populations. In 2001, the median age[2] of men and women in the White British population was 38 years and 40 years respectively. The median age of Bangladeshi men and women, by comparison, was just over half that, at 21 years for both men and women (Appendix Table A2.1).

Population pyramids (Figures 2.4–2.11) provide an instant visual overview of the age and sex profiles of ethnic groups. The vertical axis shows single years of age, ranging from one year of age (at the base) to 100 years of age (at the apex). The horizontal axis shows the percentage of the population that were of any single year of age and either male (to the left) or female (to the right). For example, the Chinese pyramid shows that men aged 21 years accounted for 1.5 per cent of the Chinese population (Figure 2.11 on page 25). The different shapes of the pyramids reflect variations in fertility rates, mortality rates and migration patterns. Younger populations have a triangular shape, with a greater proportion of people towards the base of the pyramid and a smaller proportion towards the apex. The Bangladeshi (Figure 2.8 overleaf) and Pakistani (Figure 2.7 overleaf) pyramids have the youngest age profiles and the most pronounced triangular shape. Older populations have a greater proportion of people towards the apex of the pyramid and a smaller proportion towards the base – the White Irish pyramid (Figure 2.5) is the best example of this.

Imbalances in the sex distribution produce asymmetry in the shape of the population pyramids; when a population has more women than men at certain ages the bars on the right will be longer than the bars on the left. For example, the White British population pyramid (Figure 2.4) shows more women than men over 60 years of age. By comparison, the Black Caribbean (Figure 2.9 overleaf) and Black African population pyramids (Figure 2.10 on page 25) show more women than men in the working-age population. These variations are discussed in more detail in the following profiles.

Figure **2.4**

White British population: by sex and age, April 2001

Great Britain

Percentages

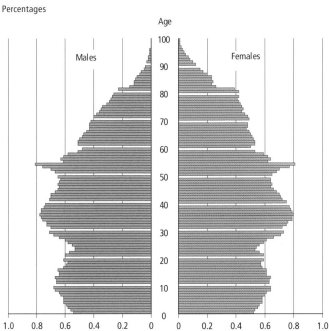

Source: Census 2001, Office for National Statistics; Census 2001, General Register Office for Scotland

Figure **2.5**

White Irish population: by sex and age, April 2001

Great Britain

Percentages

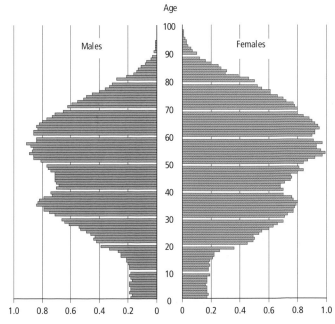

Source: Census 2001, Office for National Statistics; Census 2001, General Register Office for Scotland

Figure **2.6**

Indian population: by sex and age, April 2001

Great Britain

Percentages

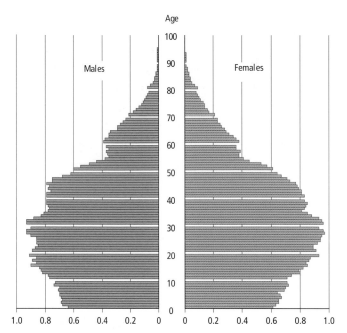

Source: Census 2001, Office for National Statistics; Census 2001, General Register Office for Scotland

Figure **2.8**

Bangladeshi population: by sex and age, April 2001

Great Britain

Percentages

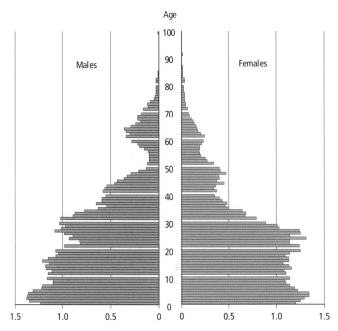

Source: Census 2001, Office for National Statistics; Census 2001, General Register Office for Scotland

Figure **2.7**

Pakistani population: by sex and age, April 2001

Great Britain

Percentages

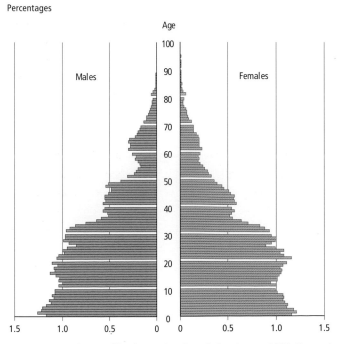

Source: Census 2001, Office for National Statistics; Census 2001, General Register Office for Scotland

Figure **2.9**

Black Caribbean population: by sex and age, April 2001

Great Britain

Percentages

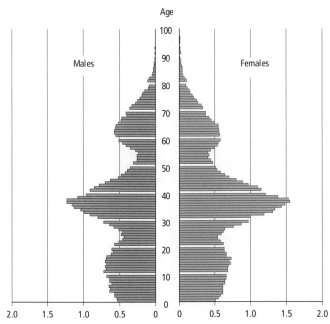

Source: Census 2001, Office for National Statistics; Census 2001, General Register Office for Scotland

Figure 2.10

Black African population: by sex and age, April 2001

Great Britain

Percentages

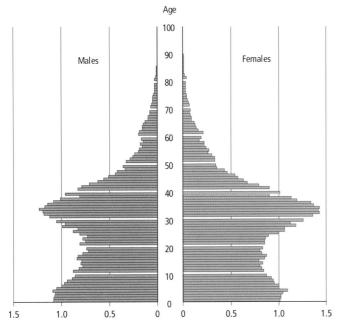

Source: Census 2001, Office for National Statistics; Census 2001, General Register Office for Scotland

Figure 2.11

Chinese population: by sex and age, April 2001

Great Britain

Percentages

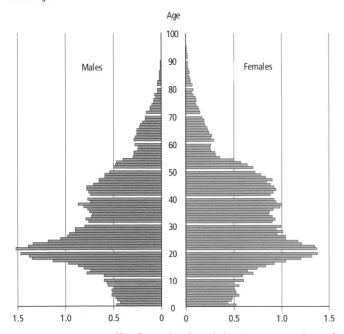

Source: Census 2001, Office for National Statistics; Census 2001, General Register Office for Scotland

In addition to differences in the age and sex structure of populations, there are also socio-economic differences between ethnic groups. As discussed previously, the proportion of people of working age in a managerial or professional occupation varies considerably. Furthermore, there is often diversity *within* individual ethnic groups as well as *between* them. Ethnic groups may encompass people from different geographic regions, who may speak different languages, follow different cultural practices and have very different educational and skill levels. The age and sex structure and socio-economic characteristics of these sub-groups will vary. The non-specific ethnic group categories – particularly the Other White, Other Asian and Other ethnic groups – have the greatest diversity. These groups include people from many different ethnic backgrounds. The people within each of these groups may have very little in common, apart from the fact that they were unable to identify with any of the main ethnic groups within the classification. Analysis of these non-specific groups, which takes account of this heterogeneity, has been published previously and is not repeated here.[3]

The Mixed ethnic group is also highly heterogeneous. Great Britain's Mixed ethnic population includes people from three separate Mixed groups – Mixed White and Black Caribbean, Mixed White and Black African and Mixed White and Asian – as well as people in the non-specific Other Mixed group. These four groups vary in many respects, including size, age structure and socio-economic characteristics. Analysis of the four mixed groups in England and Wales has been published separately and is not repeated here.[4]

The following analyses profile and compare the 8 main ethnic groups in Great Britain. These analyses exclude people living in Northern Ireland because of differences between the 2001 Census ethnic group classification used in Northern Ireland and the classifications used in the rest of the UK (Chapter 1).[5]

The White British population

Great Britain has always had a predominantly White population and as already mentioned White British people remain the majority ethnic group, 88 per cent, of the population in 2001 (Table 2.1). The vast majority (98 per cent) of White British people were born in the UK; 82 per cent were born in England, 10 per cent in Scotland, 5 per cent in Wales and 0.4 per cent in Northern Ireland. A minority (2 per cent) had been born outside of the UK (Table 2.12 overleaf).

Table 2.12

White British population: by region of birth, April 2001

Great Britain	Percentages
United Kingdom	*98.2*
England	*82.1*
Scotland	*10.2*
Wales	*5.5*
Northern Ireland	*0.4*
United Kingdom not specified[1,2]	-
Other Europe	*0.8*
Africa	*0.3*
Asia	*0.4*
North America[3]	*0.2*
South America[2]	-
Oceania	*0.1*
Other[2]	-
All White British	**50,366,497**

1 Includes respondents who didn't specify where in the United Kingdom.
2 '-' negligible (less than 0.05).
3 Includes the Caribbean and West Indies.

Source: Census 2001, Office for National Statistics; Census 2001, General Register Office for Scotland

Great Britain is historically a Christian country and three-quarters (76 per cent) of White British people shared this common religious background in 2001. A further 16 per cent had no religion (Table 2.3).

The White British population has an older age profile than most ethnic minority populations. This is reflected in their labour market characteristics which include, for example, a greater proportion of economically inactive people[6] (above retirement age) and a greater proportion of people at higher occupational levels (partly due to people having had longer to progress in their occupations) (Chapter 5). The older age profile of the White British population also has implications at the household level, including a relatively large proportion of pensioner households and fewer households with children (Chapter 4).

The age and sex structure of the White British population is typical for an indigenous population in the industrialised world. As the population pyramid demonstrates (Figure 2.4), there are more adults than children and the number of people decreases from the age of 60 onwards as mortality rises. In 2001 a fifth (20 per cent) of the population was under 16 years of age and a similar proportion was aged 65 and over (17 per cent), but the majority (63 per cent) of the population were aged around working age – that is, between 16 and 64 years.[7] The age structure of the White British population contains a few peaks,

corresponding to a greater proportion of people in their 30s and 50s. These peaks reflect the baby boom immediately after the Second World War and again in the 1960s.

The distribution of men and women differs according to age. There are equal numbers of men and women among the largely working-age population between 16 and 64, slightly more males than females at younger ages but many more women than men at older ages. For example, among White British people under 16 years of age, 51 per cent were male and 49 per cent were female; conversely, among people aged 65 and over, 42 per cent were male and 58 per cent were female, reflecting the longer life expectancy of women.[7] The slightly greater number of males than females among people under 16 is typical for most populations, including ethnic minority populations. The greater number of women among people over 65 years of age is typical for White, Mixed and Chinese populations but different to the pattern among Black and Asian populations, which generally have more men than women at older ages.

The White British population includes people from very different socio-economic backgrounds. In 2001 one in three (34 per cent) White British men of working age was in a managerial or professional occupation (Figure 2.13). This proportion is similar to that for Indian men but considerably greater than that for Pakistani or Bangladeshi men. A further one in three (35 per cent) White British men was in a routine or

Figure 2.13

White British working-age population:[1] by National Statistics Socio-economic Classification[2] and sex, April 2001

Great Britain

Percentages

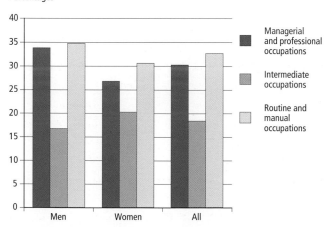

Legend:
- Managerial and professional occupations
- Intermediate occupations
- Routine and manual occupations

1 Men aged 16–64, women aged 16–59.
2 See Appendix Chapter 2.

Source: Census 2001, Office for National Statistics; Census 2001, General Register Office for Scotland

manual occupation; a proportion higher than that for Pakistani, Indian, Black African and Chinese men but smaller than that for Bangladeshi and Black Caribbean men.

The pattern was similar for White British women but the proportions in a managerial or professional (27 per cent) or routine or manual occupational group (31 per cent) were smaller than the proportions among White British men. Women were more likely than men to be in the intermediate occupational group (20 per cent and 17 per cent respectively). Although women are generally less likely than men to be in a managerial or professional occupation, White British women were among the most likely of all women to be in such an occupation, a characteristic they shared with White Irish and Black Caribbean women. These three groups were around three times as likely as Pakistani or Bangladeshi women to be in a managerial or professional occupational group (Appendix Table A2.2). The difference partly reflects the much smaller number of Pakistani and Bangladeshi women in employment in 2001 (Chapter 5).

The White Irish population

Great Britain has a long history of Irish immigration. Large-scale emigration from Ireland followed the potato famines in the 19th century and continued throughout the 20th century. The United States was the favoured destination for Irish emigrants up until the introduction of immigration quotas in the 1930s. After that, migration to Great Britain increased and then increased considerably following the Second World War.[8]

In 2001 the White Irish population accounted for 691,000 people, 1 per cent of the population of Great Britain (Table 2.1). The number of people identifying as White Irish in the 2001 Census does not appear to reflect the pattern of large-scale migration from Ireland. For example, net emigration from Southern Ireland in just the single decade between 1951 and 1961 totalled 409,000 – around 60 per cent of the total number of White Irish recorded in the 2001 Census.[8] Not all of those who emigrated from Ireland came to Great Britain and some who came may have since returned to Ireland, but these factors are unlikely to fully account for the relatively small size of the White Irish population in 2001. The size of Great Britain's White Irish population may be affected by an unwillingness of people born in Ireland, or their UK-born descendants, to identify as Irish. Surveys undertaken in preparation for the 1991 Census indicated that many people born in Ireland did not want to record their identity as Irish.[9] This may be particularly true for people born in Northern Ireland; in the 2001 Census, the majority of people born in Northern Ireland, and living in

Great Britain, identified as White British (72 per cent) rather than White Irish (26 per cent). People born in the Republic of Ireland, and living in Great Britain, were more likely to identify as White Irish (89 per cent) than White British (10 per cent).[10]

Also, analysis of households suggests that the White Irish population recorded in the 2001 Census may not include the children and grand-children of White Irish people. Many children in households headed by White Irish people were classified as White British (Chapter 1). In this respect, the White Irish population differs from many non-White immigrant populations; for example, the descendants of Indian, Black Caribbean and Pakistani immigrants generally retain their parents' ethnic group. This difference in ethnic identification between the descendants of White and non-White immigrants is partly due to the ethnic classification; it reflects the availability of White British as an ethnic category which can be selected by British-born descendants of immigrants, while Black British or Asian British are not categories available for selection. Changing ethnic identification among the descendants of White Irish people has implications for the age structure, household and labour market characteristics of the White Irish population.

The majority (64 per cent) of the White Irish population in Great Britain were born in the Republic of Ireland. A further one in five (21 per cent) had been born in England, 2 per cent in Scotland and less than 1 per cent in Wales (Table 2.14 overleaf). One in ten (10 per cent) of the White Irish population had been born in Northern Ireland.

The proportion of White Irish people born in the UK (34 per cent) is considerably smaller than for many non-White populations. For example, UK-born people accounted for around half, or more, of Indian (46 per cent), Bangladeshi (46 per cent), Pakistani (55 per cent) and Black Caribbean (58 per cent) populations in 2001. The difference reflects the tendency for Irish descendants to identify as White British rather than White Irish.

Both the Republic of Ireland and Northern Ireland have a strong historical and present-day connection to the Christian faith and this is reflected in the religious profile of Great Britain's White Irish population. They were more likely than their White British counterparts to identify as Christian (86 per cent compared with 76 per cent) and less likely to have no religion (6 per cent compared with 16 per cent) (Table 2.3).

As demonstrated by the population pyramid (Figure 2.5), the White Irish population have the oldest age structure of any ethnic group in Great Britain. In 2001, only 6 per cent of the

Table **2.14**

White Irish population: by region of birth, April 2001

Great Britain	Percentages
United Kingdom	**34.2**
England	20.9
Northern Ireland	10.2
Scotland	2.4
Wales	0.7
United Kingdom not specified[1,2]	-
Other Europe	**64.2**
Republic of Ireland	63.8
Rest of Europe	0.4
Africa	**0.4**
Asia	**0.2**
North America[3]	**0.6**
South America[2]	**-**
Oceania	**0.3**
Other[2]	**-**
All White Irish	**691,232**

1 Includes respondents who didn't specify where in the United
   Kingdom.
2 '-' negligible (less than 0.05).
3 Includes the Caribbean and West Indies.

Source: Census 2001, Office for National Statistics; Census 2001, General Register Office for Scotland

White Irish population were under 16 years of age while four times that proportion (25 per cent) was aged 65 and over.[7] As discussed previously, this is partly due to Irish descendants not being included in the White Irish population but their older age structure also partly reflects their earlier settlement compared with other ethnic minority groups.[11] In contrast to the White Irish population in Great Britain, the populations of both Northern Ireland and the Republic of Ireland have a relatively young age structure; a fifth or more of these populations being under 16 years of age.[12]

Irish migration to Great Britain differs from migration from some other regions, particularly from South Asia, in that women are just as likely as men to be primary labour migrants.[8] The sex ratio is similar to most ethnic groups in some respects; there are slightly more males than females among people under 16 years of age (51 and 49 per cent respectively) and conversely more women than men among the largely working-age population between 16 and 64 years (51 per cent and 49 per cent respectively). However, there are many more women than men in the 65 and over age group (58 per cent and 42 per cent respectively) – a pattern typical for White populations.[7]

In occupational terms, the historical stereotype of the Irish manual labourer bears no relation to the factual evidence

about the occupational structure of the White Irish population in Great Britain in 2001. More than one in three men and women of working age belonged to a managerial or professional occupational group, the highest proportion for any ethnic group (Figure 2.15).

The proportion of White Irish men in a routine or manual occupational group, at 29 per cent, was smaller than the proportion among White British, Pakistani, Bangladeshi and Black Caribbean men (Appendix Table A2.2). But it is not possible to discern the socio-economic position of the descendants of Irish immigrants because many will have been included in the White British population.

Figure **2.15**

White Irish working-age population:[1] by National Statistics Socio-economic Classification[2] and sex, April 2001

Great Britain

Percentages

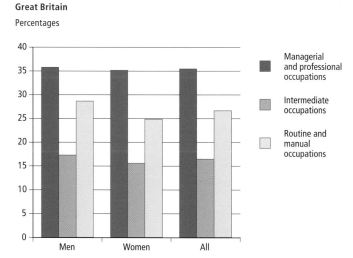

1 Men aged 16–64, women aged 16–59.
2 See Appendix Chapter 2.

Source: Census 2001, Office for National Statistics; Census 2001, General Register Office for Scotland

The Indian population

There has been an Indian presence in Great Britain since the 18th century but mass migration from the Indian subcontinent began in the 1950s.[13] The peak of Indian migration followed Black Caribbean migration but preceded Pakistani and Bangladeshi migration.[14] In 2001, together with their British-born descendants, Indians formed the largest ethnic minority group in Great Britain, numbering just over a million people. As such, they accounted for 2 per cent of the total population (Table 2.1).

The Indian population includes many different religious and regional groups. These include Sikhs and Hindus from the

Punjab region in India as well as Hindus and Muslims from the Gujarat region. The population also includes East African Indians, mainly Hindu, from Kenya, Uganda and Tanzania; these groups came to Great Britain as refugees, many years after previously having migrated from India to East Africa. The Indian population is characterised by caste membership; although castes are not covered in this report they contribute to the differentiation within the Indian population.[15]

By 2001 a third (35 per cent) of Great Britain's Indian population had been born in India, 13 per cent had been born in East Africa, particularly Kenya (8 per cent), and almost half had been born in the UK (46 per cent) (Table 2.16). The proportion born in the UK had, as expected, increased slightly since the 1991 Census, when 41 per cent had been born in the UK, 37 per cent in India and 17 per cent in the East African Commonwealth countries.[16]

Hindus formed the largest religious group within the Indian population in Great Britain in 2001 (45 per cent) but there was also a large Sikh population (29 per cent), as well as Muslim (13 per cent) and Christian (5 per cent) populations (Table 2.3).

Table **2.16**

Indian population: by region of birth, April 2001

Great Britain	Percentages
United Kingdom	**45.9**
England	44.8
Scotland	0.7
Wales	0.3
Northern Ireland[1]	-
United Kingdom not specified[2]	0.1
Other Europe	**0.2**
Africa	**16.0**
Kenya	7.9
Uganda	2.9
Tanzania	1.9
Rest of Africa	3.3
Asia	**36.6**
India	34.6
Rest of Asia	2.1
North America[3]	**0.3**
South America	**0.2**
Oceania	**0.2**
Other	**0.6**
All Indians	**1,051,844**

1 '-' negligible (less than 0.05).
2 Includes respondents who didn't specify where in the United Kingdom.
3 Includes the Caribbean and West Indies.

Source: Census 2001, Office for National Statistics; Census 2001, General Register Office for Scotland

Because the majority of Sikhs and Hindus are Indian their countries of birth follow the pattern for Indians, but there are some differences. In 2001 Sikhs were more likely than Hindus to have been born in the UK (56 per cent and 37 per cent respectively) and India (35 per cent and 30 per cent respectively) but less likely to have been born in Africa (6 per cent and 21 per cent).[17]

The Indian population is younger than the White British, White Irish and Black Caribbean populations but older than the Pakistani and Bangladeshi populations. Twenty-three per cent of Indians were under 16 years of age in 2001 while 7 per cent were aged 65 and over.[7] As the population pyramid shows (Figure 2.6), the majority of Indians are around 20 to 50 years old.

Overall, there are equal numbers of men and women in the Indian population (50 per cent respectively). The first Indian migrants were more likely to be men than women but family reunion and fertility have modified the earlier sex imbalance.[16] In common with most ethnic groups there were more males than females aged under 16 (51 per cent and 49 per cent respectively). Conversely, there were more women (51 per cent) than men (49 per cent) in the largely working-age population between 16 and 64 years.[7] Again, this was not unusual – there were slightly more women than men between the ages of 16 and 64 years in all ethnic minority groups except the Pakistani group, in which there were equal proportions of men and women, and the Other Asian group, which unusually had more men than women between 16 and 64 years.

The occupational pattern for Indian men was similar in some respects to that for White British men. In both groups, a third of working-age men (34 per cent) were in a managerial or professional occupational group and 17 per cent were in an intermediate occupational group. But Indian men were less likely than White British men to be in a routine or manual occupation, 26 per cent compared with 35 per cent (Figure 2.17 overleaf).

The pattern among women was different. Among Indian women of working age, 23 per cent were in a managerial or professional occupational group, slightly less than the proportion among White British women (27 per cent). Part of the explanation lies with the lower proportion of Indian women in employment; Indian women were more likely than their White British counterparts to be classified as Never worked or long-term unemployed (13 per cent and 4 per cent respectively) (Appendix Table A2.2). This reflects higher rates of economic inactivity among women from South Asian groups (Chapter 5).

Figure **2.17**

Indian working-age population:[1] by National Statistics Socio-economic Classification[2] and sex, April 2001

Great Britain

Percentages

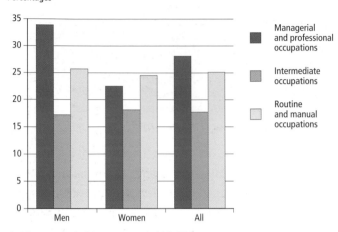

1 Men aged 16–64, women aged 16–59.
2 See Appendix Chapter 2.

Source: Census 2001, Office for National Statistics; Census 2001, General Register Office for Scotland

Indians were more likely than Pakistanis and Bangladeshis of working age to be in a managerial or professional occupational group, 28 per cent compared with 14 per cent and 11 per cent respectively. This corresponds with higher levels of educational attainment in the Indian population – in 2004 a quarter of the Indian population held a degree qualification compared with 12 per cent of the Pakistani and 8 per cent of the Bangladeshi population.[18] A relatively large proportion of Indians of working age were classified as full-time students (15 per cent) in 2001, partly reflecting the young age structure of the population. This was greater than the proportion of full-time students among White British people (7 per cent), but not greater than the proportion among Pakistani (16 per cent) and Bangladeshi people of working age (17 per cent) (Appendix Table A2.2).

The Pakistani population

Mass migration from Pakistan took place from the 1960s with the arrival of male economic migrants to the UK and continued through the 1970s and 1980s with family reunion.[19] Pakistani migrants, together with their British-born descendants, accounted for almost three-quarters of a million people (747,000) in 2001, making up 1 per cent of the Great Britain population (Table 2.1).

Much of the growth in the Pakistani population in Great Britain since the 1960s can be accounted for by births rather than immigration; by 2001 more than half (55 per cent) of Great Britain's Pakistani population had been born in the UK. The

majority had been born in England (52 per cent), with 2 per cent born in Scotland and 1 per cent in Wales, reflecting settlement patterns (Table 2.18).

Virtually all Pakistanis (92 per cent) identified as Muslim in the 2001 Census and, of the minority of cases that were not Muslim, most were classified as Religion not stated (6 per cent). It is possible that those who did not disclose their religion shared a Muslim background, as they were neither classified as having no religion nor classified as belonging to any other religion; 1 per cent of Pakistanis had no religion in 2001 and 1 per cent identified with any religion other than Islam.[20]

Although most Pakistanis are Muslim, they accounted for less than half (43 per cent) of Great Britain's Muslims in 2001; the Muslim population contains many other ethnic groups, including Bangladeshi (16 per cent), Indian (8 per cent), Black African (6 per cent), Other White (7 per cent), Other Asian (6 per cent) and White British (4 per cent) (Table 2.3).

The Pakistani population pyramid has a pronounced triangular shape, revealing a concentration of people at younger ages (Figure 2.7). In 2001, 35 per cent of Pakistanis were under 16 and only 4 per cent were aged 65 and over.[7] The median age for Pakistani men and women was 22 years (Appendix Table A2.1).

Table **2.18**

Pakistani population: by region of birth, April 2001

Great Britain

	Percentages
United Kingdom	**55.0**
England	51.9
Scotland	2.3
Wales	0.7
Northern Ireland[1]	-
United Kingdom not specified[2]	0.1
Other Europe	**0.4**
Africa	**1.0**
Asia	**43.2**
Pakistan	39.6
Rest of Asia	3.5
North America[3]	**0.1**
South America[1]	**-**
Oceania[1]	**-**
Other	**0.4**
All Pakistanis	**746,619**

1 '-' negligible (less than 0.05).
2 Includes respondents who didn't specify where in the United Kingdom.
3 Includes the Caribbean and West Indies.

Source: Census 2001, Office for National Statistics; Census 2001, General Register Office for Scotland

The sex distribution among Pakistanis under 16 years of age follows the typical pattern, with slightly more males (51 per cent) than females (49 per cent). Among the population between 16 and 64 years of age there was an equal proportion of men and women. But, as shown in the population pyramid, there were more men (55 per cent) than women (45 per cent) among those aged 65 and over.[7] This may reflect spousal age differences in the Pakistani population, wives tending to be younger than their husbands.[21]

In 2001 one in seven (14 per cent) Pakistanis of working age were in a managerial or professional group but a larger proportion (23 per cent) were in a routine or manual occupational group, the reverse of the pattern observed for most ethnic groups (Figure 2.19). There was also a significant sex difference, with Pakistani men of working age almost twice as likely as Pakistani women to be in a managerial or professional occupational group, 18 per cent compared with 10 per cent respectively. The relatively small proportion of women classified to any occupational group reflects the large proportion of Pakistani women of working age who were economically inactive.[22] More than two-fifths (44 per cent) of Pakistani women of working age were classified as Never worked or long-term unemployed (Appendix Table A2.2). The relatively high rate of economic inactivity among Pakistani women is discussed in Chapter 5.

Figure **2.19**

Pakistani working-age population:[1] by National Statistics Socio-economic Classification[2] and sex, April 2001

Great Britain
Percentages

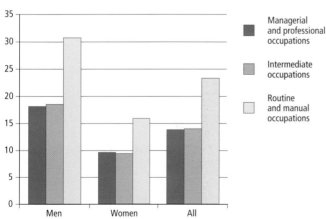

Legend:
- Managerial and professional occupations
- Intermediate occupations
- Routine and manual occupations

1 Men aged 16–64, women aged 16–59.
2 See Appendix Chapter 2.

Source: Census 2001, Office for National Statistics; Census 2001, General Register Office for Scotland

The occupational pattern for the Pakistani population contrasts with their Indian counterparts, partly reflecting the regions from which the groups originated. The majority of Pakistanis in Great Britain are of Punjabi descent, in common with some Indians. But, while parts of the Punjab are relatively developed in economic terms, many Pakistani migrants came from the less developed rural areas.[23] Related to this, Pakistani migrants tended to have fewer skills and qualifications and lower levels of English language fluency than Indian migrants.[24] These differences have had, and continue to have, a profound impact on the relative socio-economic positions of the South Asian ethnic groups resident in Great Britain.

The Bangladeshi population

Bangladesh came into existence in 1971 when it became independent from Pakistan. The majority of the Bangladeshi population in Great Britain originate from one district, Sylhet, in the north east of Bangladesh. Migration from this region began before the 1960s but increased thereafter. Male economic migrants arrived first and rapid expansion of the population occurred during the 1980s as men were joined by their wives and dependants from Bangladesh.[25]

Family reunion was accompanied by births and by 1991, 36 per cent of Great Britain's Bangladeshi population had been born in the UK.[26] Ten years later, this proportion had increased to almost half (46 per cent), close to the proportion who had been born in Bangladesh (52 per cent) (Table 2.20 overleaf). Despite relatively fast population growth, the Bangladeshi population remains the second smallest of the main ethnic groups in Great Britain, after the Chinese population. In 2001, the population accounted for 283,000 people, making it, at 0.5 per cent of the population in Great Britain, considerably smaller than the Indian and Pakistani populations (Table 2.1).

Most Bangladeshi immigrants to the UK settled in England and the countries of birth of the Bangladeshi population in 2001 reflect this – 45 per cent had been born in England, 1 per cent in Wales, and less than 0.5 per cent in either Scotland or Northern Ireland (Table 2.20 overleaf).

The Bangladeshi population is similar to the Pakistani population in terms of their religious affiliation, with nine in ten (92 per cent) Bangladeshis classified as Muslim in the 2001 Census. Virtually all of the remainder were classified as Religion not stated (6 per cent) and, as with the Pakistani population, it is possible that these people shared a Muslim background, being neither classified to another religion nor classified as having no religion.[20]

Table **2.20**

Bangladeshi population: by region of birth, April 2001

Great Britain	Percentages
United Kingdom	**46.4**
England	45.0
Wales	0.9
Scotland	0.3
Northern Ireland[1]	-
United Kingdom not specified[2]	0.2
Other Europe	**0.1**
Africa	**0.1**
Asia	**52.8**
Bangladesh	51.7
Rest of Asia	1.1
North America[1,3]	**-**
South America[1]	**-**
Oceania[1]	**-**
Other	**0.6**
All Bangladeshis	**282,811**

1 '-' negligible (less than 0.05).
2 Includes respondents who didn't specify where in the United Kingdom.
3 Includes the Caribbean and West Indies.

Source: Census 2001, Office for National Statistics; Census 2001, General Register Office for Scotland

The Bangladeshi population living in Great Britain is one of the youngest ethnic populations, 38 per cent were under the age of 16 and only 3 per cent were aged 65 and over.[7] As with the Pakistani population, their young age profile reflects a number of factors, including their recent immigration to Great Britain, a greater proportion of women of child-bearing age and a cultural preference for larger families (Chapter 4).

The population pyramid for the Bangladeshi group has the most pronounced triangular shape of all populations, highlighting a concentration of children and young people (Figure 2.8). The pyramid also reveals a greater proportion of men than women at older ages. Among those aged 65 and over, men outnumbered women by a ratio of two men to every woman, women making up only 34 per cent of this age group. This reflects both the tendency for men to emigrate before women and spousal age differences in the Bangladeshi population, with wives tending to be younger than their husbands.[21] In other respects the Bangladeshi population had a similar sex structure to most other groups, with slightly more males than females among those aged under 16 (51 per cent and 49 per cent respectively) and the exact reverse among those aged between 16 and 64.

In occupational terms, Bangladeshis were the least likely of all ethnic groups to be in a managerial or professional occupation. Just over one in ten (11 per cent) Bangladeshis of working age belonged to this group in 2001. More than twice as many were in a routine or manual occupational group (27 per cent) (Figure 2.21).

Among men, 14 per cent were in a managerial or professional occupational group, the lowest proportion among all ethnic groups, and 40 per cent were in a routine or manual occupational group, the highest among all ethnic groups. Among women, just 8 per cent were in a managerial or professional occupational group – again lowest among all ethnic groups – and 15 per cent were in a routine or manual occupational group. Half (49 per cent) of Bangladeshi women of working age were classified as Never worked or long-term unemployed, similar to Pakistani counterparts (Appendix Table A2.2). This corresponds with high rates of female economic inactivity in the Bangladeshi, and Pakistani, populations (Chapter 5).

Figure **2.21**

Bangladeshi working-age population:[1] by National Statistics Socio-economic Classification[2] and sex, April 2001

Great Britain

Percentages

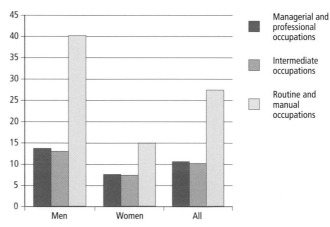

1 Men aged 16–64, women aged 16–59.
2 See Appendix Chapter 2.

Source: Census 2001, Office for National Statistics; Census 2001, General Register Office for Scotland

The Black Caribbean population

The 1950s and early 1960s were periods of mass migration from the Caribbean in response to labour shortages in Great Britain.[27] The sex distribution of migrants from the Caribbean differed from the pattern among South Asian migrants – those from the Caribbean generally came as families rather than men arriving first and being joined by wives and children later.[28] By 2001 the Black Caribbean population numbered roughly half a million people (566,000), and accounted for about 1 per cent of the population of Great Britain (Table 2.1). This was half as many as the Indian population, nearly a third smaller than the Pakistani population, and only slightly larger than the other main Black ethnic group, Black Africans.

In 2001, the main countries of birth of Great Britain's Black Caribbean population were England (57 per cent) and Jamaica (23 per cent). Much smaller proportions were born in Barbados (3 per cent), Trinidad and Tobago, Guyana and Grenada (each around 2 per cent) (Table 2.22).

Caribbean migrants differed from the majority of South Asian migrants in sharing the Christian religious background of the White British population. In 2001, 74 per cent were classified as Christian and 11 per cent had no religion, a profile very similar to the White British population (Table 2.3). Less than one in a

Table 2.22

Black Caribbean population: by region of birth, April 2001

Great Britain	Percentages
United Kingdom	**57.9**
England	57.3
Wales	0.4
Scotland	0.1
Northern Ireland[1]	-
United Kingdom not specified[1,2]	-
Other Europe	**0.2**
Africa	**0.4**
Asia	**0.1**
North America[3]	**38.5**
Jamaica	23.2
Barbados	3.4
Trinidad and Tobago	2.2
Grenada	1.6
Rest of North America	8.2
South America	**1.9**
Guyana	1.8
Rest of South America	0.1
Oceania[1]	**-**
Other	**1.0**
All Black Caribbeans	**565,621**

1 '-' negligible (less than 0.05).
2 Includes respondents who didn't specify where in the United Kingdom.
3 Includes the Caribbean and West Indies.

Source: Census 2001, Office for National Statistics; Census 2001, General Register Office for Scotland

hundred (1 per cent) Black Caribbean people identified themselves as Muslim in 2001 but they were six times more likely than White British people to do so.[20]

The Black Caribbean population is younger than the White British population, but has the oldest age profile among the non-White groups, partly reflecting their earlier settlement in Great Britain. In 2001 the median age was 35 years for men and 36 years for women (Appendix Table A2.1). One in ten (11 per cent) of the Black Caribbean population was aged 65 and over.[7]

The age/sex pyramid for the Black Caribbean population reveals three peaks, at around 60, 38 and 16 years of age (Figure 2.9). The upper segment of the pyramid reflects the peak of Black Caribbean immigration.[29] The second segment, in the middle of the pyramid, mostly reflects the second generation, who are larger in numbers than the first generation and who were predominantly born in Great Britain. The third segment, at the bottom of the pyramid, reflects the third generation, almost entirely born in Great Britain.

The Black Caribbean population pyramid shows more women than men between the ages of 20 to 60 years (Figure 2.9). This imbalance was reflected in the working-age population; women accounted for 56 per cent of the Black Caribbean population aged between 16 and 64 years. The 1991 Census showed a similar pattern.[29] Possible reasons for the imbalance include a potential undercount of Black Caribbean men in the Census as well as a greater likelihood of Black Caribbean men to emigrate.[30] There are equal numbers of males and female in the Black Caribbean population under 16 years of age (50 per cent respectively) and slightly more men than women in the population aged 65 and over (51 per cent and 49 per cent respectively).

Although many Black Caribbean migrants came to Great Britain to fill routine or manual occupations, the population in 2001 had a socio-economic distribution broadly similar to the White British population. Among the working-age population, 28 per cent belonged to a managerial or professional occupational group and 30 per cent to a routine or manual occupational group. The overall figures conceal marked variations between the sexes (Figure 2.23 overleaf).

The Black Caribbean population in Great Britain is exceptional in that women are more likely than men to be in a managerial or professional occupational group, 30 per cent compared with 24 per cent in 2001. In all other ethnic groups, either the proportion of men and women in a managerial or professional occupational group was similar or men were more likely to be in this group. Black Caribbean women were more likely than

Figure **2.23**

Black Caribbean working-age population:[1] by National Statistics Socio-economic Classification[2] and sex, April 2001

Great Britain

Percentages

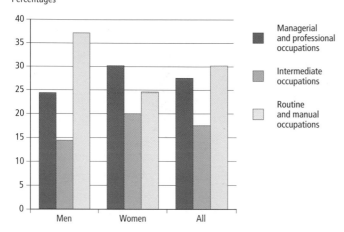

1 Men aged 16–64, women aged 16–59.
2 See Appendix Chapter 2.

Source: Census 2001, Office for National Statistics; Census 2001, General Register Office for Scotland

women from any other group, except White Irish women, to be in a managerial or professional occupational group (Appendix Table A2.2). It is possible that many of these women occupied professional or management positions within the public sector – around half (54 per cent) of Black Caribbean women in employment worked in public administration, education or health in 2004.[31] Black Caribbean women have a higher rate of economic activity than South Asian – particularly Pakistani and Bangladeshi – women (see Chapter 5, Employment and Labour Market Participation). These variations are partly related to differences in the early migration patterns of these groups; Black Caribbean women having come to Great Britain as economic migrants in their own right.

Black Caribbean men, by comparison, were concentrated in routine or manual occupations in 2001. They were one of only three populations (along with Pakistanis and Bangladeshis) where the proportion of men in a routine or manual occupation (37 per cent) exceeded the proportion in a managerial or professional occupation (24 per cent) (Appendix Table A2.2).

The Black African population

The Black African population has a long history of small-scale settlement in Great Britain with communities established from the late 1940s onwards in the seaports of Liverpool, Cardiff and London. Migration for the purposes of obtaining training and education has always been a key feature of Black African

migration to Great Britain. Since the 1970s political instability across the African continent has contributed to increased migration.[32] By April 2001, the Black African population, at 485,000 people, was approaching the size of the Black Caribbean population and accounted for just under 1 per cent of the population in Great Britain (Table 2.1).

The Black African population is one of the most diverse in terms of geographic origins. In 2001 it included people born in Nigeria (16 per cent), Ghana (10 per cent), Somalia (8 per cent), Zimbabwe (4 per cent), Uganda, Sierra Leone and Kenya (3 per cent respectively) (Table 2.24). The proportion born in the UK, at 34 per cent, was considerably smaller than the proportion among the Black Caribbean population, and smaller than the proportion among all other non-White groups except the Chinese, reflecting their later migration to the UK.

Table **2.24**

Black African population: by region of birth, April 2001

Great Britain	Percentages
United Kingdom	**33.7**
England	32.8
Scotland	0.4
Wales	0.4
Northern Ireland[1]	-
United Kingdom not specified[2]	0.1
Other Europe	**1.1**
Africa	**62.7**
Nigeria	15.9
Ghana	10.4
Somalia	8.2
Zimbabwe	3.8
Uganda	3.1
Sierra Leone	3.1
Kenya	2.8
Rest of Africa	15.4
Asia	**0.5**
North America[3]	**0.9**
South America	**0.1**
Oceania[1]	**-**
Other	**1.1**
All Black Africans	**484,783**

1 '-' negligible (less than 0.05).
2 Includes respondents who didn't specify where in the United Kingdom.
3 Includes the Caribbean and West Indies.

Source: Census 2001, Office for National Statistics; Census 2001, General Register Office for Scotland

As their countries of origin suggest, Black Africans living in Great Britain form distinct populations, different from each other on many characteristics including religious affiliation and socio-economic background. In addition, they have come to Great Britain for diverse reasons, some as economic migrants, others as students and others as refugees seeking asylum.

In 2001, seven in ten (69 per cent) Black Africans were Christian and two in ten (20 per cent) were Muslim. They were far less likely than the Black Caribbean population to have no religion, just 2 per cent of Black Africans having no religion in 2001.[20] Although Black Africans were more likely to be Christian than Muslim they made up just 1 per cent of the Christian population but 6 per cent of the Muslim population (Table 2.3).

The Black African population has a young age profile, in common with most ethnic minority populations. In 2001, the median age for Black Africans was 27 years for men and 28 for women; this was younger than the median age for White, Indian and Black Caribbean groups but older than the median age for Pakistani and Bangladeshi groups (Appendix Table A2.1). Three in ten (30 per cent) Black Africans were under 16 while only one in fifty (2 per cent) were aged 65 and over.[7]

The population pyramid shows slightly more women than men between the ages of 20 to 40 years (Figure 2.10). This was reflected in the largely working-age population between 16 and 64 years, where there were more women (53 per cent) than men (47 per cent). Conversely, there were more men (52 per cent) than women (48 per cent) among those aged 65 and over. There was no sex imbalance in the population under 16 years.

In occupational terms, the proportion of Black Africans of working age in a managerial or professional occupation (26 per cent) was larger than the proportion in a routine or manual occupation (23 per cent) (Figure 2.25). The proportion of Black Africans in a managerial or professional occupational group was similar to the proportion among Black Caribbean and Indian counterparts – they were slightly less likely than White groups, but more likely than Pakistani and Bangladeshi groups, to be in such an occupation. The Black African population of working age included a large proportion of full time students (24 per cent), second only to the Chinese population (30 per cent) (Appendix Table A2.2).

The Chinese population

The Chinese group is diverse in terms of geographic origins. Large scale migration occurred from the 1960s with economic migrants from Hong Kong, Malaysia and Singapore coming to

Figure **2.25**

Black African working-age population:[1] by National Statistics Socio-economic Classification[2] and sex, April 2001

Great Britain

Percentages

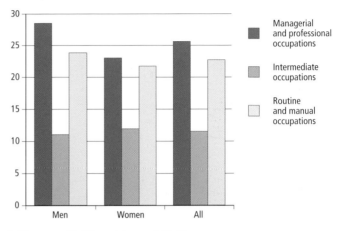

1 Men aged 16–64, women aged 16–59.
2 See Appendix Chapter 2.

Source: Census 2001, Office for National Statistics; Census 2001, General Register Office for Scotland

Great Britain – partly in response to deteriorating economic conditions in rural Hong Kong and partly as a means of obtaining better education and career opportunities.[33] Migration from mainland China started as early as the late 19th century but from the 1980s onwards there has been a resurgence of immigration, with many people coming from China to study. In 2001, the Chinese population in Great Britain numbered 243,000 people. As such, it was the smallest of the main ethnic groups identified in the 2001 Census (Table 2.1).

The countries of birth of the Chinese population in Great Britain reflect the immigration patterns described above. In 2001 the main countries of birth were Hong Kong (29 per cent), England (25 per cent) and China (19 per cent). There were smaller populations from Malaysia (8 per cent), Vietnam (4 per cent), Singapore (3 per cent) and Taiwan (2 per cent) (Table 2.26 overleaf).

The proportion born in the UK (29 per cent) was the smallest of all non-White populations and has changed very little in the decade between 1991 and 2001. While the overall Chinese population increased from 157,000 to 243,000 between 1991 and 2001, the proportion born in the UK remained almost the same – 28 per cent in 1991 and 29 per cent in 2001. Over the same period, the proportion born in Hong Kong declined from 34 per cent to 29 per cent, along with smaller declines in the proportions born in Malaysia, Singapore and Vietnam.

Table **2.26**

Chinese population: by region of birth, April 2001

Great Britain	Percentages
United Kingdom	**28.7**
England	25.2
Scotland	2.4
Wales	0.9
Northern Ireland	0.1
United Kingdom not specified[1,2]	-
Other Europe	**0.6**
Africa	**1.0**
Asia	**68.0**
Hong Kong	28.7
China	18.7
Malaysia	8.4
Vietnam	4.2
Singapore	3.2
Taiwan	2.2
Rest of Asia	2.6
North America[3]	**0.7**
South America	**0.2**
Oceania	**0.3**
Other	**0.5**
All Chinese	**243,258**

1 Includes respondents who didn't specify where in the United
  Kingdom.
2 '-' negligible (less than 0.05).
3 Includes the Caribbean and West Indies.

Source: Census 2001, Office for National Statistics; Census 2001, General Register Office for Scotland

Conversely, the proportion born in China and Taiwan increased from 13 per cent in 1991 to 21 per cent in 2001.[34]

Over half (53 per cent) of Chinese people in Great Britain had no religion in 2001 and they were the most likely of all ethnic groups to have no religion.[20] Christianity was the most common religion in the Chinese population (21 per cent). One in seven Chinese people (15 per cent) identified as Buddhist but they were not the largest ethnic group within the Buddhist population; Chinese people made up 25 per cent of the Buddhist population while White British people made up 34 per cent (Table 2.3).

The Chinese population is older than many ethnic minority groups although they are younger than the White population. Three-quarters (76 per cent) of the Chinese population in 2001 were aged between 16 and 64, a fifth (19 per cent) were under 16 years of age and 5 per cent were 65 and over.[7]

The shape of the Chinese population pyramid (Figure 2.11) reflects the various migration waves described previously. The pyramid has a narrow base and a very wide middle that grows gradually smaller towards the apex. The top of the pyramid reflects Chinese economic migrants who came over during the 1950s and 1960s. Students from mainland China are represented in the peak of young people in their early 20s.

The population pyramid for the Chinese group shows slightly more men than women in their early 20s (Figure 2.11). However, overall there are more Chinese women than men between the ages 16 to 64 years (52 per cent and 48 per cent respectively) and also in the population over 65 years of age (54 per cent and 46 per cent respectively).[7] A gender imbalance was also observed in the 1991 Census, which found more Chinese women than men; the imbalance was particularly marked among those born in South East Asia, where there were 161 women for every 100 men.[35]

In 2001 about one in four Chinese of working age was in a managerial or professional occupational group (24 per cent) and less than one in five was in an intermediate occupational group (18 per cent). The Chinese population of working age had the smallest proportion of any ethnic group in a routine or manual occupation (17 per cent) (Figure 2.27). Conversely, the Chinese population had the largest proportion of full-time students (30 per cent), corresponding with the immigration patterns described previously (Appendix Table A2.2). The pattern was similar for men and women.

Figure **2.27**

Chinese working-age population:[1] by National Statistics Socio-economic Classification[2] and sex, April 2001

Great Britain

Percentages

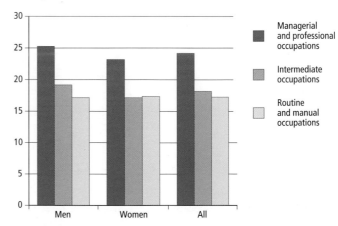

1 Men aged 16–64, women aged 16–59.
2 See Appendix Chapter 2.

Source: Census 2001, Office for National Statistics; Census 2001, General Register Office for Scotland

Notes and references

1. Although the ethnic group question in the 2001 Census in England and Wales presented a 16-group classification, five of the ethnic categories were non-specific 'Other' groups – Other White, Other Mixed, Other Asian, Other Black and Other Ethnic Group – and four were Mixed ethnic groups – Mixed White and Black Caribbean, Mixed White and Black African, Mixed White and Asian and Other Mixed. Both the Other ethnic groups and the Mixed ethnic groups have been profiled previously (see notes 3 and 4).

2. See Glossary for definition of median age.

3. Gardener D and Connolly H (2005) *Who are the 'Other' ethnic groups*? Available at: www.statistics.gov.uk/cci/article.asp?id=1291

4. Bradford B (2006) *Who are the 'Mixed' ethnic groups*? Available at: www.statistics.gov.uk/cci/article.asp?id=1580

5. Data on the ethnic populations in Northern Ireland are available on the NICA website at www.nicensus2001.gov.uk

6. See Glossary for definition of the economically inactive population.

7. Office for National Statistics (2004), 'Age and Sex', in *Focus on Ethnicity & Identity Overview report*. Available at: www.statistics.gov.uk/cci/nugget.asp?id=456 For data on age and sex by ethnic group follow links to Download data.

8. Chance J (1996) 'The Irish: invisible settlers', in Peach C (ed.) *Ethnicity in the 1991 Census, Volume 2*: The ethnic minority populations of Great Britain, HMSO: London, p 223.

9. Chance J (1996) 'The Irish: invisible settlers', in *Ethnicity in the 1991 Census, Volume 2*, HMSO: London, p 222.

10. Office for National Statistics (2004) *Census 2001 National report for England and Wales*, Table S102 Sex and country of birth by ethnic group, TSO: London, p123. Also available at: www.statistics.gov.uk/StatBase/ssdataset.asp?vlnk=7547

11. Rendall M and Salt J (2006) 'The foreign-born population', in (Chappell R ed.) *Focus on People and Migration*, Palgrave Macmillan: Basingstoke, Chapter 8, p150. Also available at: www.statistics.gov.uk/statbase/Product.asp?vlnk=12899

12. For data on the age structure of the populations in Northern Ireland and Republic of Ireland see www.nicensus2001.gov.uk and www.cso.ie/census/

13. Robinson V (1996) 'The Indians: onward and upward', in Peach C (ed.) *Ethnicity in the 1991 Census Volume 2: The ethnic minority populations of Great Britain*, HMSO: London, p 95.

14. Robinson V (1996) 'The Indians: onward and upward', in Peach C (ed.) *Ethnicity in the 1991 Census Volume 2: The ethnic minority populations of Great Britain*, HMSO: London, p 96.

15. Ballard R (1994) *Desh Pardesh: The South Asian Presence in Britain*, Hurst & Company: London.

16. Robinson V (1996) 'The Indians: onward and upward', in Peach C (ed.) *Ethnicity in the 1991 Census Volume 2: The ethnic minority populations of Great Britain*, HMSO: London, p98.

17. Office for National Statistics (2004) 'Country of Birth and National Identity', in *Focus on Religion Overview report*. Available at: www.statistics.gov.uk/cci/nugget.asp?id=958 For data on country of birth by religion follow links to Download data.

18. Office for National Statistics (2004) 'Education', in *Focus on Ethnicity & Identity Overview report*. Available at: www.statistics.gov.uk/cci/nugget.asp?id=461 For data on education by ethnic group follow links to Download data.

19. Ballard R (1996) 'The Pakistanis: stability and introspection', in Peach C (ed.) *Ethnicity in the 1991 Census Volume 2: The ethnic minority populations of Great Britain*, HMSO: London, pp 124–125.

20. Office for National Statistics (2004) 'Religion', in *Focus on Ethnicity Overview report*. Available at: www.statistics.gov.uk/cci/nugget.asp?id=460 For data on ethnicity by religion follow links to Download data.

21. Berrington A (1996) 'Marriage patterns and inter-ethnic unions', in Coleman D and Salt J (eds.) *Ethnicity in the 1991 Census Volume 1: Demographic characteristics of the ethnic minority populations*, HMSO: London, p 194.

22. See introduction of Employment and Labour Market Participation (Chapter 5) for definition of the economically inactive population.

23. Ballard R (1996) 'The Pakistanis: stability and introspection', in Peach C (ed.) *Ethnicity in the 1991 Census Volume 2: The ethnic minority populations of Great Britain*, HMSO: London, p 122.

24. Ballard R (1996) 'The Pakistanis: stability and introspection', in Peach C (ed.) *Ethnicity in the 1991 Census Volume 2: The ethnic minority populations of Great Britain*, HMSO: London, p 133.

25. Eade J, Vamplew T and Peach C (1996) 'The Bangladeshis: the encapsulated community', in Peach C (ed.) *Ethnicity in the 1991 Census Volume 2: The ethnic minority populations of Great Britain*, HMSO: London, pp 150–151.

26. Eade J, Vamplew T and Peach C (1996) 'The Bangladeshis: the encapsulated community', in Peach C (ed.) *Ethnicity in the 1991 Census Volume 2: The ethnic minority populations of Great Britain*, HMSO: London, p 151.

27. Peach C (1996) 'Black-Caribbeans: Class, gender and geography', in Peach C (ed.) *Ethnicity in the 1991 Census Volume 2: The ethnic minority populations of Great Britain*, HMSO: London, p 28.

28. Scott A, Pearce D and Goldblatt P (2001) The sizes and characteristics of the minority ethnic populations of Great Britain. *Population Trends* **105**, p 11.

29. Peach C (1996) 'Black-Caribbeans: Class, gender and geography', in Peach C (ed.) *Ethnicity in the 1991 Census Volume 2: The ethnic minority populations of Great Britain*, HMSO: London, p 31.

30. The ONS Longitudinal Study (LS) of England and Wales is available at: www.statistics.gov.uk/ls Data available on request.

31. Office for National Statistics (2004) 'Employment patterns', in *Focus on Ethnicity & Identity Overview report*. Available at: www.statistics.gov.uk/cci/nugget.asp?id=463 For data on employment by ethnic group follow links to Download data.

32. Daley P (1996) 'Black Africans: students who stayed', in Peach C (ed.) *Ethnicity in the 1991 Census Volume 2*: *The ethnic minority populations of Great Britain*, HMSO: London, p 44.

33. Cheng Y (1996) 'The Chinese: upwardly mobile', in Peach C (ed.) *Ethnicity in the 1991 Census Volume 2*: *The ethnic minority populations of Great Britain*, HMSO: London, pp 163–164.

34. Cheng Y (1996) 'The Chinese: upwardly mobile', in Peach C (ed.) *Ethnicity in the 1991 Census Volume 2*: *The ethnic minority populations of Great Britain*, HMSO: London, p 162.

35. Cheng Y (1996) 'The Chinese: upwardly mobile', in Peach C (ed.) *Ethnicity in the 1991 Census Volume 2*: *The ethnic minority populations of Great Britain*, HMSO: London, p 165.

Appendix Chapter 2: Population

National Statistics Socio-economic Classification (NS-SEC)

From 2001 the National Statistics Socio-economic Classification (NS-SEC) was adopted for all official surveys. It replaced Social Class based on Occupation (SC, formerly Registrar General's Social Class) and Socio-economic Groups (SEG).

The NS-SEC is an occupationally based classification but has rules to provide coverage of the whole adult population. The information required to create the NS-SEC is occupation coded to the unit groups (OUG) of the Standard Occupational Classification 2000 (SOC2000) and details of employment status (whether an employer, self-employed or employee; whether a supervisor; number of employees at the workplace). Similar information was previously required for SC and SEG.

The number of classes used depends both upon the analytic purposes at hand and the quality of available data. Within the conceptual model, it is possible to have eight, five and three class versions of NS-SEC. The nested relationship between the 8, 5 and 3-class versions is given below.

For complete coverage of the population, the three categories Students, Occupations not stated or inadequately described and Not classifiable for other reasons are added. These three categories are usually combined and shown as 'Not classified'. For the purpose of analysing ethnic groups, which tend to have large variations in the proportion of students, the category for 'Full-time student' is shown separately in Appendix Table A2.2.

Further information about NS-SEC can be found on the National Statistics website: www.statistics.gov.uk/methods_quality/ns_sec/default.asp

8 classes	5 classes	3 classes
1 Higher managerial and professional occupations	1 Managerial and professional occupations	1 Managerial and professional occupations
1.1 Large employers and higher managerial occupations		
1.2 Higher professional occupations		
2 Lower managerial and professional occupations		
3 Intermediate occupations	2 Intermediate occupations	2 Intermediate occupations
4 Small employees and own account workers	3 Small employers and own account workers	
5 Lower supervisory and and technical occupations	4 Lower supervisory and technical occupations	3 Routine and manual occupations
6 Semi-routine occupations	5 Semi-routine and routine occupations	
7 Routine occupations		
8 Never worked and long-term employed	Never worked and long-term employed	Never worked and long-term employed

Appendix Table A2.1

Median age:[1] by ethnic group, April 2001

Great Britain   Age

	Males	Females	All people
White British	38	40	39
White Irish	49	52	50
Other White	33	33	33
Mixed	15	16	16
Indian	30	31	31
Pakistani	22	22	22
Bangladeshi	21	21	21
Other Asian	31	30	30
Black Caribbean	35	36	35
Black African	27	28	27
Other Black	20	24	22
Chinese	27	30	29
Any other ethnic group	29	32	30
All ethnic groups	**36**	**38**	**37**

1 Median age of a population is the age that divides the population into two numerically equal groups.

Source: Census 2001, Office for National Statistics; Census 2001, General Register Office for Scotland

Appendix Table A2.2

Working-age population:[1] by National Statistics Socio-economic Classification,[2] sex and ethnic group, April 2001

Great Britain

Percentages

	Managerial and professional occupations	Intermediate occupations	Routine and manual occupations	Never worked and long-term unemployed	Full-time student	Occupation not stated or inadequately described
Men						
White British	33.8	16.7	34.7	3.0	6.6	5.4
White Irish	35.7	17.3	28.6	4.2	5.5	8.8
Other White	42.4	14.3	21.6	4.5	14.3	3.0
Mixed	28.4	12.5	26.6	8.1	20.9	3.4
Indian	33.9	17.2	25.7	3.5	15.7	4.1
Pakistani	18.1	18.5	30.7	8.7	18.2	5.8
Bangladeshi	13.6	12.9	40.1	8.5	18.8	6.2
Other Asian	30.9	15.7	23.9	9.0	16.8	3.7
Black Caribbean	24.4	14.4	37.2	9.0	9.5	5.6
Black African	28.5	11.0	23.8	10.1	24.6	2.0
Other Black	23.3	11.9	33.2	10.8	16.8	4.0
Chinese	25.3	19.3	17.2	3.4	32.9	2.0
Any other ethnic group	33.0	10.5	19.2	10.3	24.6	2.4
All men	**33.5**	**16.5**	**33.7**	**3.4**	**7.8**	**5.2**
Women						
White British	26.7	20.2	30.5	3.6	7.3	11.8
White Irish	35.1	15.5	24.8	4.9	6.2	13.5
Other White	35.5	17.3	18.7	7.1	13.4	7.9
Mixed	25.7	15.5	22.2	9.6	20.2	6.9
Indian	22.5	18.1	24.5	12.8	14.1	7.9
Pakistani	9.6	9.4	15.9	44.1	14.7	6.4
Bangladeshi	7.5	7.3	14.9	49.3	15.5	5.5
Other Asian	22.9	14.8	19.1	20.6	15.7	6.9
Black Caribbean	30.2	20.0	24.6	6.3	10.6	8.3
Black African	23.0	12.0	21.7	16.2	23.0	4.2
Other Black	24.2	17.3	25.4	9.4	16.9	6.9
Chinese	23.2	17.2	17.4	8.8	27.7	5.8
Any other ethnic group	23.5	12.5	22.2	16.1	18.7	7.1
All women	**26.7**	**19.6**	**29.3**	**5.0**	**8.2**	**11.3**
All people of working age						
White British	30.3	18.4	32.6	3.3	6.9	8.6
White Irish	35.4	16.4	26.6	4.6	5.8	11.2
Other White	38.7	15.9	20.0	5.9	13.9	5.6
Mixed	27.0	14.1	24.3	8.9	20.5	5.2
Indian	28.1	17.7	25.1	8.2	14.9	6.0
Pakistani	13.8	14.0	23.3	26.3	16.5	6.1
Bangladeshi	10.5	10.1	27.3	29.1	17.1	5.8
Other Asian	27.4	15.3	21.8	14.1	16.3	5.1
Black Caribbean	27.6	17.5	30.2	7.5	10.1	7.1
Black African	25.6	11.5	22.7	13.4	23.8	3.2
Other Black	23.8	14.8	29.0	10.0	16.9	5.6
Chinese	24.2	18.2	17.3	6.2	30.2	4.0
Any other ethnic group	27.5	11.6	21.0	13.6	21.2	5.1
All ethnic groups	**30.1**	**18.0**	**31.5**	**4.2**	**8.0**	**8.3**

1 Men aged 16–64 and women aged 16–59.
2 See Appendix Chapter 2.

Source: Census 2001, Office for National Statistics; Census 2001, General Register Office for Scotland

Geographic diversity

Frances Forsyth and David Gardener

Chapter 3

Introduction

This chapter looks at how different ethnic and religious groups are spread throughout Great Britain, and the relative sizes of their populations in each area, using data from the 2001 Census. This helps to illustrate the geographic distribution and concentration of each group. It adds to the existing literature in a number of ways, for example:

- by mapping the populations at small area level (see Box) using the most detailed ethnic and religious classifications

- by reporting on geographic variation by ethno-religious group

- by analysing the overall diversity of different areas using the Fractionalisation Index of diversity (see Ethnic and religious diversity by area)

Box 1

Geographic levels

The analysis describes the population distribution across different geographic levels: country, Government Office Region (GOR) in England, local authority areas, and smaller areas known as Middle-layer Super Output Areas (MSOAs). MSOAs, which contain on average 7,200 people, are the smallest unit used for area analysis in this chapter and are referred to as 'small areas'. More explanation of geographic terms is given in the Appendix at the end of this chapter, along with a reference map showing the position of each region and local authority.

Standard tables from the 2001 Census (published in 2002 and 2003) gave details of regional variations in the ethnic and religious composition of the population. The key differences at regional level are summarised here to provide the context for the analysis at smaller geographic levels:

- People from ethnic and religious minority groups were more highly concentrated in England than Scotland or Wales

- The London region was the most ethnically diverse of any in Great Britain, home to more than three-quarters of Great Britain's total Black African population, as well as six out of ten Black Caribbeans, half the Bangladeshi population, one in four Indians, one in three each of the White Irish, Mixed, and Chinese populations, and one in five Pakistanis

- Great Britain's Pakistani population was the least concentrated in London of any ethnic minority group, with large clusters in the West Midlands, Yorkshire and the Humber, and the North West

- Indians were also relatively well represented outside London, forming a substantial proportion of the population in several areas of the East and West Midlands

- The Mixed, Chinese and White Irish ethnic groups were generally more evenly spread out than the other ethnic minority groups

- Christians were relatively evenly spread across the regions

- More than half of Great Britain's Hindu and Jewish populations, and around a third of people from the Buddhist, Muslim and Sikh groups, lived in London

- The Sikh population was highly clustered outside London, with almost a third living in the West Midlands

- Muslims were among the more widely spread of the different religious populations at a regional level. Outside London, one in seven of Great Britain's Muslims lived in the West Midlands; one in eight lived in the North West and a further one in eight in Yorkshire and the Humber

Concentrations of specific ethnic groups within the population were more apparent at small area (MSOA) level than at local authority or regional level. In a few MSOAs, ethnic minority groups formed the majority of the local population. For example, Indians formed a majority in a small number of MSOAs in Leicester, as did Pakistanis in some MSOAs in Bradford, Birmingham and Rochdale, and Bangladeshis in some MSOAs in Tower Hamlets and Oldham. No other ethnic minority group formed a majority in any other MSOA; so, while Black Africans were to a large extent clustered in south London, they did not form a majority of the population in any MSOA. People from the Chinese and Mixed groups were the most spread out at MSOA level, making up no more than one in ten of the population of any area. While the White British ethnic group made up the majority of the population of each constituent country of Great Britain, each region, almost all local authorities, and most MSOAs, in a very small number of MSOAs less than one in ten of the population was White British, for example those around Southall in the London Borough of Ealing and Mosley in Birmingham.

Concentrations of specific religious minority populations were also more apparent at MSOA level. For instance, Muslims made up a majority of the population in MSOAs around Mosley and Yardley near the centre of Birmingham and in an MSOA near Frizinghall in Bradford. Hindus made up a majority in some MSOAs in the centre of Leicester. Similarly, the Jewish population made up almost half the population in an MSOA in Broughton in Salford, and around four in ten of the population of several MSOAs around Golders Green in the London

Borough of Barnet. Sikhs made up more than a third of the local population in MSOAs around Southall in the London Borough of Ealing and Handsworth in Birmingham.

Analysing geographic patterns by ethno-religious group shows further variation. For example, while one in four Indian Muslims lived in the North West region, the proportion of Indian Hindus or Indian Sikhs living there was lower (one in twenty and one in fifty). White British Christians were spread fairly evenly across the regions, while White British Jews and White British Muslims were highly concentrated in London, where more than half lived. Muslims belonging to different ethnic groups also tended to be concentrated in specific areas of Great Britain. Around three-quarters of Black African and Other White Muslims lived in London, compared with just over a half of Bangladeshi Muslims, around a third of Indian Muslims and a fifth of Pakistani Muslims.

The small size of the ethnic and religious minority populations in Great Britain, and their greater tendency to be clustered in small areas, meant that most local authority areas were not particularly diverse. Of the 376 local authority areas of England and Wales, 28 were found to have high ethnic diversity based on the Fractionalisation Index of diversity (see 'Ethnic and religious diversity by area' later in the chapter). Almost all these highly diverse areas were London boroughs. Brent and Newham had the highest ethnic diversity of all, while outside London, Slough had the highest ethnic diversity. People from the three Black ethnic groups and the Bangladeshi group tended to live in the most ethnically diverse MSOAs, while the White British population tended to live in the least ethnically diverse areas.

Using the same index to measure religious diversity, 11 of the 376 local authorities in England and Wales had high religious diversity. Ten of these were London boroughs, of which Harrow had the highest religious diversity; outside London, Leicester had the highest religious diversity. Hindus, Sikhs, Jews and Muslims were the most likely to be living in religiously diverse areas, whereas Christians were the least likely to be doing so.

Population distribution by ethnic group in 2001

This section illustrates spread of the population in 2001 by ethnic group, showing how the concentration of different groups varies across Great Britain. In the past, ethnic minority groups have tended to be concentrated in specific geographic areas, typically in urban areas, especially London but also in major cities in the East and West Midlands and North West of England,[1] and this pattern can still be seen in 2001. Concentration by ethnic group results from a range of different factors. Migrants from the 1950s onwards tended to settle in

areas relatively close to their point of arrival, though the precise location was influenced by availability of jobs and access to housing.[2] Among the White population there was an overall trend of movement away from cities to suburban and rural areas from the 1970s onwards. Thus between 1971 and 1981, the overall population of all Great Britain's major cities shrank, but then stabilised during the 1980s as the growth in their ethnic minority populations compensated for the reduced White population.[3] The continuing growth and concentration of ethnic minority populations in metropolitan areas is partly the result of expanding households following the birth of children, new households tending to form close to existing communities from the same ethnic group, and migrants from outside the UK joining existing communities.[4]

The tendency of different ethnic and religious groups to concentrate in particular geographic areas has prompted much public debate about the integration of the diverse communities in Great Britain. The role of National Statistics is to inform the debate by providing statistics showing the patterns of residential population distribution, not to participate in the debate. Research has found that residential concentration can occur for reasons of both positive choice and negative constraint. Positive factors that have led to the residential concentration of ethnic minority groups in Great Britain include the desire to maintain family and social networks and to live in a community large enough to support culturally specific shops, religious institutions and possibly language learning.[5] Negative factors include the racial discrimination in housing allocation by both private and social landlords, which was prevalent in the 1950s and 1960s and continued for some years afterwards despite the introduction of race equality legislation,[5] and a tendency for people from ethnic minorities living in areas where there are low concentrations of people from their own ethnic group to experience higher levels of prejudice, harassment and deliberate damage to property.[6]

The analysis focuses on nine of the ethnic groups defined in the 2001 classification, combining the four Mixed groups into one, but excluding those classified as an 'other' ethnic group (Other White, Other Asian, Other Black and Other Ethnic group).[7] It describes two different aspects of the geographic concentration of the population:

- The proportion of a specific group within the total population of an area, for example 'Bangladeshis made up 2 per cent of London's population in 2001'. This gives an indication of the size of one ethnic group relative to the other groups in the same area

- The proportion of a specific group's total population that is contained within a smaller area, for example '54 per cent of Great Britain's Bangladeshi population lived in London in 2001'. This gives an indication of the distribution of a specific group's members across different areas

Before looking in depth at the geographic distribution of each ethnic group, the proportion of each ethnic group's population in each country of Great Britain and in the English regions is outlined below.

In 2001, 86 per cent of Great Britain's population lived in England, 9 per cent lived in Scotland and 5 per cent lived in Wales (Table 3.1). People from ethnic minority groups were highly concentrated in England, for example almost all people from the Black groups lived in England (99 per cent of Black Africans and 98 per cent of Black Caribbeans).

Among the Asian groups, 98 per cent of Indians, 97 per cent of Bangladeshis and 95 per cent of Pakistanis lived in England. Pakistanis were more likely than other Asian groups to live in Scotland, 4 per cent lived there, compared with 1 per cent of Indians and Bangladeshis. Two per cent of the Bangladeshi population and 1 per cent of each of the Indian and Pakistani populations of Great Britain lived in Wales.

The White Irish and Chinese populations most closely matched the distribution of the White British population by country and region. The proportion of Great Britain's White Irish and Chinese populations who lived outside England was higher than that of the remaining ethnic minority groups, with 7 per cent of each group living in Scotland and 3 per cent in Wales.

Table 3.1

Ethnic group: by country and Government Office Region, April 2001

Great Britain

Percentages

	White British	White Irish	Other White	Mixed	Indian	Pakistani	Bangladeshi	Other Asian	Black Caribbean	Black African	Other Black	Chinese	Other Ethnic group	All people
North East	4.8	1.3	1.5	1.8	1.0	1.9	2.2	1.3	0.2	0.5	0.4	2.5	1.8	4.4
North West	12.3	11.2	5.3	9.3	6.9	15.7	9.2	5.9	3.6	3.3	5.5	11.1	5.8	11.8
Yorkshire and the Humber	9.0	4.7	4.0	6.7	4.9	19.6	4.4	5.0	3.8	2.0	3.4	5.1	4.1	8.7
East Midlands	7.6	5.1	4.0	6.4	11.6	3.7	2.4	4.8	4.7	1.9	3.7	5.3	3.2	7.3
West Midlands	9.0	10.6	4.4	10.9	17.0	20.7	11.1	8.5	14.5	2.5	10.0	6.6	6.1	9.2
East of England	9.8	8.9	9.6	8.6	4.9	5.2	6.5	5.4	4.6	3.5	5.4	8.4	6.3	9.4
London	8.5	31.9	41.8	33.6	41.5	19.1	54.4	53.8	60.7	78.2	62.1	33.0	49.3	12.6
South East	14.5	11.9	15.6	12.7	8.5	7.8	5.4	9.5	4.9	5.1	5.0	13.6	12.8	14.0
South West	9.3	4.7	5.7	5.5	1.6	0.9	1.7	2.0	2.2	1.3	2.4	5.2	4.1	8.6
England	84.9	90.3	91.9	95.5	97.8	94.6	97.4	96.1	99.2	98.2	98.1	90.7	93.6	86.1
Wales	5.5	2.6	2.6	2.6	0.8	1.1	1.9	1.4	0.5	0.8	0.8	2.6	2.2	5.1
Scotland	9.6	7.2	5.5	1.9	1.4	4.3	0.7	2.5	0.3	1.1	1.2	6.7	4.2	8.9
Great Britain = 100% (numbers)	50,366,497	691,232	1,423,471	673,798	1,051,844	746,619	282,811	247,470	565,621	484,783	97,198	243,258	229,325	57,103,927

Source: Census 2001, Office for National Statistics, Census 2001, General Register Office for Scotland

Maps and ranges

The ranges on the maps in this chapter have been determined using the Jenks Optimisation method (see the Appendix at the end of this chapter for more information). The discussion in the text generally refers to the same ranges shown on the maps, but sometimes it also draws attention to specific areas that particularly stand out at the top or bottom of each range.

White British population distribution by area

There were 50.4 million White British people living in Great Britain in 2001, 88 per cent of the population. The South East contained a slightly higher proportion of the White British population than other areas, 15 per cent, while the North East and Wales had the lowest proportions, 5 per cent and 6 per cent (Table 3.1).

In most local authority areas of Great Britain the White British made up a large proportion (over 94 per cent) of the population (Map 3.2), but each region contained some local authorities with a lower proportion of White British people, typically in cities and urban areas. The White British population made up less than 66 per cent of the population in most London boroughs, as well as in Slough, Leicester, Luton and Birmingham.

The local authority areas containing the highest proportion of White British people relative to other ethnic groups were Easington, Sedgefield, Derwentside, Berwick-upon-Tweed, and Wear Valley, all in the North East region. In these local authority areas almost all (99 per cent) people were White British. In contrast, in 9 of the 32 London boroughs, less than half were White British, of which the lowest proportions were in Newham (34 per cent) and Brent (29 per cent).

The White British population was unevenly distributed within certain local authority areas. For instance, although more than 81 per cent of people were White British in most MSOAs in the local authorities of Birmingham, Sandwell and Walsall (Map 3.3), these areas contained two clusters where White British people accounted for less than 36 per cent of the local population. The first of these clusters was located around the centre of Birmingham north of Mosley, and the second was around Handsworth and included parts of neighbouring Sandwell. In contrast, in MSOAs around Mere Green in north Birmingham, and Lonbridge Rubery and Northfield in south west Birmingham, more than nine out of ten people were White British.

In certain MSOAs in Birmingham the proportion of White British residents was among the lowest in England and Wales. In two MSOAs near Mosley in Birmingham 9 per cent of the population was White British, the lowest proportion outside London.

In parts of London the White British population was unevenly distributed between neighbouring MSOAs. For instance, the London Borough of Ealing's population was 45 per cent White British overall, but in MSOAs in and around Southall the proportion was between 8 per cent and 14 per cent. In other MSOAs in Ealing, including those around Hanger Lane and Bedford Park, around two-thirds of the population was White British (68 per cent and 66 per cent).

White Irish population distribution by area

In 2001 there were 691,000 White Irish people in Great Britain, making up 1.2 per cent of the population.

While almost a third (32 per cent) of the White Irish lived in London (Table 3.1), they were not as heavily concentrated there as many other ethnic minority groups. Outside London, the White Irish population was more concentrated in some regions than others, specifically the South East, North West and West Midlands, where 12 per cent, 11 per cent and 11 per cent of Great Britain's total White Irish population lived.

Even in areas where the White Irish were most highly concentrated, such as London and the surrounding areas, they made up a relatively small proportion of the local population (Map 3.4). For instance, they accounted for 7 per cent of the population in Brent and 6 per cent in Islington, the local authorities with largest proportions in Great Britain. There were few areas outside London where the concentration was higher than 2.3 per cent; these were Luton (5 per cent) and Watford (3 per cent) in the East of England, Manchester (4 per cent) and Trafford (3 per cent) in the North West, and Birmingham (3 per cent) and Coventry (3 per cent) in the West Midlands.

The White Irish population was concentrated to some extent in specific MSOAs in the north and west of London, where they formed between 7 per cent and 14 per cent of the local population, for example in the boroughs of Brent, Harrow, Ealing, Islington and Camden (Map 3.5). A cluster of three MSOAs around Dollis Hill and Cricklewood in the north east of Brent contained the highest proportion of White Irish of any in Great Britain, where they made up between 11 per cent and 14 per cent of the local population.

Map **3.2**

White British population[1]: by local authority area, April 2001

Great Britain

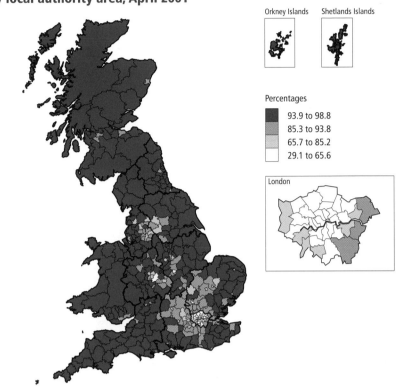

Orkney Islands   Shetlands Islands

Percentages

- 93.9 to 98.8
- 85.3 to 93.8
- 65.7 to 85.2
- 29.1 to 65.6

London

1 White British includes those who ticked White Scottish in Scotland.

Source: Census 2001, Office for National Statistics; Census 2001, General Register Office for Scotland

Map **3.3**

White British population of Birmingham, Walsall and Sandwell: by MSOA,[1] April 2001

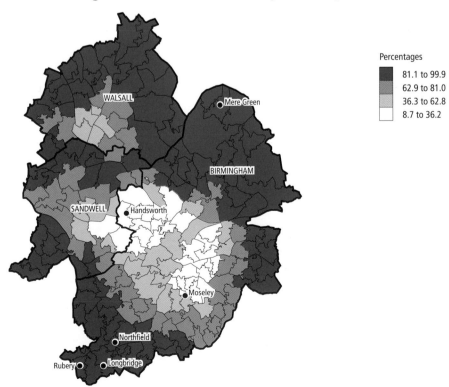

Percentages

- 81.1 to 99.9
- 62.9 to 81.0
- 36.3 to 62.8
- 8.7 to 36.2

1 Middle layer super output area.

Source: Census 2001, Office for National Statistics

Map **3.4**

White Irish population: by local authority area, April 2001
Great Britain

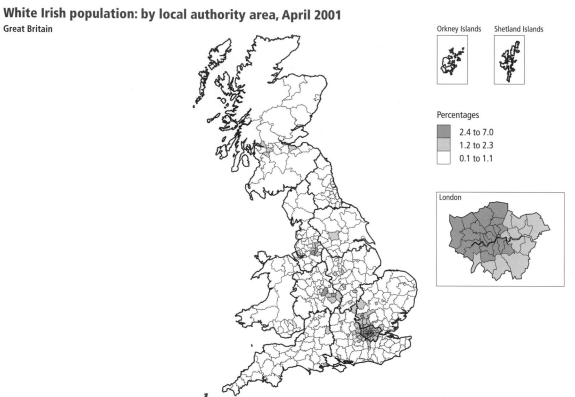

Orkney Islands   Shetland Islands

Percentages

2.4 to 7.0
1.2 to 2.3
0.1 to 1.1

London

Source: Census 2001, Office for National Statistics; Census 2001, General Register Office for Scotland

Map **3.5**

White Irish population of London: by MSOA,¹ April 2001

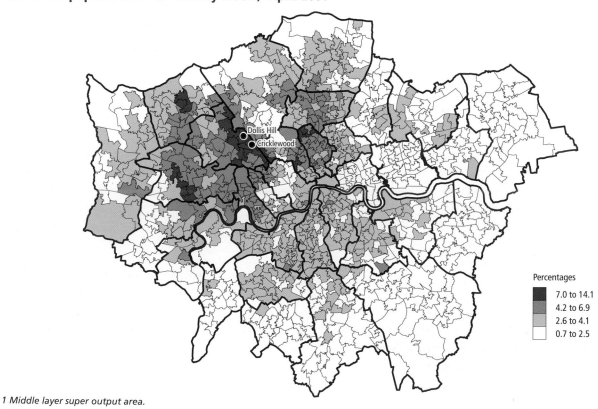

Dollis Hill
Cricklewood

Percentages

7.0 to 14.1
4.2 to 6.9
2.6 to 4.1
0.7 to 2.5

1 Middle layer super output area.
Source: Census 2001, Office for National Statistics

Indian population distribution by area

Great Britain's 1.1 million Indians made up 2 per cent of the population in 2001. They were concentrated in particular regions of England, for instance, more than four out of ten lived in London (42 per cent) and a further three out of ten lived in the two Midlands regions (17 per cent in the West Midlands and 12 per cent in the East Midlands) (Table 3.1).

Indians accounted for 1.6 per cent or less of the population in most areas of Great Britain (Map 3.6). They were concentrated in particular areas, most notably in Leicester and parts of north and west London. Leicester had the highest proportion of Indians of any local authority area in Great Britain, where they made up a quarter (26 per cent) of the population, followed by the London Boroughs of Harrow (22 per cent), Brent (18 per cent), Hounslow (17 per cent) and Ealing (17 per cent). There were further concentrations in Barnet, Redbridge and Newham in north London and Hillingdon in west London, where Indians accounted for up to 14 per cent of the population. Outside London, there were also concentrations in areas in the South East, West Midlands, North West and East Midlands, with the highest of these concentrations in Slough (14 per cent), Wolverhampton (12 per cent), Oadby and Wigston (11 per cent) and Blackburn with Darwen (11 per cent).

Indians in Leicester were clustered in nine MSOAs around Belgrave and the city centre, where they formed between 46 per cent and 71 per cent of the local population (Map 3.7). In contrast, they made up less than 9 per cent of the population in several other areas of Leicester, particularly in the southern parts of Leicester and neighbouring Oadby and Wigston.

Similarly, Indians in the London Borough of Harrow tended to be clustered in particular areas, ranging from over 40 per cent of the local population in three MSOAs near Kenton, to less than one in ten (9 per cent) in an MSOA in Pinner.

Pakistani population distribution by area

In 2001, 747,000 Pakistanis lived in Great Britain, forming 1 per cent of the population. They were concentrated in several English regions, most notably the West Midlands, Yorkshire and the Humber, and London, which each contained around one fifth of Great Britain's Pakistani population. The Pakistani population was the least concentrated in London of any ethnic minority group (Table 3.1).

Pakistanis formed between 5 per cent and 15 per cent of the local population in the local authority areas where they were most highly concentrated. These were around the border of the North West and Yorkshire and the Humber, as well as areas of north east London, the West Midlands and the South East (Map 3.8).

The local authority areas containing the highest proportion of Pakistanis were Bradford (15 per cent of the population), Pendle (13 per cent), Slough (12 per cent) and Birmingham (11 per cent).

Pakistanis made up 6.1 per cent or less of the population in most MSOAs in Bradford (Map 3.9). However, they were highly clustered in a few areas where they made up between 46 per cent and 73 per cent of the population. In one MSOA near Frizinghall, Pakistanis made up three-quarters of the population (73 per cent), the highest concentration in England and Wales, and more than 45 per cent in several MSOAs near Manningham.

Bangladeshi population distribution by area

There were 283,000 Bangladeshis in Great Britain in 2001, 0.5 per cent of the population. London was home to more than half the Bangladeshi population of Great Britain (54 per cent) (Table 3.1). Outside London, around one in ten Bangladeshis (11 per cent) lived in the West Midlands region and a further one in ten (9 per cent) lived in the North West region.

Although Bangladeshis formed 2 per cent of London's population, they were mainly concentrated in two East London boroughs, Tower Hamlets where they made up a third of the population (Map 3.10) and neighbouring Newham where they accounted for 9 per cent of the population. Other areas of London with a relatively high proportion of Bangladeshis were Camden (6 per cent) and the boroughs bordering Tower Hamlets and Newham (2.2 per cent or more).

Outside London, Bangladeshis made up 5 per cent of the population of Oldham in the North West and 4 per in Luton in the East of England.

The Bangladeshi population in Tower Hamlets made up between 28 per cent and 61 per cent of the local population in two-thirds of its MSOAs (Map 3.11). They were not evenly spread across the borough, forming more than half the population in several MSOAs in the west of Tower Hamlets (around Stepney and Spitalfields), and less than 15 per cent in MSOAs around Bow and the Isle of Dogs. In some MSOAs in neighbouring Newham they constituted between 11 per cent and 28 per cent of the population.

In one MSOA in Oldham Bangladeshis formed 61 per cent of the local population, the highest proportion in any MSOA outside Tower Hamlets. However, in most MSOAs in Oldham, Bangladeshis made up 2 per cent or less of the local population.

Map **3.6**

Indian population: by local authority area, April 2001
Great Britain

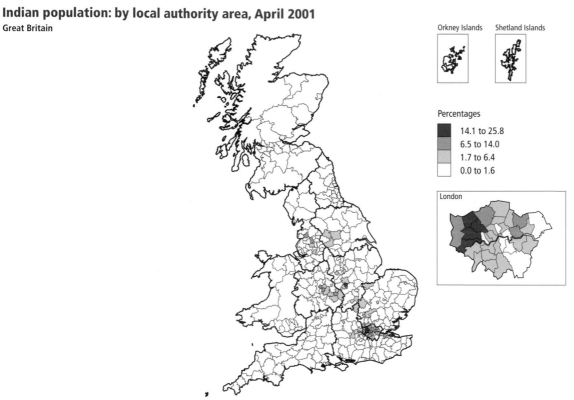

Orkney Islands   Shetland Islands

Percentages

- 14.1 to 25.8
- 6.5 to 14.0
- 1.7 to 6.4
- 0.0 to 1.6

London

Source: Census 2001, Office for National Statistics; Census 2001, General Register Office for Scotland

Map **3.7**

Indian population of Leicester and Oadby & Wigston: by MSOA,[1] April 2001

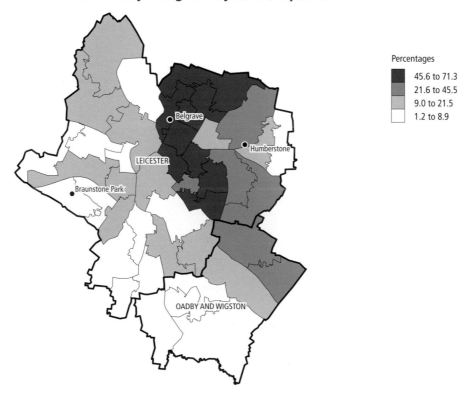

Percentages

- 45.6 to 71.3
- 21.6 to 45.5
- 9.0 to 21.5
- 1.2 to 8.9

1 Middle layer super output area.
Source: Census 2001, Office for National Statistics

Map **3.8**

Pakistani population: by local authority area, April 2001
Great Britain

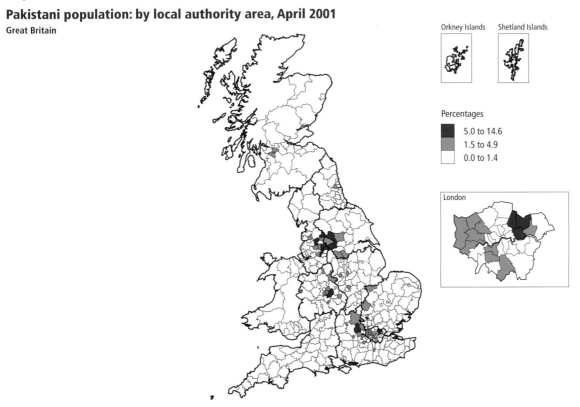

Source: Census 2001, Office for National Statistics; Census 2001, General Register Office for Scotland

Map **3.9**

Pakistani population of Bradford: by MSOA,[1] April 2001

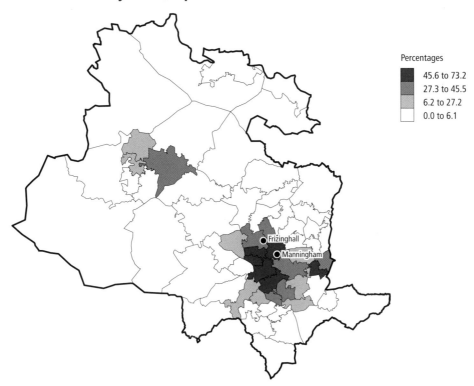

1 Middle layer super output area.
Source: Census 2001, Office for National Statistics

Map **3.10**

Bangladeshi population: by local authority area, April 2001
Great Britain

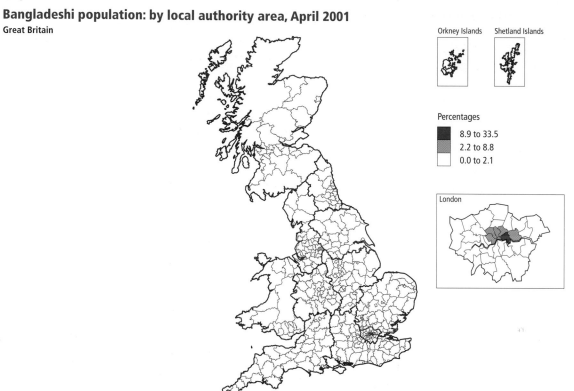

Orkney Islands   Shetland Islands

Percentages

- 8.9 to 33.5
- 2.2 to 8.8
- 0.0 to 2.1

London

Source: Census 2001, Office for National Statistics; Census 2001, General Register Office for Scotland

Map **3.11**

Bangladeshi population of London: by MSOA,[1] April 2001

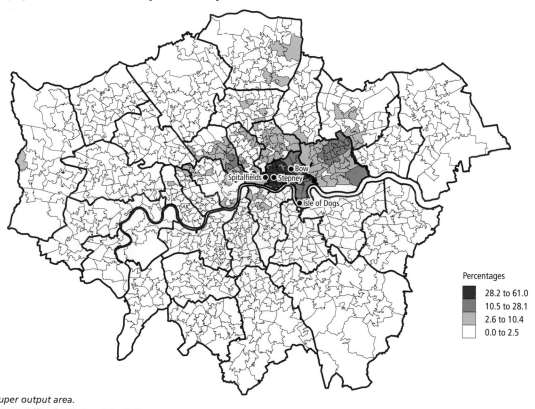

Percentages

- 28.2 to 61.0
- 10.5 to 28.1
- 2.6 to 10.4
- 0.0 to 2.5

1 Middle layer super output area.
Source: Census 2001, Office for National Statistics

Black Caribbean population distribution by area

The 566,000 Black Caribbeans in Great Britain made up 1 per cent of the population in 2001. The Black Caribbean population was concentrated in two regions of England; London was home to 61 per cent of the Black Caribbean population of Great Britain, while a further 15 per cent lived in the West Midlands (Table 3.1).

Map 3.12 shows Black Caribbeans formed between 5.4 per cent and 12.3 per cent of the local population in the areas where they were most concentrated, in particular Lewisham and Lambeth (12 per cent) in south London and Brent, Hackney and Haringey (10 per cent) in north London. There were clusters of Black Caribbeans in the West Midlands, where they made up 5 per cent of the population of Birmingham, 4 per cent in Wolverhampton and 3 per cent in Sandwell. Black Caribbeans also made up 4 per cent of the population in Luton.

The Black Caribbean population was clustered more heavily at MSOA level, for example in Brent, Haringey and Waltham Forest in north London and Lambeth, Southwark, Lewisham and Croydon in south London (Map 3.13). Each of these boroughs contained MSOAs where Black Caribbeans formed between 14 per cent and 23 per cent of the local population. They were especially highly concentrated in five MSOAs around Catford in Lewisham and Brixton in Lambeth, where they made up around one in five of the population.

Outside London, Black Caribbeans were highly concentrated in an MSOA around Rusholme in Manchester, where they accounted for almost one in four of the population, and in several MSOAs near the Handsworth area of Birmingham, where they constituted one in five of the population.

Black African population distribution by area

The 485,000 Black Africans in Great Britain made up 1 per cent of the population in 2001. At a regional level, Black Africans were the most heavily concentrated of the ethnic minority groups. More than three-quarters (78 per cent) lived in London (Table 3.1), with 40 per cent living in seven boroughs.

Several London boroughs contained high concentrations of Black Africans, in particular Southwark (where they formed 16 per cent of the population), Lambeth (12 per cent) and Lewisham (9 per cent) in south London, and Newham (13 per cent), Hackney (12 per cent), and Haringey (9 per cent) in the east and north of London (Map 3.14). Black Africans formed 2 per cent or less of the local population in every local authority area outside London.

Black Africans were heavily concentrated in specific MSOAs in the London boroughs of Lambeth, Southwark and Lewisham in the south and Brent, Newham, Hackney and Haringey in the north (Map 3.15), where they made up between 16 per cent and 41 per cent of the local population in several MSOAs. The highest proportions of Black Africans were found in several Southwark MSOAs around Camberwell and Peckham; in one MSOA in Camberwell they made up 41 per cent of the local population, compared with 2 per cent in a neighbouring MSOA covering parts of Herne Hill and Dulwich Village.

Chinese population distribution by area

There were 243,000 Chinese people living in Great Britain in 2001, 0.4 per cent of the population. They were concentrated mainly in London and the South East, home to 33 per cent and 14 per cent of Great Britain's total Chinese population (Table 3.1).

Relative to other ethnic groups, the Chinese population was spread fairly evenly throughout England, with additional small clusters in areas of Scotland and Wales (Map 3.16).

In most areas the Chinese made up less than 0.4 per cent of the local population and in no local authority area in Great Britain did they form more than 2.2 per cent. They accounted for 1 per cent or more of the population of several London boroughs such as Westminster, City of London and Barnet, along with Cambridge, Oxford, Manchester and Liverpool.

The Chinese population made up 1 per cent of the population of London with little variation at borough level. There was greater variation at the smaller MSOA level; for example, they formed between 2.7 per cent and 7.2 per cent of the population in numerous MSOAs across London (Map 3.17). At their most heavily concentrated they made up 7 per cent of the population of one MSOA near Colindale in the London Borough of Barnet, 6 per cent in two MSOAs near Canary Wharf in Tower Hamlets and 6 per cent in an MSOA near Deptford in Lewisham. Outside London, the Chinese population made up one in eleven (9 per cent) of the local population in an MSOA toward the centre of Manchester, the highest proportion of Chinese people of any MSOA in England and Wales.

Map **3.12**

Black Caribbean population: by local authority area, April 2001
Great Britain

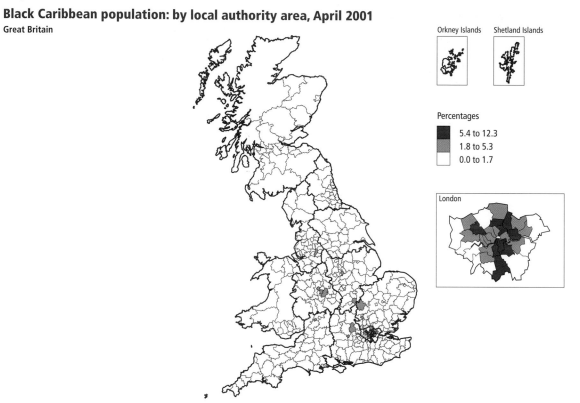

Source: Census 2001, Office for National Statistics; Census 2001, General Register Office for Scotland

Map **3.13**

Black Caribbean population of London: by MSOA,[1] April 2001

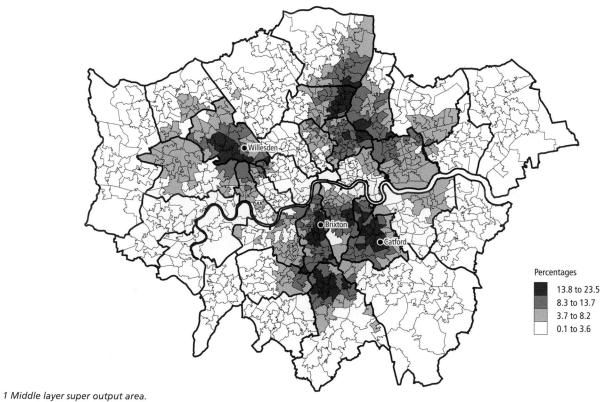

1 Middle layer super output area.
Source: Census 2001, Office for National Statistics

Map **3.14**

Black African population: by local authority area, April 2001

Great Britain

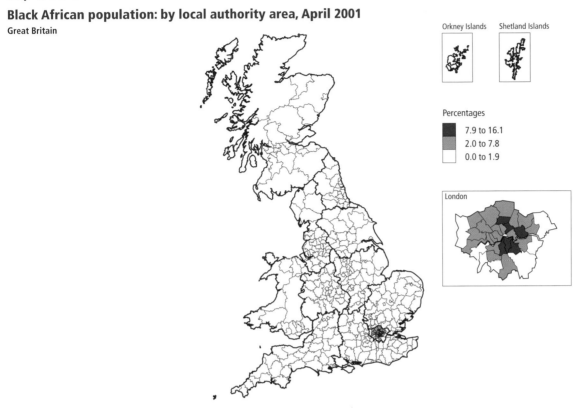

Source: Census 2001, Office for National Statistics; Census 2001, General Register Office for Scotland

Map **3.15**

Black African population of London: by MSOA,[1] April 2001

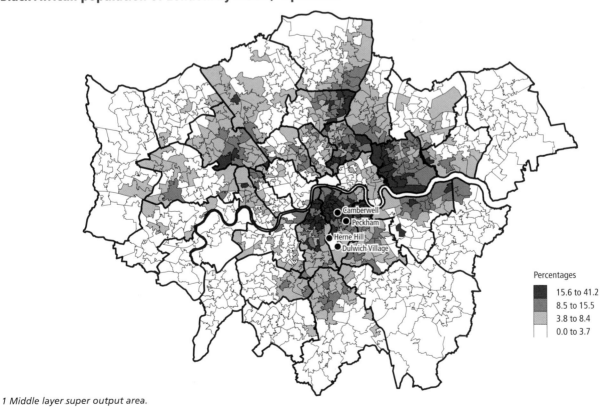

1 Middle layer super output area.

Source: Census 2001, Office for National Statistics

Map **3.16**

Chinese population: by local authority area, April 2001

Great Britain

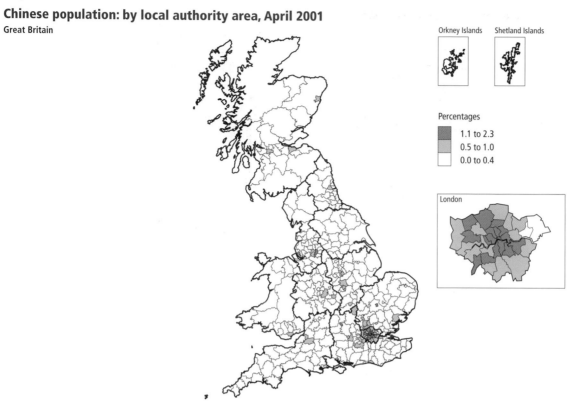

Source: Census 2001, Office for National Statistics; Census 2001, General Register Office for Scotland

Map **3.17**

Chinese population of London: by MSOA,[1] April 2001

1 Middle layer super output area.

Source: Census 2001, Office for National Statistics

Map **3.18**

Mixed population: by local authority area, April 2001

Great Britain

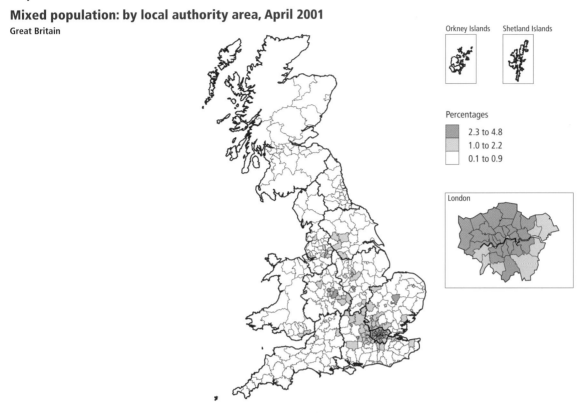

Orkney Islands   Shetland Islands

Percentages

- 2.3 to 4.8
- 1.0 to 2.2
- 0.1 to 0.9

London

Source: Census 2001, Office for National Statistics; Census 2001, General Register Office for Scotland

Map **3.19**

Mixed population of Manchester, Salford and Trafford: by MSOA,[1] April 2001

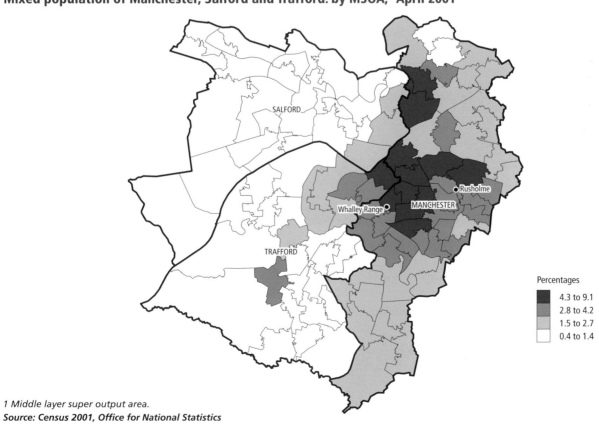

Percentages

- 4.3 to 9.1
- 2.8 to 4.2
- 1.5 to 2.7
- 0.4 to 1.4

1 Middle layer super output area.
Source: Census 2001, Office for National Statistics

Mixed population distribution by area

The 674,000 people with a Mixed ethnic identity constituted 1 per cent of the population of Great Britain in 2001.

While a third (34 per cent) of people with a Mixed ethnic identity lived in London (Table 3.1), they were not as heavily concentrated there as many other ethnic minority groups. Outside London, people with a Mixed ethnic identity tended to be concentrated in the South East and the West Midlands, where 13 per cent and 11 per cent lived.

People with a Mixed ethnic identity accounted for less than 1 per cent of the local population in most local authority areas of Great Britain, and no more than 5 per cent even in areas where they were most highly concentrated such as London, Manchester, Nottingham, Birmingham and Wolverhampton (Map 3.18).

Outside the London region, Manchester was home to the highest concentration of people with a Mixed ethnic identity, where they made up 3 per cent of the local population. Within Manchester, the Mixed ethnic group was concentrated in particular MSOAs in the centre and north of Manchester, forming between 4.3 per cent and 9.1 per cent of the local population (Map 3.19). The highest concentration was in an MSOA near Rusholme and one towards the city centre, where

almost one in ten (9.0 per cent) were from the Mixed ethnic group. Conversely, in over half of MSOAs in Manchester, 2.7 per cent or less of the population had a Mixed ethnic identity. In most areas of neighbouring Salford and Trafford the Mixed population made up 1.4 per cent or less of the local population.

The MSOA containing the highest proportion of people with a Mixed ethnic identity of any in Great Britain was located near Princes Park in Liverpool, where 11 per cent belonged to a Mixed ethnic group.

Population distribution by religion in 2001

This section illustrates the population distributions of the main religious groups[8] in 2001, showing how their concentration varied across different areas of Great Britain.

Before looking in depth at the geographic distribution of each religious group, the proportion of each group's population in the different countries of Great Britain and in the English regions is outlined to set the context.

People from all the minority religions were more likely than Christians to live in England than in Wales or Scotland (Table 3.20). Hindus were the most concentrated in England of all religious groups; 98 per cent lived there, with 1 per cent living in

Table 3.20

Religion: by country and Government Office Region, April 2001

Great Britain
Percentages

	Christian	Buddhist	Hindu	Jewish	Muslim	Sikh	Other	No Religion	Not Stated	All people
North East	4.9	2.1	0.8	1.2	1.7	1.4	2.4	3.2	4.0	4.4
North West	12.8	7.9	4.9	10.5	12.9	1.9	6.7	8.2	11.0	11.8
Yorkshire and The Humber	8.9	4.8	2.8	4.3	11.9	5.6	6.1	8.1	8.7	8.7
East Midlands	7.3	5.1	12.0	1.5	4.4	10.0	6.2	7.7	7.0	7.3
West Midlands	9.3	6.5	10.2	1.9	13.6	30.9	6.9	7.5	8.9	9.2
East of England	9.5	8.1	5.6	11.4	5.0	4.0	9.7	10.5	9.4	9.4
London	10.2	36.4	52.3	56.0	38.2	31.0	23.0	13.2	14.0	12.6
South East	14.2	14.8	8.0	7.1	6.8	11.2	18.0	15.4	13.5	14.0
South West	8.9	7.6	1.5	2.5	1.5	1.4	11.5	9.6	8.7	8.6
England	86.0	93.2	98.0	96.4	96.0	97.4	90.4	83.4	85.2	86.1
Wales	5.1	3.6	1.0	0.8	1.4	0.6	4.3	6.3	5.3	5.1
Scotland	9.0	3.2	1.1	2.8	2.7	2.0	5.3	10.3	9.5	8.9
All people = (100%) (numbers)	41,014,811	149,157	558,342	267,373	1,588,890	336,179	159,167	8,596,488	4,433,520	57,103,927

Source: Census 2001, Office for National Statistics, Census 2001, General Register Office for Scotland

each of Scotland or Wales. Similarly, 97 per cent of Sikhs lived in England with 2 per cent living in Scotland and 1 per cent in Wales. The concentration of Jews and Muslims by country was also similar; 96 per cent lived in England, 3 per cent in Scotland, and 1 per cent in Wales.

Buddhists were the least concentrated in England of the minority religions, although 93 per cent of Buddhists lived there, while 3 per cent lived in Scotland and 3 per cent in Wales.

Those with no religion were slightly more likely than the overall population to be living in Scotland and Wales (10 per cent and 6 per cent compared with 9 per cent and 5 per cent of the Christian population).

Christian population distribution by area

In 2001, 41 million people living in Great Britain were Christian, 72 per cent of the population. Christians were less likely than any other religious group to live in London; one in ten (10 per cent) did so, compared with at least a third of those from other religious groups and 13 per cent of those with no religion (Table 3.20). Christians formed the majority of the population, and therefore the distribution of the overall population of Great Britain generally reflects the distribution of the Christian population.

Christians formed more than 70 per cent of the population in almost all areas of Great Britain in 2001 (Map 3.21), and between 78 per cent and 87 per cent in most areas of the North East, North West, Yorkshire and the Humber, East Midlands and West Midlands. However, in the majority of north London boroughs, 57.7 per cent or less of the population was Christian. Tower Hamlets had the lowest proportion of Christians of any local authority (39 per cent) and Christians were in a minority in six other London boroughs (Hackney, Newham, Camden, Harrow, Barnet and Brent). Leicester contained the lowest proportion of Christians outside London (45 per cent).

The Christian population was unevenly distributed within certain local authority areas. For instance, although in most MSOAs in Birmingham, Sandwell and Walsall more than 59 per cent of people were Christian (Map 3.22), there were two distinct areas near Handsworth and Mosley where they accounted for between 11 per cent and 39 per cent of the local population. Several MSOAs near Mosley contained the lowest concentration of Christians of any in England and Wales, where no more than 13 per cent of the local population was Christian.

Christians also formed a low proportion of the local population in several MSOAs in Bradford, Leicester and the London Boroughs of Tower Hamlets, Ealing and Barnet (less than 20 per cent).

Buddhist population distribution by area

In 2001 there were 149,000 Buddhists living in Great Britain, 0.3 per cent of the total population. More than a third of Great Britain's Buddhists lived in London (36 per cent) with a further 15 per cent living in the South East. They were spread fairly evenly across most of the other English regions (which each contained between 5 per cent and 8 per cent of the Buddhist population) except in the North East, where only 2 per cent lived (Table 3.20).

Buddhists made up less than 0.6 per cent of the population in almost all areas of Great Britain outside London. They were spread fairly evenly across most London boroughs and accounted for no more than around 1.4 per cent of the population of any borough (Map 3.23). The largest concentrations of Buddhists lived in Camden and Westminster where they made up 1.3 per cent of the local population. Outside London, they accounted for 1.1 per cent of the population of Cambridge, 0.8 per cent in Oxford and 0.7 per cent in Brighton and Hove.

Buddhists made up 1.2 per cent or less of the population in most MSOAs in London (Map 3.24). While there were larger concentrations across several boroughs, they were not especially clustered in any particular area as they did not account for more than 5.3 per cent of the population in any MSOA. In two MSOA areas of Deptford in Lewisham Buddhists made up 4 per cent and 5 per cent of the local population, the largest concentration at MSOA level in England and Wales. They also made up 4 per cent of the local population in an MSOA in Manchester.

Hindu population distribution by area

There were 558,000 Hindus living in Great Britain in 2001, accounting for 1 per cent of the population. Hindus were particularly concentrated in three English regions; around half (52 per cent) lived in London, 12 per cent lived in the East Midlands and 10 per cent in the West Midlands (Table 3.20).

Hindus accounted for 1.2 per cent or less of the population in almost all areas of Great Britain outside London. In London, Hindus formed between 8 per cent and 20 per cent of the local population in specific boroughs (Map 3.25). Harrow and Brent contained the highest proportion of Hindus of any London boroughs (20 per cent and 17 per cent). Hindus formed a relatively high proportion of the local population in other areas of London, including Ealing (8 per cent), Hounslow (8 per cent) and Redbridge (8 per cent).

Outside London, Hindus made up one in fifty (2 per cent) of the population of the East Midlands. They mainly lived in Leicester, where they made up one in seven of the local

Map **3.21**

Christian population: by local authority area, April 2001

Great Britain

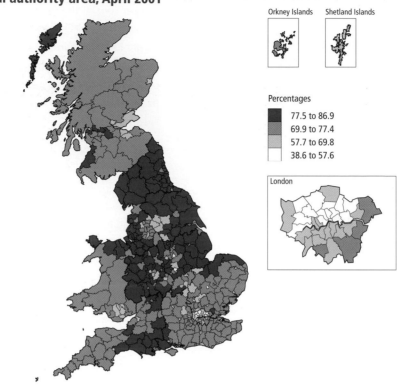

Orkney Islands   Shetland Islands

Percentages

- 77.5 to 86.9
- 69.9 to 77.4
- 57.7 to 69.8
- 38.6 to 57.6

London

Source: Census 2001, Office for National Statistics; Census 2001, General Register Office for Scotland

Map **3.22**

Christian population of Birmingham, Walsall and Sandwell: by MSOA,[1] April 2001

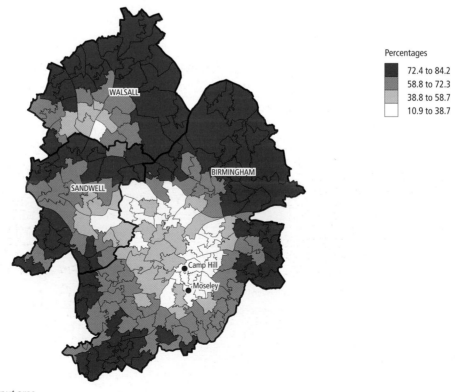

Percentages

- 72.4 to 84.2
- 58.8 to 72.3
- 38.8 to 58.7
- 10.9 to 38.7

1 Middle layer super output area.

Source: Census 2001, Office for National Statistics

Map **3.23**

Buddhist population: by local authority area, April 2001
Great Britain

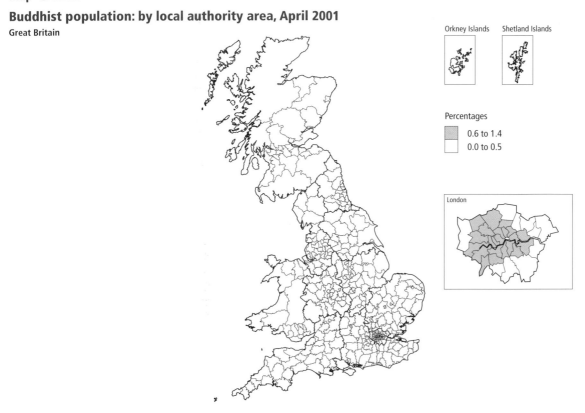

Orkney Islands   Shetland Islands

Percentages

0.6 to 1.4

0.0 to 0.5

London

Source: Census 2001, Office for National Statistics; Census 2001, General Register Office for Scotland

Map **3.24**

Buddhist population of London: by MSOA,[1] April 2001

Deptford

Percentages

1.3 to 5.3

0.5 to 1.2

0.0 to 0.4

1 Middle layer super output area.
Source: Census 2001, Office for National Statistics

Map **3.25**

Hindu population: by local authority area, April 2001
Great Britain

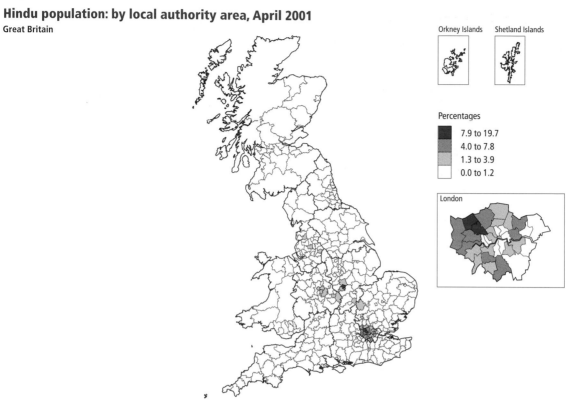

Source: Census 2001, Office for National Statistics; Census 2001, General Register Office for Scotland

Map **3.26**

Hindu population of London: by MSOA,[1] April 2001

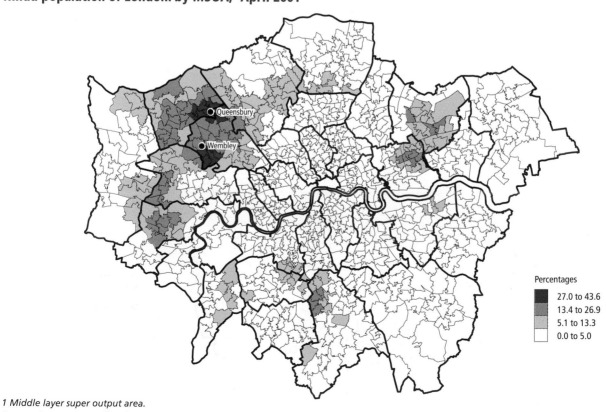

1 Middle layer super output area.
Source: Census 2001, Office for National Statistics

Map **3.27**

Jewish population: by local authority area, April 2001
Great Britain

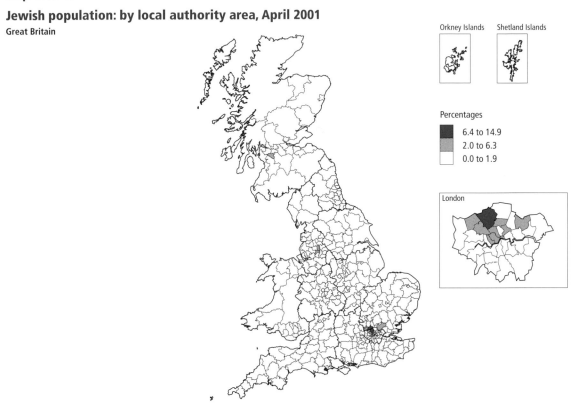

Source: Census 2001, Office for National Statistics; Census 2001, General Register Office for Scotland

Map **3.28**

Jewish population of London: by MSOA,[1] April 2001

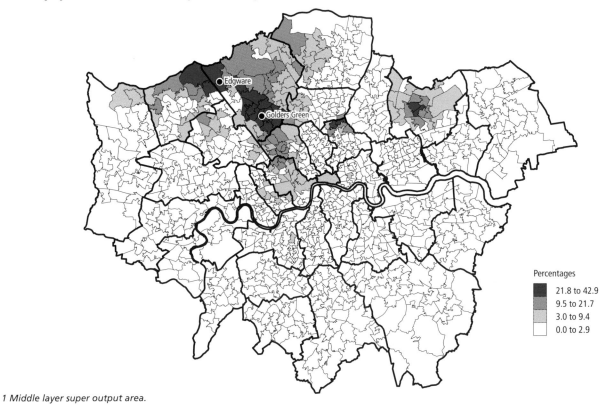

1 Middle layer super output area.
Source: Census 2001, Office for National Statistics

population (15 per cent), and Oadby and Wigston, where they accounted for 6 per cent of the population. In Slough, in the South East, Hindus constituted 4 per cent of the population.

Hindus made up 5.0 per cent or less of the population in most areas of London (Map 3.26). The Hindu population was particularly clustered in areas of the neighbouring boroughs of Harrow and Brent, where they accounted for between 27 per cent and 44 per cent of the local population in some MSOAs, reaching more than four in ten of the population in two MSOAs near Queensbury in Harrow and one near Wembley in Brent.

Hindus were most highly concentrated within three MSOAs in Leicester, where they made up around 60 per cent of the local population. In most other MSOAs in Leicester, they represented less than 10 per cent of the local population.

Jewish population distribution by area

There were 267,000 Jews living in Great Britain in 2001, making up 0.5 per cent of the population. They were concentrated in the London region, with more than half (56 per cent) living there. A further 11 per cent lived in the East of England and 10 per cent in the North West, similar to the Christian distribution (Table 3.20).

Map 3.27 shows a concentration of Jewish people in the London Borough of Barnet and neighbouring Hertsmere, where they accounted for 15 per cent and 11 per cent of the local population. There were additional smaller clusters of between 2 per cent and 6 per cent of the local population in several London boroughs and local authority areas in the East of England, many of which had borders adjoining Barnet and Hertsmere. Elsewhere in Great Britain, Bury (5 per cent) and Salford (2 per cent) in the North West, and East Renfrewshire (4 per cent) in Scotland, contained a relatively high proportion of Jewish people.

The Jewish population accounted for 2.9 per cent or less of the population in most MSOAs in London (Map 3.28). They were highly concentrated in small areas in several boroughs of north London, notably Harrow, Barnet, Hackney and Redbridge, where they formed between 22 per cent and 43 per cent of the population in some MSOAs. In London they were most heavily concentrated in three MSOAs in Golders Green in Barnet and one near Edgware, where they accounted for more than 40 per cent of the population. In contrast, in around half of Barnet's MSOAs less than one in ten of the population was Jewish.

The highest concentration of Jewish people at an MSOA level occurred in an MSOA in Broughton in Salford, where they formed almost half the population (49 per cent).

Muslim population distribution by area

There were 1.6 million Muslims living in Great Britain in 2001, 3 per cent of the population. Like other minority religions, Muslims tended to be concentrated in particular English regions. More than a third (38 per cent) of Great Britain's Muslims lived in London, 14 per cent lived in the West Midlands, 13 per cent in the North West and 12 per cent in Yorkshire and the Humber (Table 3.20).

Muslims made up less than 2.8 per cent of the population in most areas of Great Britain (Map 3.29). However, in the areas with the highest concentrations of Muslims, Tower Hamlets and Newham in London, they made up more than a third (36 per cent) and a quarter (24 per cent) of the local populations respectively. Muslims formed more than 8 per cent of the population in several other areas, notably around the border between the North West and Yorkshire and the Humber. In the North West Muslims accounted for around one in five of the population of Blackburn with Darwen (19 per cent), one in eight in Pendle (13 per cent), and around one in nine in each of Oldham, Manchester and Rochdale. In Yorkshire and the Humber they accounted for one in six of the population in Bradford (16 per cent) and one in ten in Kirklees (10 per cent). Other areas containing a relatively high concentration of Muslims were Birmingham in the West Midlands (14 per cent); east London boroughs such as Waltham Forest (15 per cent) and Hackney (14 per cent); Luton (15 per cent) in the East of England; and Slough (13 per cent) in the South East.

Muslims made up 6.4 per cent or less of the population in most MSOAs in Birmingham and in the neighbouring areas of Sandwell and Walsall (Map 3.30). They were highly clustered in areas of Birmingham where they formed between 42 per cent and 76 per cent of the population. Muslims made up three-quarters of the local population in four MSOAs around Mosley and Camp Hill near the centre of Birmingham, among the highest concentrations in England and Wales. There were smaller clusters (where they made up more than 17 per cent of the population) in several neighbouring MSOAs, along with areas in Walsall and Sandwell.

Several other areas of the country contained a high concentration of Muslims. They made up around three-quarters of the population in one MSOA near Frizinghall in Bradford. Similarly, in the London Borough of Tower Hamlets, Muslims made up almost two-thirds of the local population in two MSOAs (one in Spitalfields and one in Whitechapel) and around half the population in seven other MSOAs in the borough. In Blackburn with Darwen, Muslims made up two-thirds of the population in two MSOAs to the north of Lower Darwen.

Sikh population distribution by area

There were 336,000 Sikhs in Great Britain in 2001, 1 per cent of the population. Sikhs were mainly concentrated in two English regions; London and the West Midlands (31 per cent in each), with smaller groups living in the South East (11 per cent) and the East Midlands (10 per cent) (Table 3.20).

Sikhs accounted for 0.5 per cent or less of the local population in almost all areas of Great Britain (Map 3.31). In the areas containing the highest concentration of Sikhs they formed between 6 per cent and 9 per cent of the local population. Almost one in ten (9 per cent) of the population in the west London Boroughs of Ealing and Hounslow were Sikh. There were smaller concentrations in the adjoining borough of Hillingdon, and also in Redbridge and Newham in east London where they constituted up to 5 per cent of the population.

There were similar concentrations of Sikhs in some areas outside London, including Slough (9 per cent) and Gravesham in the South East (7 per cent), and Wolverhampton and Sandwell in the West Midlands (8 per cent and 7 per cent). Smaller concentrations of Sikhs were located on the outskirts of London and in the East and West Midlands, the East of England, and Yorkshire and the Humber.

As with other religions, the Sikh population tended to be concentrated in specific MSOAs. In most MSOAs in Birmingham, Walsall and Sandwell they made up 1.9 per cent or less of the population (Map 3.32). They were more heavily clustered in several MSOAs on the border of Sandwell and Birmingham, where they formed between 14 per cent and 31 per cent of the local population. The MSOA containing the highest proportion of Sikhs was located near the Handsworth area of Birmingham, where they made up nearly a third of the population (31 per cent).

The Sikh population was also heavily concentrated in certain MSOAs in London. They formed more than a third of the population in five MSOAs around Southall in Ealing.

Population distribution of those with no religion by area

In 2001 8.6 million people (15 per cent of the population of Great Britain) said they had no religion. Although their distribution across Scotland, Wales and the English regions was similar to that of the majority Christian population, there were some area variations, notably in London and the North West (Table 3.20). People with no religion were more likely than Christians to live in London, one in eight (13 per cent) compared with one in ten (10 per cent). People with no religion were less likely than Christians to live in the North West (8 per cent compared with 13 per cent).

In areas of eastern Scotland, South Wales, and England, between 20 per cent and 30 per cent of people had no religion (Map 3.33). In contrast, in most areas of the North East, North West, Yorkshire and the Humber, and the West Midlands, less than 12 per cent of the population had no religion.

More than one in four people living in Aberdeen (30 per cent), Norwich (28 per cent), Brighton and Hove (27 per cent) and Cambridge (27 per cent) had no religion, between four and five times the proportion living in St Helens and Knowsley, which had the lowest concentrations (6 per cent in each). People with no religion were to some extent clustered within small areas, for instance, in six MSOAs around the centre of Brighton, 40 per cent or more of the local population had no religion.

Population distribution by ethnicity and religion

Some ethnic groups contained people with a variety of religious affiliations while others were more homogeneous in this respect. For instance, in 2001 there was little religious diversity among Pakistanis and Bangladeshis, of whom nine out of ten were Muslims (92 per cent). In contrast, there was considerably more religious diversity among Indians: 45 per cent were Hindu, 29 per cent were Sikh, 13 per cent were Muslim and 5 per cent were Christian. The Black African group were predominantly Christian (69 per cent) with a substantial minority of Muslims (20 per cent). (Chapter 2)

This section examines population clustering by religion:

- among the ethnic groups with the most religious diversity (White British, Indian, Black African and Chinese)

- by ethnic group among the religious group that had most ethnic diversity (Muslims).

The analysis is based on data from the 2001 Census in England and Wales, rather than Great Britain or the UK, because the Northern Irish and Scottish census questions on ethnic group and religion differed slightly from those asked in England and Wales, and are therefore not directly comparable (Chapter 1).

White British population distribution by religion

In 2001, three-quarters (76 per cent) of the White British group in England and Wales were Christian, 0.5 per cent were Jewish, 0.1 per cent were Muslim and 0.1 per cent were Buddhist.

White British Christians were spread more evenly across England and Wales than White British Buddhists, Muslims and Jews, who were more highly concentrated in London (Table 3.34). More than half of White British Jews and Muslims lived in the London region (56 per cent and 52 per cent), compared with 8 per cent of White British Christians. Within London, the

Map **3.29**

Muslim population: by local authority area, April 2001
Great Britain

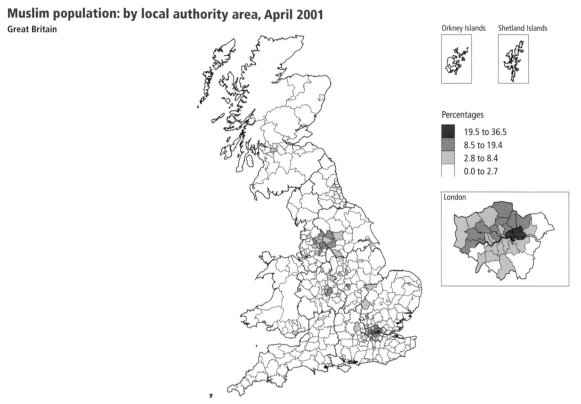

Orkney Islands   Shetland Islands

Percentages
- 19.5 to 36.5
- 8.5 to 19.4
- 2.8 to 8.4
- 0.0 to 2.7

London

Source: Census 2001, Office for National Statistics; Census 2001, General Register Office for Scotland

Map **3.30**

Muslim population of Birmingham, Walsall and Sandwell: by MSOA,[1] April 2001

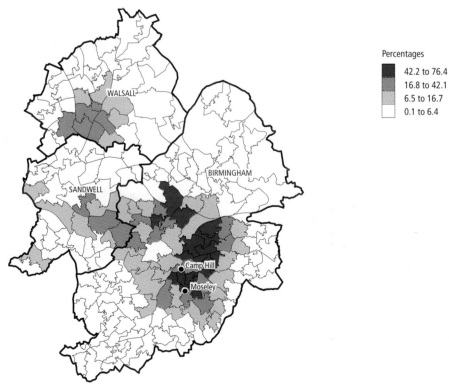

Percentages
- 42.2 to 76.4
- 16.8 to 42.1
- 6.5 to 16.7
- 0.1 to 6.4

1 Middle layer super output area.
Source: Census 2001, Office for National Statistics

Map **3.31**

Sikh population: by local authority area, April 2001
Great Britain

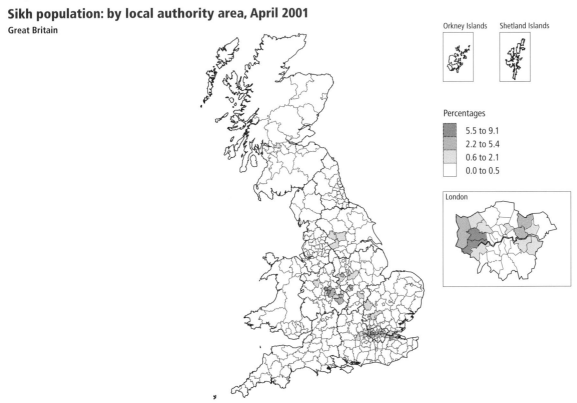

Orkney Islands   Shetland Islands

Percentages

5.5 to 9.1
2.2 to 5.4
0.6 to 2.1
0.0 to 0.5

London

Source: Census 2001, Office for National Statistics; Census 2001, General Register Office for Scotland

Map **3.32**

Sikh population of Birmingham, Walsall and Sandwell: by MSOA,[1] April 2001

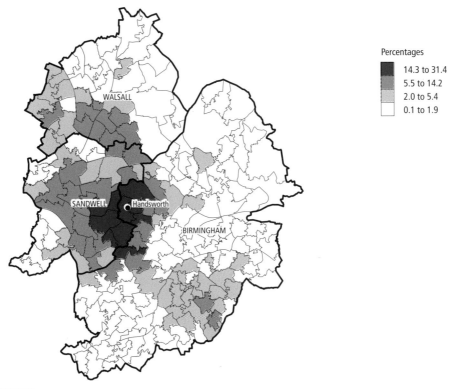

Percentages

14.3 to 31.4
5.5 to 14.2
2.0 to 5.4
0.1 to 1.9

1 Middle layer super output area.

Source: Census 2001, Office for National Statistics

Map **3.33**

Population distribution of those with no religion: by local authority area, April 2001

Great Britain

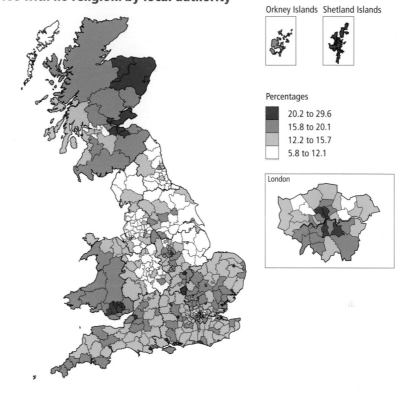

Orkney Islands   Shetland Islands

Percentages

- 20.2 to 29.6
- 15.8 to 20.1
- 12.2 to 15.7
- 5.8 to 12.1

London

Source: Census 2001, Office for National Statistics; Census 2001, General Register Office for Scotland

Table **3.34**

Geographic distribution of White British group: by selected religion, country and Government Office Region, April 2001

England and Wales

Percentages

	Christian	Buddhist	Muslim	Jewish	All White British[1]
North East	5.7	3.1	1.9	1.0	5.3
North West	14.6	10.3	8.6	11.4	13.6
Yorkshire and the Humber	10.2	7.1	6.7	4.8	10.0
East Midlands	8.3	6.2	3.4	1.6	8.4
West Midlands	10.4	6.7	6.6	1.9	10.0
East of England	10.6	9.8	6.7	12.6	10.8
London	8.3	19.1	52.2	56.2	9.4
South East	15.9	18.1	8.5	7.1	16.0
South West	10.2	13.2	3.1	2.6	10.3
England	94.1	93.7	97.6	99.1	93.9
Wales	5.9	6.3	2.4	0.9	6.1
England and Wales = (100%) (numbers)	34,576,389	50,408	63,042	218,324	45,533,741

1 *Total includes all White British of any religion, including those with no religion and whose religion was 'Not Stated'.*
Source: Census 2001, Office for National Statistics

Borough of Enfield had the largest concentration of White British Muslims (8 per cent). The White British Jewish population was particularly concentrated, with almost one in five (18 per cent) living in the Borough of Barnet. Around one in five White British Buddhists (19 per cent) lived in the London region and a further 18 per cent lived in the South East, though they were not concentrated in any particular boroughs or local authority areas.

Indian population distribution by religion

Indians of different religions tended to live in different areas of the country (Table 3.35). In 2001, while four out of ten Indians overall lived in London, this proportion varied according to religion. Indian Hindus and Christians were most likely to live in London, half did so (50 per cent) compared with around a third of Indian Sikhs (32 per cent) and Indian Muslims (31 per cent). A substantial proportion of the Indian Hindus of England and Wales lived in the London boroughs of Brent (8 per cent) and Harrow (7 per cent), while Indian Sikhs in London were concentrated in the boroughs of Ealing and Hounslow, which contained 8 per cent and 6 per cent of the Indian Sikh population of England and Wales.

Indian Muslims were less highly concentrated in London boroughs than Indians of other religions, although 5 per cent lived in the Borough of Newham and 3 per cent lived in Hackney. More than a quarter of Indian Muslims lived in the North West region of England (27 per cent), predominantly in the three local authority areas of Blackburn with Darwen (home to 10 per cent of the Indian Muslims of England and Wales), Bolton (8 per cent) and Preston (5 per cent). In contrast, 2 per cent of Indian Sikhs and 5 per cent of Indian Hindus lived in the North West region.

Leicester was home to 7 per cent of England and Wales's Indian population in 2001, including the largest concentration of Indian Muslims (14 per cent) and Indian Hindus (8 per cent) of all the local authority areas in England and Wales.

The West Midlands was home to a third of Indian Sikhs (32 per cent) in England and Wales, with most living in Birmingham (9 per cent), Sandwell (6 per cent) and Wolverhampton (6 per cent). In contrast, a lower proportion of Indian Hindus (11 per cent) and Indian Muslims (8 per cent) lived in the West Midlands region.

Table 3.35

Geographic distribution of Indian population: by selected religion, country and Government Office Region, April 2001

England and Wales   Percentages

	Christian	Hindu	Muslim	Sikh	All Indians[1]
North East	1.3	0.8	0.3	1.5	1.0
North West	3.9	5.3	26.6	1.8	7.0
Yorkshire and the Humber	2.8	3.0	11.8	5.7	5.0
East Midlands	4.3	13.5	15.2	10.1	11.8
West Midlands	9.3	11.4	8.2	32.2	17.2
East of England	7.8	5.7	2.4	4.0	4.9
London	50.9	50.2	30.8	31.6	42.1
South East	14.7	7.8	2.6	11.5	8.6
South West	3.4	1.4	1.7	1.3	1.6
England	98.5	99.0	99.6	99.5	99.2
Wales	1.5	1.0	0.4	0.5	0.8
England and Wales =100% (numbers)	50,652	466,597	131,662	301,295	1,036,807

1   Total includes all Indians of any religion, including those with no religion and whose religion was 'Not Stated'.
Source: Census 2001, Office for National Statistics

Black African population distribution by religion

Black Africans in England and Wales mainly belonged to one of two religious groups, Christians (69 per cent) and Muslims (20 per cent). More than three quarters of the Black African population lived in the London region (79 per cent), and similar proportions of both Christians and Muslims lived there (80 per cent and 77 per cent) (Table 3.36).

Black African Christians and Muslims tended to be spread across many London boroughs, and no one borough contained more than 10 per cent of the Black African population of England and Wales. Southwark was home to 9 per cent of Black African Christians and 6 per cent of Black African Muslims, and Newham was home to 7 per cent of Black African Christians and 6 per cent of Black African Muslims. Outside these two boroughs there was evidence of a slight tendency for Black African Christians and Muslims to be living in different areas; for example, Black African Christians were more concentrated in Lambeth, Hackney and Lewisham (where 7 per cent, 6 per cent and 5 per cent of the Black African Christian population lived), while Black African Muslims were more concentrated in the Borough of Brent, home to 6 per cent of the Black African Muslim population.

Chinese population distribution by religion

Just over half the Chinese population in England and Wales had no religion (53 per cent), 22 per cent were Christian and 15 per cent were Buddhist. Chinese Buddhists and Chinese Christians were more likely than those with no religion to live in the London region (42 per cent and 38 per cent compared with 32 per cent) (Table 3.37). There was little difference in the proportion of Chinese people in different religious groups in other regions of England and Wales.

Muslim population distribution by ethnic group

Muslims were the most ethnically diverse group in England and Wales in 2001. Three quarters of Muslims (74 per cent) were from an Asian ethnic background, predominantly Pakistani (43 per cent). Bangladeshis, Indians and Other Asians made up 16 per cent, 8 per cent and 6 per cent respectively. Just over one in ten Muslims in England and Wales (11 per cent) were from a White ethnic group; 4 per cent were of White British origin and 7 per cent from another White background. A further 6 per cent of Muslims were of Black African origin.

Nearly four in ten Muslims in England and Wales (39 per cent) lived in the London region in 2001, with further concentrations in the West Midlands (14 per cent), the North West (13 per cent) and Yorkshire and the Humber (12 per cent). However, Muslims from different ethnic groups tended to live in different parts of the country.

Table 3.36

Geographic distribution of Black African population: by selected religion, country and Government Office Region, April 2001

England and Wales

Percentages

	Christian	Muslim	Other	All Black African[1]
North East	0.5	0.5	0.9	0.5
North West	2.9	4.4	4.7	3.3
Yorkshire and the Humber	1.6	2.9	3.0	2.0
East Midlands	1.5	2.8	3.8	1.9
West Midlands	2.3	2.7	5.0	2.5
East of England	4.0	2.1	5.3	3.5
London	80.3	76.8	64.5	79.0
South East	5.3	4.5	8.6	5.1
South West	1.1	1.6	2.7	1.3
England	99.5	98.5	98.1	99.2
Wales	0.5	1.5	1.6	0.8
England and Wales = 100%	330,369	96,136	14,109	479,665

1 Total includes all Black Africans of any religion, including those with no religion and whose religion was 'Not Stated'.
Source: Census 2001, Office for National Statistics

Table **3.37**

Geographic distirbution of the Chinese population: by selected religion, country and Government Office Region, April 2001

England and Wales

Percentages

	Christian	Buddhist	No Religion	All Chinese[1]
North East	3.5	1.6	2.5	2.7
North West	11.0	9.8	12.7	11.8
Yorkshire and the Humber	4.9	4.6	5.9	5.4
East Midlands	5.0	5.5	6.1	5.7
West Midlands	5.5	7.4	7.5	7.1
East of England	8.7	8.7	9.2	9.0
London	37.8	42.0	32.5	35.3
South East	15.7	12.8	14.8	14.6
South West	5.5	4.9	5.8	5.6
England	97.5	97.3	97.1	97.2
Wales	2.5	2.7	2.9	2.8
England and Wales = 100% (numbers)	48,936	34,304	119,382	226,948

1 Total includes all Chinese of any religion, including those whose religion was 'Not Stated'.
Source: Census 2001, Office for National Statistics

Around three-quarters of Black African and Other White Muslims lived in London in 2001 (77 per cent and 72 per cent) (Table 3.38). More than half of Bangladeshi Muslims lived in London (55 per cent) while around one in ten lived in the West Midlands (11 per cent) and North West (9 per cent).

Bangladeshi Muslims were concentrated within particular local authorities and boroughs; 24 per cent lived in Tower Hamlets in London and 7 per cent lived in Birmingham.

Pakistani Muslims were the least likely of the Muslim groups to live in London. Pakistani Muslims were fairly evenly split between the West Midlands (22 per cent), Yorkshire and the Humber (20 per cent) and London (20 per cent) with a further 16 per cent living in the North West. As with Bangladeshi Muslims, Pakistani Muslims tended to live in particular local authorities.

The highest concentrations of Indian Muslims were in London (31 per cent) and the North West (27 per cent) with smaller clusters in the East Midlands (15 per cent) and Yorkshire and Humber (12 per cent).

More than half of White British Muslims lived in London, with 7 per cent living in the Borough of Enfield and 4 per cent living in

the boroughs of Haringey and Hackney. High proportions of Other White Muslims lived in these boroughs (9 per cent, 9 per cent and 8 per cent).

Ethnic and religious diversity by area

So far this chapter has illustrated the geographic distribution of people from specific ethnic and religious groups, focusing on each group separately and looking at how its population is spread throughout Great Britain. This section examines the picture from the other way round, looking at specific areas and summarising the level of ethnic and religious diversity within them, taking account of the many different groups living there. This is done to show which areas of England and Wales were the most and the least diverse in 2001. The overall level of ethnic and religious diversity has been calculated using the Fractionalisation Index, which is one of several indices that can be used to measure the diversity of the population in a given geographic area.[9]

The Fractionalisation Index produces a single 'score' based on the relative sizes of all the different groups within a given area. In this chapter these Fractionalisation Index scores are referred to as 'diversity scores' (see Box 3 overleaf).

Table **3.38**

Geographic distribution of Muslims: by selected ethnic group, country and Government office region, April 2001

England and Wales

Percentages

	White British	Other White	Mixed	Indian	Pakistani	Bangladeshi	Other Asian	Black African	All Muslims[1]
North East	1.9	1.1	2.6	0.3	2.0	2.2	2.1	0.5	1.7
North West	8.6	3.8	10.8	26.6	16.5	9.3	11.0	4.4	13.2
Yorkshire and the Humber	6.7	3.2	8.4	11.8	20.4	4.3	8.9	2.9	12.2
East Midlands	3.4	2.7	4.4	15.2	3.9	2.5	5.6	2.8	4.5
West Midlands	6.6	3.1	8.2	8.2	21.9	11.2	11.8	2.7	14.0
East of England	6.7	4.9	5.8	2.4	5.4	6.5	5.0	2.1	5.1
London	52.2	71.6	44.1	30.8	19.9	55.0	43.6	76.8	39.3
South East	8.5	6.9	9.8	2.6	8.2	5.5	8.1	4.5	7.0
South West	3.1	1.8	3.2	1.7	0.8	1.6	2.0	1.6	1.5
England	97.6	99.1	97.3	99.6	98.9	98.1	98.2	98.5	98.6
Wales	2.4	0.9	2.7	0.4	1.1	1.9	1.8	1.5	1.4
England and Wales =100% (numbers)	**63,042**	**115,841**	**64,262**	**131,662**	**657,680**	**259,710**	**90,013**	**96,136**	**1,546,626**

1 Includes Muslims from all ethnic groups.
Source: Census 2001, Office for National Statistics

Box 3

How to interpret the Fractionalisation Index of diversity

The Fractionalisation Index of diversity is relatively straightforward to calculate and interpret. It produces scores that represent the probability that two people chosen at random within a given area will belong to different groups. A high score means that there is a high probability that two people drawn randomly from the area will belong to different groups, and therefore that the area is highly diverse. For example, the London Borough of Brent had an ethnic diversity score of 0.85, representing an 85 per cent chance that two people drawn at random from Brent would be from different ethnic groups. A low score means that the area is not diverse, or in other words that it is homogeneous in terms of its ethnic or religious composition. For example, Easington local authority in the North East had an ethnic diversity score of 0.02, representing a 2 per cent chance that two people drawn at random from Easington would be from different ethnic groups. If the diversity score was zero, this would indicate that there was no chance of two people being from different groups as there was only one group in the area. See the Appendix at the end of this chapter for more details.

For this analysis, scores are classed as highly diverse if they are 0.5 or higher, as this indicates a 50 per cent chance or above that two people drawn at random would be from a different ethnic group.

Ethnic diversity by area

Most local authority areas in England and Wales were not particularly ethnically diverse (Map 3.39). Some 223 local authorities (59 per cent) had diversity scores of 0.11 or less, representing a lower than 11 per cent chance in most areas that two people drawn at random would be from different ethnic groups. Of these, 80 (21 per cent) were particularly homogeneous, with diversity scores of 0.05 or lower. Easington in the North East had the lowest ethnic diversity score of all areas (0.02), representing a 2 per cent chance that two people chosen at random would belong to different ethnic groups.

Of the 376 local authorities in England and Wales, 28 (7 per cent) were highly diverse, with diversity scores greater than 0.50. The great majority (24) of these highly diverse areas were London boroughs. Brent and Newham were the most ethnically diverse local authority areas in the country with scores of 0.85 and 0.83 respectively, representing an 85 per cent and 83 per cent chance that two people chosen at random would be from different ethnic groups. Brent's predominant ethnic groups

Map **3.39**

Ethnic diversity: by local authority area, April 2001
England and Wales

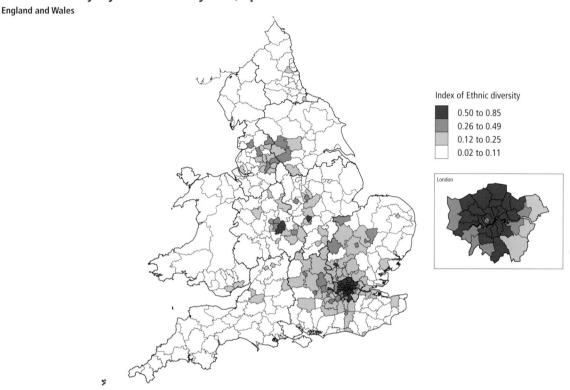

Index of Ethnic diversity
- 0.50 to 0.85
- 0.26 to 0.49
- 0.12 to 0.25
- 0.02 to 0.11

Source: Census 2001, Office for National Statistics

were White British (29 per cent), Indian (18 per cent), Black Caribbean (10 per cent), Other White (9 per cent) and Black African (8 per cent). In Newham, White British formed the largest ethnic group (34 per cent), followed by Black Africans (13 per cent), Indians (12 per cent), Bangladeshis (9 per cent) and Pakistanis (8 per cent).

Havering had the lowest ethnic diversity score of any London borough (0.15). Nine out of ten (92 per cent) of the Havering population was White British.

Slough was the most ethnically diverse local authority area outside London, with a diversity score of 0.62. White British people made up the majority (58 per cent) of the population, but there were substantial proportions of Indians (14 per cent) and Pakistanis (12 per cent) who formed the next largest ethnic groups. Leicester and Luton were also highly diverse (ethnic diversity scores of 0.57 and 0.56). Both contained a majority of White British people, though the remaining population of each area contained different ethnic minority groups in different proportions. Leicester was 61 per cent White British and 26 per cent Indian, while no other ethnic group formed more than 2 per cent of its population. In contrast, Luton was 65 per cent White British and contained relatively small populations from several other ethnic groups, such as Pakistanis (9 per cent),

White Irish (5 per cent), Indians, Bangladeshis and Black Caribbeans (each forming 4 per cent of its population).

Ethnic diversity scores varied across smaller geographic areas. The London boroughs of Brent and Newham contained the MSOAs with the highest diversity scores in England and Wales. In Brent ethnic diversity scores varied from 0.72 to 0.87, and in Newham from 0.62 to 0.87. In contrast, the MSOA with the lowest ethnic diversity score in England and Wales (0.01) was located in Sedgefield in the North East.

Average diversity by ethnic group

This section compares the extent to which members of different ethnic groups tended to live in ethnically diverse areas. It reports average ethnic diversity scores of the MSOAs, by ethnic group. The average ethnic diversity score for each group can be seen as a measure of that group's exposure to ethnic diversity at MSOA level. (The method used to calculate average diversity is explained in the Appendix at the end of this chapter.)

As White British are by far the largest group in the UK and tend to live in areas where they form a majority, a large proportion of White British people in any given area would typically reduce the diversity score of the area. People from ethnic minority

Figure **3.40**

Average ethnic diversity of middle layer super output areas of residence: by ethnic group, April 2001

England and Wales
Ethnic diversity scores

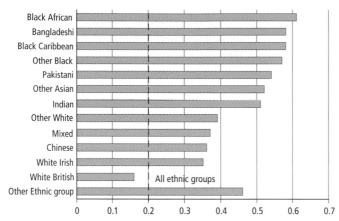

Source: Census 2001, Office for National Statistics

groups tended to form a minority in most (though not all) areas. Therefore, a high proportion of people from any ethnic minority groups in an area would usually raise the diversity score of the area, unless the group formed an absolute majority.

People from the three Black ethnic groups and the Bangladeshi group tended to live in the most ethnically diverse MSOAs (Figure 3.40). Black Africans lived in MSOAs with, on average, ethnic diversity scores of 0.61. This represents a 61 per cent chance that two people drawn at random from the area in which they lived would be from different ethnic groups. Among people from Black Caribbean, Other Black and Bangladeshi ethnic groups, the average ethnic diversity score of the areas in which they lived was above 0.55. Those from White Irish, Other White, Chinese, and Mixed ethnic groups tended to live in less ethnically diverse areas, with average scores between 0.30 and 0.40. The White British population tended to live in the least ethnically diverse areas; on average, White British people lived in areas with an ethnic diversity score of 0.16. Thus, people from ethnic minority groups were more likely to live in ethnically diverse areas than the White British.

Religious diversity by area

In 2001 most areas in England and Wales had low religious diversity[10] (Map 3.41). Three-quarters (76 per cent) of local authorities in England and Wales had religious diversity scores of 0.10 or less, meaning that there was a 10 per cent or less chance that two people chosen at random from these areas would belong to different religions. In 7 per cent of local

Map **3.41**

Religious diversity: by local authority area, April 2001
England and Wales

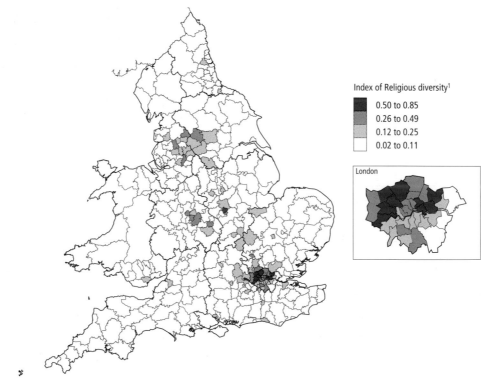

1 Index excludes No Religion and Not Stated.
Source: Census 2001, Office for National Statistics

authorities the religious diversity score was 0.01. The local authority areas with the lowest levels of religious diversity were located in the North West, including Allerdale and Knowsley; the North East, including Sedgefield and Berwick upon Tweed; and Yorkshire and the Humber, including Ryedale.

Religious diversity scores of 0.50 or higher were found in 11 (3 per cent) of the 376 local authorities in England and Wales. Almost all these areas were located in north London; the others were Leicester and Slough. Areas of moderately high religious diversity (up to 0.50) were found around the border of the North West and Yorkshire and the Humber, and in London and the surrounding areas.

The London Borough of Harrow had the highest religious diversity score in England and Wales, 0.62. Just under half of the local population of Harrow were Christian (47 per cent), 20 per cent were Hindu, 7 per cent were Muslim and 6 per cent were Jewish. Within London, the boroughs of Brent, Redbridge, Barnet, Newham, Ealing and Tower Hamlets also had high religious diversity. Outside London, Leicester had the highest religious diversity score, 0.59. Leicester's local population included Christians (45 per cent), Hindus (15 per cent) and Muslims (11 per cent).

The London Borough of Redbridge contained MSOAs with the highest religious diversity scores in England and Wales (0.77), but there was a large variation between different areas of this borough. Three areas of Redbridge had religious diversity scores of 0.75 or higher, while its least diverse MSOA had a score of 0.15. Around half the population of Redbridge were Christian (51 per cent), while Muslims made up the next largest group (12 per cent), followed by Hindus (8 per cent), Jews (6 per cent) and Sikhs (5 per cent).

Some MSOAs of Birmingham, Leicester and the London Borough of Brent also had high religious diversity scores (0.75, 0.74 and 0.74). Again, there was a large variation between neighbouring MSOAs within these three boroughs. For example, in Birmingham the religious diversity scores ranged from 0.75 in one MSOA to 0.03 in three MSOAs. Birmingham's population was 59 per cent Christian and 14 per cent Muslim, while no other religious group formed more than 3 per cent.

Average diversity by religious group

This section looks at the extent to which members of different religious groups tended to live in religiously diverse areas. It reports average religious diversity scores of the MSOAs by religious group. As with ethnic diversity, the average religious diversity score for each group can also be thought of as a measure of its exposure to religious diversity at MSOA level.

As Christians are by far the largest group in the UK and tended to live in areas where they formed a vast majority, a large proportion of Christians in an area would typically reduce the diversity score of the area. People from smaller religious groups tended to form a minority in most (though not all) areas. Therefore a high proportion of people from any minority religious groups would typically raise the diversity score of the area, unless the group was large enough to form an absolute majority in that area.

Hindus, Sikhs, Jews and Muslims tended to live in MSOAs with higher religious diversity than Buddhists, Christians and people from other religions (Figure 3.42). On average, Hindus, Sikhs, Jews and Muslims lived in MSOAs where there was around a 40 per cent chance that two people drawn at random would be from different religions (mean religious diversity scores of around 0.40). Buddhists and people from other non-Christian religions tended to live in areas with slightly lower average diversity scores (0.21 and 0.17). Christians tended to live in areas of relatively low religious diversity; the average religious diversity score of the areas in which they lived was 0.09.

Figure **3.42**

Average religious diversity of middle layer super output areas of residence by religion, April 2001

England and Wales

Religious diversity scores

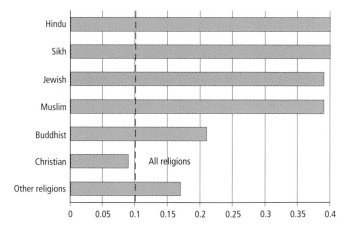

Source: Census 2001, Office for National Statistics

Population distribution in urban and rural areas

This section gives an overview of the extent to which different ethnic groups tended to live in urban or rural areas, based on the urban and rural area classification of Census output areas. Details of the urban and rural area classification can be found in the Appendix at the end of this chapter.

Figure **3.43**

Proportion of people living in rural areas: by ethnic group, April 2001

England and Wales

Percentages

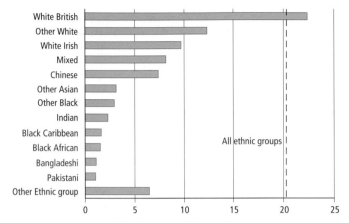

Source: Census 2001, Office for National Statistics

Although one in five people in England and Wales lived in a rural area in 2001 (20 per cent), the rural population contained a very low proportion of people from ethnic minority groups (Figure 3.43). White British people were much more likely to live in rural areas than people of any other ethnic group; 22 per cent lived there, as did 12 per cent of the Other White group and 10 per cent of the White Irish group. Pakistanis and Bangladeshis were the least likely ethnic groups to live in rural areas, only 1 per cent of each group did so, followed by 2 per cent of people from each of the Indian, Black Caribbean and Black African groups.

The White British population formed a majority in both urban and rural areas. In rural areas 96 per cent of people were White British, higher than in urban areas where 85 per cent were White British. In rural areas the Other White ethnic group accounted for 2 per cent of the population. Collectively the remaining ethnic groups made up 2 per cent of the rural population of England and Wales.

Even in regions where a relatively large proportion of the population lived in rural areas and the overall population was ethnically diverse, people from ethnic minority groups tended to live in urban areas. For example, one in six people in the West Midlands lived in a rural area (16 per cent), and it was ethnically diverse, containing more than one in five (22 per cent) of the Pakistani population, one in six (17 per cent) of the Indian population and one in seven (15 per cent) of the Black Caribbean population of England and Wales. Yet while almost one in five (18 per cent) of the White British population of the West Midlands lived in a rural area, one in a hundred (1 per cent) of the Pakistanis, Indians and Black Caribbeans in the West Midlands lived in a rural area.

Notes and references

1. Owen D (1996) 'Size, structure and growth of the ethnic minority populations', in Coleman D and Salt J (eds.) *Ethnicity in the 1991 Census, Vol 1: Demographic characteristics of the ethnic minority populations*, HMSO: London.

2. Peach C (1997) Pluralist and Assimilationist models of ethnic settlement in London 1991. *Tijdschrift voor economische en sociale geografie* **88(2)**, 130–134.

3. Owen D (1999) Geographical patterns of recent migration and population change for minority ethnic groups within Great Britain. *Revue Europeene des Migrations Internationales* **15**, 7–12.

4. Rees P and Phillips D (1996) 'Geographical spread: the national picture' in Ratcliffe P (ed.) *Social geography and ethnicity in Britain: geographical spread, spatial concentration and internal migration*, HMSO: London, 23–110.

5. Peach C (1996) Does Britain Have Ghettoes? *Transactions of the Institute of British Geographers* **22 (1)**, 216–235.

6. Halpern D and Nazroo J (2000) The ethnic density effect: results from a national community survey of England and Wales. *International Journal of Social Psychiatry*, **46**, 1, 34–46.

7. This chapter does not report on the 'Other' ethnic groups (other White, Other Asian, Other Black and Other Ethnic). The 'Other' groups are particularly heterogeneous, including people with a diverse range of ethnicities, religions, countries of birth and languages. For more information see Connolly H and Gardener D (2005) '*Who are the 'Other' ethnic groups?*' Available at: ww.statistics.gov.uk/cci/article.asp?id=1291

8. This chapter does not report on the 'Other' religious groups. This group is particularly heterogeneous, comprising people belonging to many different religions. For information on this group see Focus on Religion Overview (2004), 'Religious Populations'. Available at: www.statistics.gov.uk/cci/nugget.asp?id=954

9. For an overview of the various measures of diversity see Reardon S F and Firebaugh G (2002) Measures of Multigroup Segregation, *Sociological Methodology* **32** and Tong Y L (1983) Some distribution properties of sample species diversity indices and their applications. *Biometrics* **39**.

10. Religious diversity has been calculated based on the seven substantive religious categories in the 2001 classification (Christian, Buddhist, Hindu, Jewish, Muslim and Sikh), excluding No religion and Not Stated.

Appendix: Chapter 3 Geographic Diversity

Geographic areas

More details of the geographic areas mentioned in this chapter.

Government Office Regions

Government Offices for the Regions were established across England in 1994. In 1996 the regions covered, known as Government Office Regions (GORs), became the primary classification for the presentation of regional statistics.

GORs are built up of complete counties/unitary authorities so although they are subject to change they always reflect administrative boundaries as at the end of the previous year. Scotland and Wales are not subdivided into GORs but are listed with them in GB-wide statistical comparisons.

Local authorities, unitary authorities and boroughs

In the context of this chapter, the term 'local authority' includes areas categorised as counties, unitary authorities, non-metropolitan districts and metropolitan districts. London boroughs have a similar structure to metropolitan districts and so are also included in the term 'local authority'. In England there are currently 46 unitary authorities; 34 shire counties split into 239 (non-metropolitan) districts; 36 metropolitan district councils, 32 London boroughs and the City of London authority. Scotland has 32 unitary authorities and Wales has 22 unitary authorities.

For more information on UK Geography, see the 'ONS Beginners Guide to UK Geography' at: www.statistics.gov.uk/geography/beginners_guide.asp

Census Output Areas

Super Output Areas (SOAs) are a new geographic hierarchy designed to improve the reporting of small area statistics in England and Wales. Their first statistical application was for the Indices of Deprivation 2004. They have been increasingly used for datasets on the ONS Neighbourhood Statistics (NeSS) website and are intended to become a standard across National Statistics.

Up to 2004 the standard unit for presenting local statistical information was the electoral ward/division. This has the following drawbacks:

- Electoral wards/divisions vary greatly in size, from fewer than 100 residents to more than 30,000. This is not ideal for nationwide comparisons, and also means that data that can safely be released for larger wards may not be released for smaller wards due to disclosure requirements (i.e. the need to protect the confidentiality of individuals)

- Electoral wards/divisions are subject to regular boundary changes. This creates problems when trying to compare datasets from different time periods

It was therefore decided to develop SOAs, a range of areas that would be of consistent size and whose boundaries would not change. These were built from groups of the Output Areas (OAs) used for the 2001 Census.

Middle-layer Super Output Areas (MSOAs)

In this chapter, the main unit for small-area analysis is the Middle-layer Super Output Area (MSOA). The average MSOA has a residential population of 7,200 and the minimum population is 5,000. MSOAs are built from groups of Census Output Areas and constrained by the boundaries of the 2003 local authority boundaries used for 2001 Census outputs.

For more information see: www.statistics.gov.uk/geography/soa.asp

Reference map of local authority areas

See overleaf.

Types of area

Urban and rural

The 2001 Census Output Areas have been classified as urban or rural depending on the population density.[A] They are described as 'urban' if the majority of the population falls inside a settlement of population 10,000 or more, and 'rural' if not.

Statistical measurement

Determining ranges on maps using the Jenks Optimisation method

The ranges on the maps have been determined using the Jenks Optimisation method. This method has advantages for:

- classifying data that contain extreme values or that look very different from a normal distribution; and

- arranging data into a small number of ranges or classes (i.e. less than five).

This method arranges values into classes by determining natural break points between the classes and assigning the data to classes based upon their position along the data distribution relative to all other data values. It is done by comparing the sum of the squared differences of values from the mean avreages of their classes and arranging the break points between the classes, to minimise the squared deviations of the class means and maximise the goodness of variance fit.[B]

Local and Unitary Authorities
Great Britain

1 Dundee City
2 Clackmannanshire

3 Inverclyde
4 West Dunbartonshire
5 East Dunbartonshire
6 North Lanarkshire
7 Renfrewshire
8 East Renfrewshire
9 Glasgow City
10 City of Edinburgh

11 Wansbeck
12 Newcastle upon Tyne
13 North Tyneside
14 Gateshead
15 South Tyneside
16 Derwentside
17 Chester-le-Street
18 Durham
19 Sedgefield
20 Darlington
21 Stockton-on-Tees
22 Middlesbrough

23 Ballymoney
24 Carrickfergus
25 Newtownabbey
26 Belfast
27 Castlereagh
28 North Down

29 Blackpool
30 Preston
31 South Ribble
32 Chorley
33 Blackburn with Darwen
34 Hyndburn
35 Rossendale
36 Burnley
37 Pendle
38 Calderdale
39 West Lancashire
40 Bolton
41 Bury
42 Rochdale

43 Liverpool
44 Knowsley
45 St. Helens
46 Wigan
47 Salford
48 Manchester
49 Oldham
50 Tameside
51 Halton
52 Warrington
53 Trafford
54 Stockport
55 Ellesmere Port and Neston

56 City of Kingston upon Hull
57 Rotherham
58 Chesterfield
59 Bolsover
60 North East Derbyshire
61 Ashfield
62 Mansfield
63 Newark and Sherwood
64 Lincoln
65 Amber Valley
66 Broxtowe
67 Gedling
68 Derby
69 Erewash
70 Nottingham
71 South Derbyshire
72 North West Leicestershire
73 Charnwood

74 Macclesfield
75 Congleton
76 Crewe and Nantwich
77 Newcastle-under-Lyme
78 Stoke-on-Trent
79 Staffordshire Moorlands
80 Oswestry
81 East Staffordshire
82 Telford and Wrekin
83 South Staffordshire
84 Cannock Chase
85 Lichfield
86 Tamworth

87 Wolverhampton
88 Walsall
89 Dudley
90 Sandwell
91 Birmingham
92 Solihull
93 North Warwickshire
94 Nuneaton and Bedworth
95 Coventry
96 Wyre Forest
97 Bromsgrove
98 Redditch
99 Worcester

100 Hinckley and Bosworth
101 Blaby
102 Leicester
103 Oadby and Wigston
104 Corby
105 Peterborough
106 Norwich
107 Kettering
108 East Northamptonshire
109 East Cambridgeshire
110 Northampton
111 Wellingborough
112 Cambridge
113 South Northamptonshire
114 Milton Keynes
115 Mid Bedfordshire
116 South Cambridgeshire
117 Ipswich
118 West Oxfordshire
119 South Bedfordshire
120 Luton
121 North Hertfordshire
122 Stevenage
123 East Hertfordshire
124 Oxford
125 South Oxfordshire
126 Wycombe
127 Chiltern
128 Dacorum
129 St. Albans
130 Welwyn Hatfield
131 Broxbourne
132 Harlow
133 Three Rivers
134 Watford
135 Hertsmere
136 Epping Forest
137 Brentwood
138 Chelmsford
139 Colchester
140 Basildon
141 Castle Point
142 Southend-on-Sea
143 Thurrock
144 Medway

145 Wychavon
146 Tewkesbury
147 Rhondda, Cynon, Taff
148 Merthyr Tydfil
149 Blaenau Gwent
150 Caerphilly
151 Torfaen
152 Newport
153 Forest of Dean
154 Gloucester
155 Cheltenham
156 City of Bristol
157 South Gloucestershire
158 Bath and North East Somerset
159 Swindon

160 Weymouth and Portland
161 Bournemouth
162 Poole
163 Eastleigh
164 Southampton
165 Fareham
166 Havant
167 Reading
168 Wokingham
169 Hart

170 Windsor and Maidenhead
171 South Bucks
172 Slough
173 Bracknell Forest
174 Runnymede
175 Spelthorne
176 Elmbridge
177 Surrey Heath
178 Rushmoor

179 Woking
180 Guildford
181 Waverley
182 Mole Valley
183 Epsom and Ewell
184 Reigate and Banstead
185 Tandridge
186 Crawley
187 Mid Sussex

188 Worthing
189 Adur
190 Dartford
191 Gravesham
192 Tonbridge and Malling
193 Tunbridge Wells
194 Maidstone
195 Hastings
196 Canterbury

A Kingston upon Thames
B Hammersmith and Fulham
C Kensington and Chelsea
D Westminster
E City of London
F Islington
G Hackney
H Waltham Forest

Fractionalisation Index of diversity

The diversity scores in this report are based on the Fractionalisation Index of diversity. The Fractionalisation Index is a measure of the variation of a population according to a classification system. It measures the probability that two individuals chosen at random in a population will belong to two different groups.[c] It can also be used to show how balanced the distribution of a population is across a fixed set of categories.

The Fractionalisation Index has been applied to the standard classifications of both ethnic group and religion to produce separate 'scores' for ethnic and religious diversity.

Points to bear in mind when interpreting the diversity scores:

- The diversity scores do not provide precise details of the population composition in a given area. For example, an area whose population was made up of equal proportions of people from two groups would have a diversity score of 0.50 (a 50 per cent chance that two people drawn at random belonged to different ethnic groups). An area where there was one predominant group and several smaller groups could also have a diversity score of 0.50. This can be an advantage, as the diversity scores are neutral about the nature of the group that is in the majority. Low diversity scores would be found in any area where a single ethnic group formed a large majority, whether that majority was White British, Black African, Pakistani or any other

- People classified in the residual 'Other, please specify' group are not treated as being different from each other for the purposes of the diversity scores. People in the 'Other' category may have different ethnicities, for example the Other ethnic group category is made up of people from many different groups such as Arab, Japanese and South American, but the ethnic group classification did not identify them separately so these differences would not contribute to the calculation of the diversity scores. If a large proportion of the population was composed of diverse people classified as 'Other', any diversity scores based on the standard ethnic group classification would underestimate the true diversity of that area. However in most areas of Great Britain the 'Others' make up a small proportion of the population, therefore the overall results are unlikely to be significantly affected

- The more groups there are in the classification, the greater the maximum possible value of the diversity score. The maximum possible diversity score would occur if the population of an area contained an equal

proportion of people from each of the groups measured. If there were two groups included in the classification, the maximum possible diversity score would be 0.50. If there were 8 groups in the classification (as there are in the religion classification), the maximum possible diversity score would be 0.88, and if there were 16 groups in the classification (as there are in the ethnicity classification), the maximum possible diversity score would be 0.94

The Fractionalisation Index is calculated as one minus the sum of the squared proportion of each group, and is represented as follows in mathematical notation, where the Fractionalisation Index is F:

$$F = 1 - \sum_{i=1}^{k} p_i^2$$

i = ethnic group category

p_i = fraction of population belonging to category i

k = the number of categories of the chosen classification system

An index equal to zero means that there is only one group in that area. If the index is at its maximum value, then all groups have equal size. By definition, the maximum F value is:

$$F_{max} = \frac{(k-1)}{k}$$

Maximum value of F for a chosen number of categories

Number of groups in classification system	Maximum possible value for F
2	0.500
3	0.667
4	0.750
5	0.800
6	0.833
7	0.858
8	0.875
9	0.888
10	0.900
....	....
16	0.938

The more groups are defined in a classification, the more likely it is for two people to belong to two different groups.

Indices for measuring diversity have been developed by economists, sociologists, demographers, ecologists and statisticians throughout the 20th century. The Fractionalisation Index used in this analysis has been referred to using different names, such as the Diversity Index,[D,E,F] the Fractionalisation Index[G] and the Fragmentation Index.[H] Some variants of the index are known as the Index of Qualitative Variation (IQV) or Simpson's Index.[I]

Average Fractionalisation Indices of diversity

To calculate an average diversity index, the index for each area is weighted by the population in that area as a proportion of the total population.

In the case of averages for each ethnic group, this means the index for an area is weighted by the number of people from that group as a proportion of the total number of people in that group. For example, if 1,000 out of a total 100,000 Black Caribbeans lived in a specific area, the weight assigned to that area would be 1000/100,000 or 0.01. The index for that area is then multiplied by the weight. The weighted indices are then summed to give the average index for members of that group.

$$\bar{F} = \sum_{i=1}^{i=k} \frac{N_{ei} * F_i}{N_e}$$

Where:

i = area

k = number of areas

N = number of individuals

e = a given ethnic group

F = Fractionalisation Index of diversity

Notes and references

A. Countryside Agency, Department for the Environment Food and Rural Affairs, ODPM (renamed Department for Communities and Local Government in 2006), ONS and Welsh Assembly Government (2004) *Rural and Urban Area Classification 2004: An Introductory Guide*. Available at: www.statistics.gov.uk/ geography/nrudp.asp

B. Jenks G F (1967) The Data Model Concept in Statistical Mapping. *International Yearbook of Cartography* **7**, 186–190.

C. Lieberson S (1969) Measuring Population Diversity. *American Sociological Review* **34**.

D. Religious diversity has been calculated based on the seven substantive religious categories in the 2001 classification (Christian, Buddhist, Hindu, Jewish, Muslim and Sikh), excluding No religion and Not Stated.

E. Agresti A and Agresti B F (1978) Statistical Analysis of Qualitative Variation. *Sociological Methodology* **9**, 205.

F. Greenberg J H (1956) The measurement of linguistic diversity. *Language* **32**.

G. Easterly W and Levine R (1997) Africa's Growth Tragedy: Policies and Ethnic Divisions. *Quarterly Journal of Economics* **111**, 4.

H. Alesina A, La Ferrara E (2000) Participation in Heterogeneous Communities. *Quarterly Journal of Economics* **115**, 3.

I. Simpson E H (1949) Measurement of Diversity. *Nature* **163**. Note that a different measure of diversity using the natural logarithm of the sum of powers of proportions is also known as Simpson's index. Agresti and Agresti (1978) and Lieberson (1969) provide an overview of the history and variants of the Fractionalisation index.

Households and families

Helen Connolly and Camellia Raha

Chapter 4

Introduction and overview

This chapter explores some of the key household characteristics that differentiate ethnic and religious groups. Households are classified according to the ethnic or religious group of the household reference person (HRP) and, for simplicity, are referred to as, for example, 'White British' or 'Christian' households.[1] However, it should be noted that households may contain people classified to different ethnic or religious groups (see Chapter 1 for a detailed discussion of the ethnic and religious homogeneity within households).

The chapter shows many differences between ethnic and religious groups. These include variations in the proportion of one-person households, pensioner households and lone-parent families with dependent children; variations in household size and, related to that, the presence of dependent children and extended families; and key measures of deprivation including overcrowding and the proportion of households with no working adults.

Where possible, results are compared with data from the 1991 Census to examine the evidence for change over the ten-year period. For example, average household size fell across all groups between 1991 and 2001 with the greatest change among Asian households, which have the largest households on average. But the direction of change was not always the same for all ethnic groups. Home ownership increased among White households between 1991 and 2001 but decreased among Asian households. Over the same period, lone-parent households with dependent children increased among White and Asian groups but decreased among Black groups.

The extent to which differences between ethnic and religious groups reflect other differences, for example differences in the age structure of the populations, is also considered. The younger age structure of Indian, Pakistani and Bangladeshi populations is associated with larger households and a greater proportion of households with dependent children. Conversely, White British and White Irish populations have an older age structure and have a greater number of pensioner households, one-person households and a greater rate of home ownership.

However, differences in the age structure of populations do not fully account for variations between households. Mixed, Black African, Chinese and Indian populations have young age profiles but households headed by these groups were less likely than Bangladeshi and Pakistani households to contain dependent children.

Ethnic differences are reflected, to some extent, in variations between religious groups. The majority of both Christian and Jewish populations are White British and many findings for

Christian and Jewish households reflect the pattern among White British households. Similarly, findings for Muslim households often mirror the pattern among Pakistani and Bangladeshi households while results for Hindu and Sikh households reflect the pattern among Indian households.

However, differences between religious groups are not fully explained by their ethnic distribution. Religion can exert a strong influence, sometimes being more important than ethnic group in determining household characteristics. For example, in all ethnic groups, Muslims tended to have larger average household sizes and a greater number of dependent children.

Other factors, for example variations in household tenure, also contribute to differences between groups. Larger households were related to high rates of overcrowding in Bangladeshi households but to a lesser extent in Pakistani households, possibly reflecting differences in tenure – Bangladeshis were far more likely than Pakistanis to live in socially rented accommodation.

Regional differences may also contribute to household variations. Black African households contained fewer dependent children than Pakistani households but had higher levels of overcrowding. The difference may be related to the concentration of Black Africans in London, which had the highest rates of overcrowding in 2001 – 78 per cent of Black Africans lived in London compared with 20 per cent of Pakistanis.

These findings suggest that, while definite patterns exist, the household characteristics of ethnic and religious groups result from more than simply their ethnicity or religion. The rest of this chapter discusses these findings, and others, in more detail.

Family households and one-person households

The 2001 Census classified households into family households, one-person households, and 'other' households. The majority of households (63 per cent) were family households, containing 'one family and no others' (see Table 4.4 on page 87).[2] A further three in ten households (30 per cent) were one-person households, about half above pension age. 'Other' households, which included extended family households and shared households, accounted for 7 per cent of all households in Great Britain in 2001. These distributions differed by ethnic group.

Changing trends in contemporary British society have implications for household and family structure. The trend towards living alone has contributed to an increase in the number of one-person households. Between 1961 and 2004, the proportion of one-person households increased three-fold for adults below pension age and doubled for people of pension age.[3] However, the majority of households are still family households.

Family households

Households containing one family and no others accounted for around two-thirds of Bangladeshi (68 per cent), Indian (66 per cent), Pakistani (65 per cent) and White British households (64 per cent) in 2001. Black African households (50 per cent) were least likely to contain one family (Figure 4.1).

Across all religious groups more than half of households contained one family. Buddhist households were least likely to contain one family (52 per cent). In other religious groups the proportion of one-family households ranged from 57 per cent (Jewish) to 66 per cent (Hindu and Sikh) (Figure 4.2).

There was greater variation in the type of family household, whether comprising: a married couple (with or without children); cohabiting couple (with or without children); lone-parent (with children); or pensioner family (usually a couple without children). 'Children' in a family household are those who share the home with a parent, irrespective of their age. Hence a family may be classified as a family household where adult children and their parent(s) live together. A minority of pensioner families may contain children but all people in the household, including the children must be above pension age. The variations by type of family household are discussed below.

Figure **4.1**

One-family households:[1] by ethnic group,[2] April 2001

Great Britain

Percentages

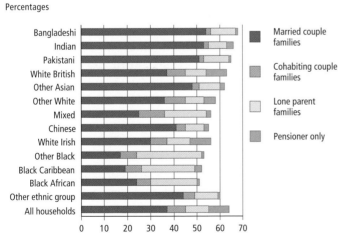

1 Living in 'one family and no others' households.
2 Of household reference person.

Source: Census 2001, Office for National Statistics; Census 2001, General Register Office for Scotland

Figure **4.2**

One-family households:[1] by religion,[2] April 2001

Great Britain

Percentages

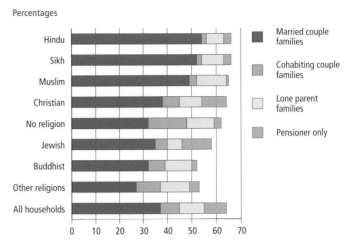

1 Living in 'one family and no others' households.
2 Of household reference person.

Source: Census 2001, Office for National Statistics; Census 2001, General Register Office for Scotland

Married couple families

Indian, Pakistani and Bangladeshi households were most likely to contain a married couple family below pension age. More than half of Bangladeshi (54 per cent), Indian (53 per cent) and Pakistani households (51 per cent) in Great Britain contained this type of family (see Table 4.4 on page 87). This was greater than the proportion among Chinese (41 per cent), White British (37 per cent) or White Irish households (30 per cent). Although the proportion of married couple families among White British and White Irish households was smaller than the proportion among Asian groups, the difference largely reflects variations in the age structure; 9 per cent of White British and White Irish households were pensioner families and the vast majority of these comprised a married couple above pension age. Black African (24 per cent) and Black Caribbean households (19 per cent) were least likely to contain a married couple family. In the case of these groups, the relatively small proportion of married couple families reflected the relatively large proportion of lone-parent families (see Table 4.4 on page 87).

There was a similar pattern for religion. Married couple families below pension age accounted for about half of Hindu (54 per cent), Sikh (52 per cent) and Muslim households (49 per cent), similar to Indian, Pakistani and Bangladeshi households. The households least likely to contain a married couple family below pension age were Buddhist (32 per cent), Jewish (35 per cent), Christian (38 per cent) and those headed by someone with no religion (32 per cent), reflecting the pattern among White groups. The smaller proportion of married couple families among Jewish and Christian households reflects the age structure of these groups: one in ten Jewish (12 per cent) and Christian households (10 per cent) were pensioner families, the majority comprising a married couple (Table 4.5).

Cohabiting couple families

In 2001 cohabiting couple families in Great Britain were most common in households headed by someone from a Mixed ethnic group (11 per cent), followed by White British (8 per cent), White Irish (7 per cent), Black Caribbean (7 per cent) and Black African households (6 per cent) (Table 4.4). Cohabiting couple families made up 4 per cent of Chinese households and 2 per cent of Indian, Pakistani and Bangladeshi households.

There were large variations between religious groups. Households with no religion were the most likely to be a cohabiting couple family (16 per cent) (Table 4.5). Cohabiting couple families were least common among Hindu (2 per cent), Sikh (2 per cent) and Muslim households (3 per cent). The proportion of cohabiting households ranged from 5 per cent (Jewish) to 7 per cent (Christian and Buddhist) in other groups.

Cohabiting couple families increased in most ethnic groups between 1991 and 2001. They increased from 5 per cent to 8 per cent of White households, from 2 per cent to 4 per cent of Chinese households and from 5 per cent to 6 per cent of Black African households.[4] Indian, Pakistani and Bangladeshi households were least likely to contain a cohabiting couple family, in both 1991 and 2001, but the percentage of these households increased from 1 per cent to 2 per cent for these groups between 1991 and 2001. Among Black Caribbean

households, by comparison, the proportion of cohabiting couple families remained stable, at 7 per cent, over the ten-year period (Table 4.3). Data for 1991 are not available for the Mixed ethnic group as this category was not included in the ethnic group classification for the 1991 Census (Chapter 1).

Lone-parent families

In 2001, 10 per cent of households in Great Britain had a lone-parent family but not all of these had dependent children (Table 4.4). From a policy perspective, there is greater interest in lone-parent families with dependent[5] children as they are particularly vulnerable to economic deprivation.

Among households with dependent children, those headed by someone from a Black ethnic group were most likely to be a lone-parent family. About half of Other Black and Black Caribbean households with dependent children were headed by a lone parent (52 per cent and 48 per cent respectively), as were 36 per cent of Black African households (Figure 4.6). The Other Black group contains predominantly young Black people, the majority having been born in the UK.[6] Lone-parent families were less common among White British (22 per cent), Chinese (15 per cent), Pakistani (13 per cent), Bangladeshi (12 per cent) and Indian households with dependent children (10 per cent). White British children accounted for the vast majority of children growing up in a lone-parent family in 2001 due to the greater population size of the White British group.

Table 4.3

Cohabiting family households:[1] by ethnic group,[2] April 1991 and April 2001

Great Britain

Percentages

	1991	2001
White	5	8
Indian	1	2
Pakistani	1	2
Bangladeshi	1	2
Black Caribbean	7	7
Black African	5	6
Chinese	2	4

1 With or without children.
2 Of household reference person.

Source: Census 2001, Office for National Statistics; Census 2001, General Register Office for Scotland; Peach, C. (1996)

Figure 4.6

Households with dependent children headed by a lone parent:[1] by ethnic group,[2] April 2001

Great Britain

Percentages

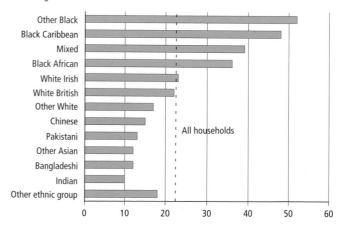

1 Living in 'one family and no others' households.
2 Of household reference person.

Source: Census 2001, Office for National Statistics; Census 2001, General Register Office for Scotland

Table **4.4**

Household type: by ethnic group,[1] April 2001

Great Britain　　Percentages

	One person			One family and no others					Other households	
	Pensioner	Other	All one person households	Pensioner families[2]	Married couple families[3]	Cohabiting couple families[3]	Lone parent families[3]	All one family households	Other households	All households = (100%) (numbers)
White British	15	15	31	9	37	8	9	64	6	21,439,962
White Irish	18	20	37	9	30	7	10	55	8	383,805
Other White	9	20	28	5	36	9	8	58	14	587,947
Mixed	5	25	31	2	25	11	18	56	13	149,508
Indian	4	12	15	3	53	2	8	66	19	319,887
Pakistani	3	9	12	1	51	2	11	65	23	180,349
Bangladeshi	2	7	9	1	54	2	11	68	24	62,505
Other Asian	4	15	19	2	48	3	9	62	20	82,943
Black Caribbean	10	28	38	3	19	7	23	53	9	276,404
Black African	3	27	30	1	24	6	20	50	20	178,452
Other Black	5	29	34	1	17	7	28	53	12	31,631
Chinese	4	23	28	2	41	4	8	56	16	82,784
Other ethnic group	3	21	24	1	44	5	10	60	16	76,544
All households	**14**	**16**	**30**	**9**	**37**	**8**	**10**	**63**	**7**	**23,852,721**

1　Of household reference person.
2　One family consisting only of related people of pensionable age (men aged 65 and over and women aged 60 and over).
3　One family in which at least one person is below pensionable age with or without dependent children.

Source: Census 2001, Office for National Statistics; Census 2001, General Register Office for Scotland

Table **4.5**

Household type: by religion,[1] April 2001

Great Britain　　Percentages

	One person			One family and no others					Other households	
	Pensioner	Other	All one person households	Pensioner families[2]	Married couple families[3]	Cohabiting couple families[3]	Lone parent families[3]	All one family households	Other households	All households = (100%) (numbers)
Christian	17	14	30	10	38	7	9	64	5	17,728,972
Buddhist	5	31	36	2	32	7	11	52	12	66,001
Hindu	3	11	14	3	54	2	7	66	19	174,625
Jewish	19	17	36	12	35	5	6	57	7	119,957
Muslim	2	13	15	1	49	3	12	65	20	423,348
Sikh	4	9	13	3	52	2	9	66	21	95,194
Other religions	8	30	38	4	27	10	12	52	10	79,674
No religion	4	25	29	3	32	16	11	62	9	3,435,551
Religion not stated	17	20	38	8	29	8	10	55	7	1,729,399
All households	**14**	**16**	**30**	**9**	**37**	**8**	**10**	**63**	**7**	**23,852,721**

1　Of household reference person.
2　One family consisting only of related people of pensionable age (men aged 65 and over and women aged 60 and over).
3　One family in which at least one person is below pensionable age with or without dependent children.

Source: Census 2001, Office for National Statistics; Census 2001, General Register Office for Scotland

The relatively small percentage of lone-parent families among Indian, Pakistani and Bangladeshi households with dependent children was reflected in the pattern for religion. Muslim (15 per cent), Sikh (11 per cent) and Hindu households with dependent children (8 per cent) were among the least likely to be a lone-parent family (Figure 4.7). Lone-parent families were also relatively uncommon among Jewish households with dependent children (12 per cent). They were more common among Buddhist (25 per cent) and Christian households with dependent children (21 per cent) and in those with no religion (26 per cent). Lone-parent families were most common among Other religion households with dependent children (32 per cent). The Other religion group in England and Wales contains people classified to diverse groups, the largest being Spiritualist (21 per cent), Pagan (20 per cent), Jain (10 per cent), Humanist and Wicca (6 per cent and 5 per cent respectively).[7]

Figure **4.7**

Households with dependent children headed by a lone parent:[1] by religion,[2] April 2001

Great Britain

Percentages

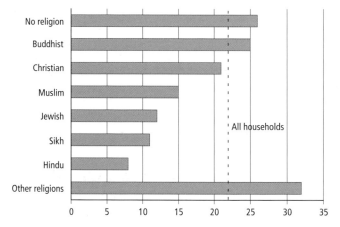

1 Living in 'one family and no others' households.
2 Of household reference person.

Source: Census 2001, Office for National Statistics; Census 2001, General Register Office for Scotland

Lone-parenthood results from many different circumstances. Sometimes it reflects a life style choice but often it results from the end of a relationship or, less often, the death of a spouse. The marital status of the lone-parent provides some insight into the reasons for lone parenthood.

In the majority of lone-parent families with dependent children the lone parent was divorced or separated (53 per cent). A further 39 per cent were single and 5 per cent were widowed. Three per cent gave their marital status as 'married' but there was no partner living in the household. These distributions varied by ethnic and religious group.

Half or more of Pakistani (59 per cent), Indian (56 per cent), White British (55 per cent), White Irish (52 per cent) and Chinese lone parents with dependent children (50 per cent) were divorced or separated (Figure 4.8).

Figure **4.8**

Lone parents with dependent children who were divorced or separated:[1] by ethnic group,[2] April 2001

England and Wales

Percentages

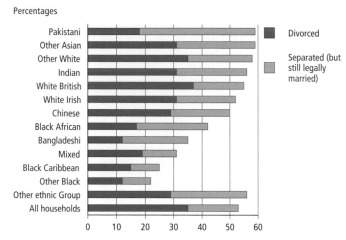

1 Living in 'one family and no others' households.
2 Of household reference person.

Source: Census 2001, Office for National Statistics

Divorce or separation was less common among Bangladeshi (35 per cent) and Black Caribbean lone parents with dependent children (25 per cent) but their respective marital statuses were very different (Table 4.9). Black Caribbean lone parents with dependent children were among the most likely to be single (71 per cent) whereas Bangladeshi lone parents with dependent children were least likely to be single (5 per cent).

Bangladeshi lone parents with dependent children were the most likely to be widowed (29 per cent) or to give their marital status as married (30 per cent). The relatively high rates of widowhood among Bangladeshi lone parents may reflect larger than average spousal age differences in the Bangladeshi population as well as cultural attitudes discouraging remarriage among widowed women.[8] Lone parents who reported their status as married also accounted for relatively large proportions of Chinese (26 per cent), Indian (17 per cent) and Black African lone parents with dependent children (16 per cent). The relatively large proportion giving their marital status as 'married' may indicate a partner who was not living at the household at the time of the 2001 Census or it may reflect a reluctance by those whose marriages have broken down to revise their marital status.

Table **4.9**

Marital status of lone parents with dependent children:[1] by ethnic group,[2] April 2001

England and Wales   Percentages

	Single (never married)	Married (first and remarried)	Separated (but still legally married)	Divorced	Widowed	Lone parent households with dependent children (=100%) (Numbers)
White British	39	2	18	37	5	1,193,526
White Irish	37	3	21	31	8	17,253
Other White	28	7	23	35	7	28,307
Mixed	64	3	12	19	3	23,407
Indian	11	17	25	31	16	15,089
Pakistani	8	20	41	18	12	14,923
Bangladeshi	5	30	23	12	29	5,383
Other Asian	14	16	28	31	12	4,850
Black Caribbean	71	2	10	15	2	48,880
Black African	35	16	25	17	7	30,469
Other Black	74	3	10	12	2	7,672
Chinese	14	26	21	29	10	4,375
Other ethnic group	19	16	27	29	9	5,805
All lone parent households with dependent children	**39**	**3**	**18**	**35**	**5**	**1,399,939**

1 Living in 'one family and no others' households.
2 Of household reference person.

Source: Census 2001, Office for National Statistics

Among all religions, the majority of lone parents with dependent children were divorced or separated, these proportions being highest among Jewish (65 per cent) and Sikh (61 per cent) lone parents (Figure 4.10).

Lone parents with no religion were least likely to be divorced or separated (43 per cent) and most likely to be single (53 per cent) (Table 4.11 overleaf). Hindu, Sikh and Muslim lone parents with dependent children were, conversely, least likely to be single (8 per cent, 9 per cent and 13 per cent respectively) and were most likely to be married or widowed. One in five Hindu (21 per cent) and Muslim lone parents with dependent children (20 per cent) gave their marital status as married, as did 14 per cent of Sikh lone parents. Similar proportions were widowed: Hindu (19 per cent), Sikh (16 per cent) and Muslim (13 per cent). In comparison, 2 per cent of Christian lone parents with dependent children were married and 5 per cent were widowed.

Figure **4.10**

Lone parents with dependent children who were divorced or separated:[1] by religion,[2] April 2001

England and Wales

Percentages

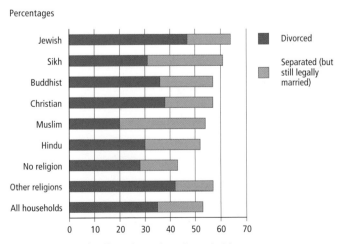

1 Living in 'one family and no others' households.
2 Of household reference person.

Source: Census 2001, Office for National Statistics

Table **4.11**

Marital status of lone parents with dependent children:[1] by religion,[2] April 2001

England and Wales

Percentages

	Single (never married)	Married (first and remarried)	Separated (but still legally married)	Divorced	Widowed	Lone parent households with dependent children (=100%) (Numbers)
Christian	36	2	19	38	5	942,166
Buddhist	28	9	21	36	6	5,129
Hindu	8	21	22	30	19	6,744
Jewish	21	5	17	47	9	3,573
Muslim	13	20	34	20	13	39,192
Sikh	9	14	30	31	16	5,584
Other religions	36	2	15	42	4	6,605
No religion	53	2	15	28	2	287,209
Religion not stated	45	4	16	31	5	103,737
All lone parent households with dependent children	**39**	**3**	**18**	**35**	**5**	**1,399,939**

1 Living in 'one family and no others' households.
2 Of household reference person.

Source: Census 2001, Office for National Statistics

Between 1991 and 2001, lone-parent households with dependent children increased slightly among Pakistani (7 per cent to 9 per cent), Bangladeshi (8 per cent to 9 per cent), Chinese and White households (5 per cent to 6 per cent

respectively).[4] Conversely, lone-parent households with dependent children decreased among Black African (21 per cent to 17 per cent) and Black Caribbean households (20 per cent to 18 per cent) (Figure 4.12).

Pensioner families

Almost one in ten households (9 per cent) was a pensioner family in 2001, usually consisting of a couple above pension age without children (a pensioner family might include children if they were also above pension age) (Table 4.4). White British and White Irish households were most likely to be pensioner families (9 per cent respectively), reflecting the older age structure of these groups. By comparison, 1 per cent of Pakistani, Bangladeshi and Black African households, and no more than 3 per cent of other non-White households, were pensioner families (Figure 4.13).

Variations in age structures were also reflected in the pattern for religion. Around one in ten Jewish and Christian households was a pensioner family (12 per cent and 10 per cent respectively) compared with 1 per cent of Muslim households and no more than 4 per cent among other households (Figure 4.14).

Many pensioners lived alone rather than in a pensioner family. The next section discusses one-person households, including one-person pensioner households.

Figure **4.12**

Lone parents with dependent children:[1] by ethnic group,[2] April 1991 and April 2001

Great Britain

Percentages

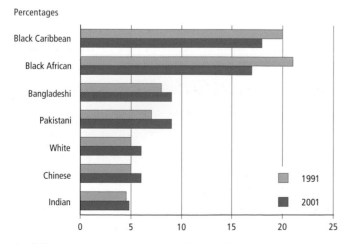

1 Living in 'one family and no others' households.
2 Of household reference person.

Source: Census 2001, Office for National Statistics; Census 2001, General Register Office for Scotland; Peach C. (1996)

Figure **4.13**

Pensioner family households:[1] by ethnic group,[2] April 2001

Great Britain

Percentages

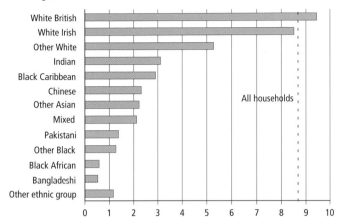

1 One family consisting only of related people of pensionable age (men aged 65 and over and women aged 60 and over).
2 Of household reference person.

Source: Census 2001, Office for National Statistics; Census 2001, General Register Office for Scotland

Figure **4.14**

Pensioner family households:[1] by religion,[2] April 2001

Great Britain

Percentages

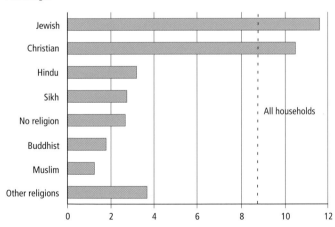

1 One family consisting only of related people of pensionable age (men aged 65 and over and women aged 60 and over).
2 Of household reference person.

Source: Census 2001, Office for National Statistics; Census 2001, General Register Office for Scotland

One-person households

In 2001 almost a third (30 per cent) of households consisted of one person living alone. Black Caribbean and White Irish households were most likely to be one-person households (38 per cent and 37 per cent respectively). Conversely, Indian, Pakistani and Bangladeshi households were least likely to be

one-person households: 15 per cent of Indian households, 12 per cent of Pakistani and just 9 per cent of Bangladeshi households consisted of one person living alone (Table 4.4).

This was reflected in the pattern for religion. Religious groups associated with Indian, Pakistani and Bangladeshi populations were the least likely to contain one person living alone: 13 per cent of Sikh households, 14 per cent of Hindu households and 15 per cent of Muslim households were one-person households compared with 30 per cent of Christian and 36 per cent of Jewish and Buddhist households (Table 4.5).

One-person households may contain someone above or below pension age. The distribution varies, reflecting differences in the age structure of ethnic and religious populations. Figure 4.15 illustrates the variation by ethnic group. The following section discusses the variations for ethnic and religious groups in more detail.

Figure **4.15**

One-person households: by ethnic group,[1] and age,[2] April 2001

Great Britain

Percentages

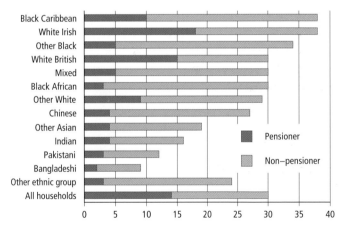

1 Of household reference person.
2 Pensioners are men aged 65 and over and women aged 60 and over.

Source: Census 2001, Office for National Statistics; Census 2001, General Register Office for Scotland

One-person households above pension age

White Irish and White British households were most likely to contain a pensioner living alone (18 per cent and 15 per cent respectively), reflecting the older age structure of these groups. Among non-White groups, Black Caribbean households were most likely to consist of a pensioner living alone (10 per cent). The Black Caribbean population has a younger age structure than White British and White Irish populations but has the oldest age structure of the non-White groups (Chapter 2). Among the other non-White households, between 2 per cent and 5 per cent contained a pensioner living alone (Table 4.4).

The relatively low proportion of one-person pensioner households among Indian (4 per cent), Pakistani (3 per cent) and Bangladeshi households (2 per cent) partly reflects the younger age structure of these populations, and the correspondingly small proportion of pensioners. It may also reflect the greater tendency for elderly people in these ethnic groups to live with their extended family. Extended families are discussed later in this chapter.

There was a similar pattern for religion, with the highest proportion of one-person pensioner households in households headed by someone from a predominantly White religious group. Around a fifth of Jewish (19 per cent) and Christian households (17 per cent) contained a pensioner living alone. Muslim (2 per cent), Hindu (3 per cent) and Sikh households (4 per cent) were least likely to contain a pensioner living alone (Table 4.5). Again, the younger age structure of these groups and the greater tendency for Muslim, Hindu and Sikh elderly people to live in an extended family account for the small proportion of one-person pensioner households among these groups.

One-person households below pension age

Analysis of one-person households containing someone below pension age shows a very different pattern. Black Caribbean, Black African, Mixed and Chinese households were most likely to contain one person below pension age living alone (28 per cent, 27 per cent, 25 per cent and 23 per cent respectively) (Table 4.4). This type of household was less common among White Irish (20 per cent) and White British households (15 per cent). They were least common among Indian, Pakistani and Bangladeshi households: 12 per cent of Indian, 9 per cent of Pakistani and 7 per cent of Bangladeshi households contained one person below pension age living alone.

Similarly for religion, Muslim (13 per cent), Hindu (11 per cent) and Sikh households (9 per cent) were least likely to contain someone below pension age living alone, followed by Christian (14 per cent) and Jewish households (19 per cent). Buddhist households were most likely to contain one person below pension age living alone (31 per cent) (Table 4.5).

The number of one-person households has almost quadrupled over the last four decades.[9] The increase has occurred across all ethnic groups although the increase has been greater for some groups than for others. In 1991 one-person households were most common among Black Caribbean (28 per cent), White (27 per cent) and Black African households (25 per cent).[4] In 2001 the proportion of one-person households had increased for all 3 groups but the increase was greater for Black Caribbean (38 per cent) than White (31 per cent) and Black African households (30 per cent) (Figure 4.16).

Figure 4.16

One-person households: by ethnic group,[1] April 1991 and April 2001

Great Britain

Percentages

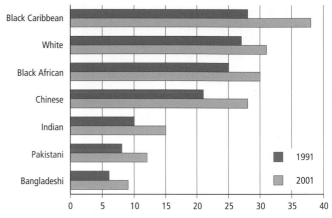

1 Of household reference person.

Source: Census 2001, Office for National Statistics; Census 2001, General Register Office for Scotland; Peach C. (1996)

Indian, Pakistani and Bangladeshi households were less likely to be one-person households but the increase for these groups between 1991 and 2001 was proportionately greater than for Black or White groups: from 10 per cent to 15 per cent of Indian households; from 8 per cent to 12 per cent of Pakistani households; and from 6 per cent to 9 per cent of Bangladeshi households.

Average household size, dependent children and extended families

Variations in the age profiles of different ethnic groups, as well as tendencies in some groups to have larger families and to live in extended families, all contribute to differences in household size. It is well documented that some ethnic minority households, particularly Indian, Pakistani and Bangladeshi households, are more likely to contain both dependent children and extended families, and that they have larger households as a consequence.[10, 11] Households headed by White groups tend towards smaller family sizes and their populations contain a greater number of older people, often living alone, resulting in smaller households.

Household size

In 2001 Indian, Pakistani and Bangladeshi households contained more people, on average, than households from any other ethnic background (Figure 4.17). Bangladeshi households were largest, with an average of 4.5 people in a household, followed by Pakistani (4.1) and Indian households (3.3).

White Irish, White British and Black Caribbean households were the smallest in 2001 with an average size of 2.3 people for White British and Black Caribbean households and 2.2 people for White Irish households. White British, Black Caribbean and White Irish households have an older age structure than the other ethnic groups and, as the previous section discussed, more than three in ten households headed by these groups were one-person households.

Figure 4.17

Average household size: by ethnic group,[1] April 2001

Great Britain

People per household

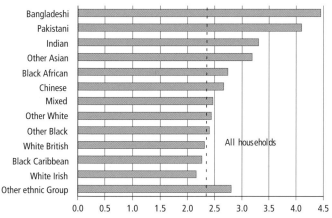

1 Of household reference person.

Source: Census 2001, Office for National Statistics; Census 2001, General Register Office for Scotland

The pattern for religion reflected the pattern by ethnicity, with the largest households among the religious populations associated with Indian, Pakistani and Bangladeshi populations and the smallest households among religious groups populated by White groups. Muslim households in Great Britain were largest, with an average of 3.8 people. Sikh and Hindu households also had on average more than 3 people (3.6 and 3.2 people respectively). Christian, Jewish and Buddhist households were among the smallest households, with 2.3 people on average (Figure 4.18).

The variations were not entirely explained by the ethnicity of the respective religious populations. Across all ethnic groups in England and Wales households headed by a Muslim contained a greater number of people on average than households headed by someone from any other religion. Among White British households, for example, Muslim households were the

Figure 4.18

Average household size: by religion,[1] April 2001

Great Britain

People per household

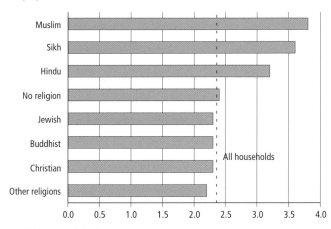

1 Of household reference person.

Source: Census 2001, Office for National Statistics; Census 2001, General Register Office for Scotland

largest on average (2.8 people), followed by Christian (2.3), Jewish (2.2) and Buddhist households (2.0). Similarly, among Indian households, Muslim households contained the greatest average number of people (3.7), followed by Sikh (3.6), Hindu (3.2) and Christian households (2.6) (Appendix Table A4.3).

Labour market and employment patterns may contribute to the greater household size of Pakistani, Bangladeshi and Muslim households. Unemployment rates among these groups are consistently among the highest in the general population and unemployment rates among young people are particularly high (Chapter 5). Lack of resources to live independently may prevent young people from leaving home, thereby contributing to the larger size of households.

As the ethnic minority populations age, their average household size could be expected to fall unless, in the case of the Indian, Pakistani and Bangladeshi groups, older adults continue to live with their children and grand-children in an extended family household. Comparison of data from the 1991 and 2001 Censuses suggests that the trend to smaller household sizes is occurring across all ethnic groups, particularly in the Asian groups, which have the largest households. Between 1991 and 2001 the largest decreases in average household size were in Pakistani (from 4.8 to 4.1), Bangladeshi (from 5.2 to 4.5) and Indian households (from 3.8 to 3.3) (Table 4.19 overleaf).[12]

Table 4.19

Average household size: by ethnic group,[1] April 1991 and April 2001

Great Britain

	People per household	
	1991	2001
White	2.4	2.3
Indian	3.8	3.3
Pakistani	4.8	4.1
Bangladeshi	5.2	4.5
Black Caribbean	2.5	2.3
Black African	2.9	2.7
Chinese	3.0	2.7

1 Of household reference person.

Source: Census 2001, Office for National Statistics; Census 2001, General Register Office for Scotland; Murphy, M. (1996)

Households with dependent children

Variations in household size often reflect the number of children in the home. In 2001 Bangladeshi and Pakistani households were most likely to contain dependent children; 74 per cent of Bangladeshi households and 66 per cent of Pakistani households. They were significantly more likely to contain dependent children than the next highest groups, Indian (50 per cent) and Black African households (48 per cent). White Irish and White British households were the least likely to contain dependent children (21 per cent and 28 per cent respectively) (Figure 4.20).

Bangladeshi and Pakistani households also contained the largest number of dependent children. Around a half of Bangladeshi (56 per cent) and Pakistani households (48 per cent) contained two or more dependent children. These proportions were quite a bit higher than the next highest groups, Indian (31 per cent) and Black African households (29 per cent). Among White Irish households 11 per cent contained two or more children.

Variations in the presence and number of dependent children reflect the age structures of these populations. White Irish and White British populations have the oldest age structure of all groups while Pakistani and Bangladeshi populations are among the youngest (Chapter 2). Older populations contain fewer women of childbearing age and, conversely, more pensioners.

For example, 17 per cent of the White British population and 25 per cent of the White Irish population were aged 65 and over in 2001 compared with 4 per cent of Pakistanis and 3 per cent of Bangladeshis.[13] The Black Caribbean population also has an older age structure than other ethnic minority populations. However, age differences do not fully account for the variations. Indian, Chinese, Mixed and Black African populations have young age structures and very few pensioners but households headed by these groups were less likely than Pakistani and Bangladeshi households to contain dependent children.

Other variations between groups contribute to the differences. The Chinese and Black African working age populations included the largest proportion of full-time students in 2001 (30 per cent and 24 per cent respectively) (Chapter 2). Some will have come from overseas in order to study. Pakistani and Bangladeshi populations, by comparison, are largely comprised of settled communities.

Data from the ONS General Household Survey (GHS) also indicate differences between ethnic groups in attitudes to *intended* family size. Bangladeshi and Pakistani women had the highest average *intended* number of children, 3.6 and 3.4 respectively, followed by 2.7 for Black African, 2.4 for Indian, 2.4 for Black Caribbean, 2.1 for White and 2.0 for Chinese women of child-bearing age.[14]

Figure 4.20

Households with dependent children:[1] by number of dependent children and ethnic group,[2] April 2001

Great Britain

Percentages

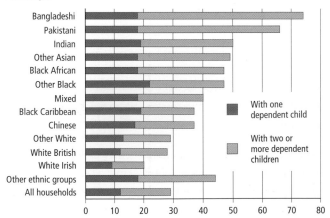

1 A dependent child is a person aged 0 to 15 in a household or aged 16 to 18 in full-time education and living with his or her parents.
2 Of household reference person.

Source: Census 2001, Office for National Statistics; Census 2001, General Register Office for Scotland

Given these findings, it is not surprising that Muslim households were most likely to contain dependent children in 2001 (63 per cent) (Figure 4.21). The next highest rates were found among Sikh (55 per cent) and Hindu households (49 per cent). By comparison, about a quarter of Jewish and Christian households contained dependent children, again largely reflecting the older age structure of these populations.

Muslim, Sikh and Hindu households also had a larger number of dependent children than other households. Forty-four per cent of Muslim households, 35 per cent of Sikh households and 28 per cent of Hindu households had two or more dependent children. These groups were around two to three times more likely than Christian (16 per cent) and Jewish households (15 per cent) to contain two or more dependent children.

Figure **4.21**

Households with dependent children:[1] by number of dependent children and religion,[2] April 2001

Great Britain

Percentages

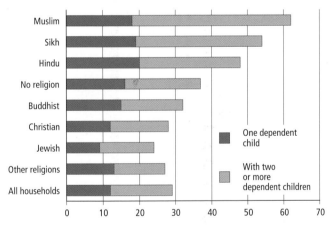

1 A dependent child is a person aged 0 to 15 in a household or aged 16 to 18 in full-time education and living with his or her parents.
2 Of household reference person.

Source: Census 2001, Office for National Statistics; Census 2001, General Register Office for Scotland

In all ethnic groups, Muslim households were most likely to contain dependent children. For example, almost half (48 per cent) of White British Muslim households contained dependent children, compared with around a quarter (27 per cent) of White British Christian households (Appendix Table A4.2). This is partly because of differences in the age structure of the populations. White British Christian households have more pensioner households than White British Muslim households (28

per cent and 9 per cent respectively) (Appendix Table A4.1). However, the greater prevalence of dependent children in Muslim households was observed in populations with younger age structures. Six in ten (60 per cent) Indian Muslim households contained dependent children, a greater proportion than for Indian Sikh (56 per cent), Indian Hindu (49 per cent) or Indian Christian households (36 per cent). Pensioner households accounted for a larger proportion of Indian Christian households (13 per cent) but Muslim (5 per cent), Sikh and Hindu households (6 per cent respectively) had similar proportions of pensioner households (Appendix Table A4.1).

Muslim households also contained a larger number of dependent children than other households. Over two fifths (42 per cent) of Indian Muslim households contained two or more dependent children, a higher proportion than among Indian Sikh (36 per cent), Indian Hindu (28 per cent) and Indian Christian households (21 per cent). Similarly, almost four in ten (37 per cent) Black African Muslim households contained two or more dependent children in 2001 compared with three in ten (29 per cent) Black African Christians households (Appendix Table A4.2).

Extended family households

One factor that contributes to the size of Indian, Pakistani and Bangladeshi households is the greater proportion of extended family households. These have implications for housing provision, social services, health and care and labour market participation. Living in an extended family unit may present individuals with advantages including access to child care, care of the elderly, emotional and financial support. On the other hand, there may be disadvantages such as overcrowding.

A household contains an extended family where it contains three or more generations in direct descent.[15] This would typically include a couple with children sharing their home with an elderly parent or parents. In 2001 less than 2 per cent of households in England and Wales were extended family households. However, non-White groups, particularly Indian, Pakistani and Bangladeshi groups contained a higher proportion of such households. About one in ten Indian (9 per cent), Pakistani (10 per cent) and Bangladeshi households (10 per cent) contained an extended family (Table 4.22 overleaf).

There was a similar pattern for religion. Sikh households (12 per cent) were most likely to contain an extended family followed by Hindu (9 per cent) and Muslim households (8 per cent) (Table 4.23 overleaf). Two per cent of Christian and Buddhist households and 1 per cent of Jewish households contained an extended family.

Table 4.22

Households with three or more generations:[1] by ethnic group,[2] April 2001

England and Wales   Percentages

	Households with three or more generations	All household (Numbers)
White British	2	19,336,648
White Irish	2	357,289
Other White	1	556,180
Mixed	2	146,309
Indian	9	314,952
Pakistani	10	172,510
Bangladeshi	10	61,939
Other Asian	5	80,748
Black Caribbean	3	275,628
Black African	3	176,436
Other Black	3	31,218
Chinese	3	77,384
Other ethnic group	2	73,234
All households	**2**	**21,660,475**

1 Based on relationships within the household.
2 Of household reference person.

Source: Census 2001, Office for National Statistics

Table 4.23

Households with three or more generations:[1] by religion,[2] April 2001

England and Wales   Percentages

	Households with three or more generations	All households (Numbers)
Christian	2	15,995,596
Buddhist	2	64,360
Hindu	9	172,379
Jewish	1	116,330
Muslim	8	411,415
Sikh	12	93,188
Other religions	2	76,190
No religion	1	3,140,413
Religion not stated	1	1,590,604
All households	**2**	**21,660,475**

1 Based on relationships within the household.
2 Of household reference person.

Source: Census 2001, Office for National Statistics

Household deprivation

The larger size of Indian, Pakistani and Bangladeshi households is related to the number of dependent children within the household and the number of extended family households. These characteristics are associated with higher rates of overcrowding, although they do not fully account for it. Differences in household tenure and area of residence also have implications for overcrowding.

Household tenure and overcrowding are 2 measures of household deprivation. A household may also be deprived if there are no adults in employment. The deprivation may be greater where a non-working household contains dependent children. The next section looks at 3 key measures of deprivation: household tenure; overcrowding; and workless households with dependent children.

Tenure

Housing tenure (that is the right or title under which property is held) is often used as a measure of relative disadvantage, with households in socially rented accommodation generally experiencing greater economic deprivation than owner-occupied households. The Poverty and Social Exclusion Survey (2000) defines households as 'poor' if they do not have two or more items from a list of things perceived as necessary by most people.[16] According to this definition, 25 per cent of the adult population in Great Britain were poor in 2001, with variations by housing tenure. Almost two-thirds (61 per cent) of households in the social rented sector were classified as poor compared with 17 per cent of households that were buying their home with a mortgage and 15 per cent of households that owned their home outright.

In 2001, 68 per cent of households in Great Britain owned their own homes outright or with a mortgage or as part of a shared ownership scheme (Figure 4.24). Indian (76 per cent), White British (70 per cent) and Pakistani households (67 per cent) were most likely to own their own homes.

Black African households were least likely to be owner-occupiers (26 per cent) followed by Bangladeshi households (37 per cent). Around half of Black African (50 per cent) and Bangladeshi households (48 per cent) lived in accommodation rented from a council or housing association (Table 4.25).

Although Indian households were most likely to own their own homes, Sikhs (82 per cent) were more likely than Hindus (74 per cent) to do so (Figure 4.26). The proportions were slightly lower among Christian households (70 per cent), while Muslim and Buddhist households were least likely to own their homes (52 per cent and 54 per cent respectively).

Figure **4.24**

Home ownership:[1] by ethnic group,[2] April 2001

Great Britain

Percentages

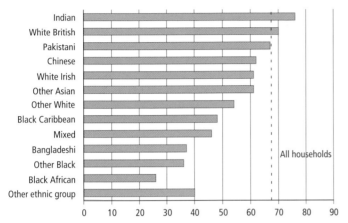

1 Owned outright or owned with a mortgage.
2 Of household reference person.

Source: Census 2001, Office for National Statistics; Census 2001, General Register Office for Scotland

Figure **4.26**

Home ownership:[1] by religion,[2] April 2001

Great Britain

Percentages

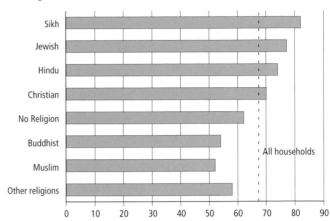

1 Owned outright or owned with a mortgage.
2 Of household reference person.

Source: Census 2001, Office for National Statistics; Census 2001, General Register Office for Scotland

Table **4.25**

Household tenure: by ethnic group,[1] April 2001

Great Britain   Percentages

	Owner occupied[2]	Social rented	Private rented	Lives rent free	All households (=100%) (Numbers)
White British	70	19	9	2	21,439,962
White Irish	61	26	11	2	383,805
Other White	54	14	29	3	587,947
Mixed	46	32	19	3	149,508
Indian	76	10	13	2	319,887
Pakistani	67	16	15	3	180,349
Bangladeshi	37	48	12	3	62,505
Other Asian	61	16	19	4	82,943
Black Caribbean	48	43	8	1	276,404
Black African	26	50	20	3	178,452
Other Black	36	50	11	3	31,631
Chinese	62	13	21	4	82,784
Other ethnic group	40	22	34	5	76,544
All households	**68**	**20**	**10**	**2**	**23,852,721**

1 Of household reference person.
2 Owned outright or owned with a mortgage

Source: Census 2001, Office for National Statistics; Census 2001, General Register Office for Scotland

Muslim households were the most likely to be living in socially rented accommodation in 2001 (28 per cent) (Table 4.27).

The lower rates of home ownership among some ethnic minority groups compared with their White British counterparts may be partly related to the concentration of ethnic minority populations in London. Rates of home ownership tend to be lower in London than in other Government Office Regions, possibly reflecting house prices in London, which tend to be among the highest in the country.[17]

Even in London, rates of home ownership were generally lower for ethnic minority households compared with White British households (62 per cent) although the highest rate of home ownership in London was among Indian households (74 per cent) (Table 4.28). Black African and Bangladeshi households in London were least likely to own their own homes (23 per cent and 26 per cent respectively).

Between 1991 and 2001, home ownership increased among White households from 66 per cent to 69 per cent (Table 4.29).[18] Home ownership remained stable for Black Caribbean and Chinese households while decreasing among the Indian, Pakistani and Bangladeshi groups over the same period. The greatest decrease was among Pakistani households, the proportion owning their own homes falling from 76 per cent in 1991 to 67 per cent in 2001.

The fall in home ownership among Pakistani and Bangladeshi households was accompanied by an increase in the proportion

living in socially rented accommodation, a pattern that was not observed among Indian households. In 1991, 43 per cent of Bangladeshi households lived in socially rented accommodation. In 2001 this had risen to 48 per cent. Pakistani households were less likely than Bangladeshi households to live in socially rented accommodation but the proportion of Pakistani households living in socially rented accommodation increased between 1991 and 2001 from 12 per cent to 16 per cent. The proportion of Pakistani households living in privately rented accommodation also increased over this period, from 10 per cent to 15 per cent.[19] There was no similar movement into private rented accommodation among the Bangladeshi population at this time but among Indian households the proportion living in privately rented accommodation increased from 9 per cent to 13 per cent between 1991 and 2001.

It is not clear from the data whether these differences result from movements out of owned accommodation into rented accommodation or whether they indicate that more recent migrants have been less able to enter the housing market, thus increasing the proportion of the population in social and private rented accommodation. In addition, young people from these communities may experience problems buying their own homes and this may account for some of the increase in the proportion in social and privately rented accommodation. These problems may be particularly acute for people living in London. While young White people may face similar difficulties, there are proportionately fewer.

Table 4.27

Household tenure: by religion,[1] April 2001

Great Britain

Percentages

	Owner occupied[2]	Social rented	Private rented	Lives rent free	All households (=100%) (Numbers)
Christian	70	20	8	2	17,728,972
Buddhist	54	19	24	3	66,001
Hindu	74	9	16	2	174,625
Jewish	77	9	13	2	119,957
Muslim	52	28	17	4	423,348
Sikh	82	8	8	2	95,194
Other religions	58	21	19	2	79,674
No Religion	62	20	16	2	3,435,551
Religion not stated	63	24	11	3	1,729,399
All households	**68**	**20**	**10**	**2**	**23,852,721**

1 Of household reference person.
2 Owned outright or owned with a mortgage.

Source: Census 2001, Office for National Statistics; Census 2001, General Register Office for Scotland

Table 4.28

Household tenure in London: by ethnic group,[1] April 2001

Percentages

	Owner occupied[2]	Social rented	Private rented	Lives rent free	All households in London (=100%) (Numbers)
White British	62	23	13	1	1,950,689
White Irish	52	33	14	2	122,938
Other White	45	18	35	3	247,309
Mixed	41	37	20	3	55,640
Indian	74	11	13	2	136,151
Pakistani	58	20	20	2	38,951
Bangladeshi	26	63	9	3	33,510
Other Asian	57	19	21	3	43,187
Black Caribbean	45	47	8	1	162,203
Black African	23	57	16	3	137,030
Other Black	31	58	10	2	17,655
Chinese	58	17	21	4	30,719
Other ethnic group	36	27	32	4	40,015
All households	**57**	**26**	**15**	**2**	**3,015,997**

1 Of household reference person.
2 Owned outright or owned with a mortgage.

Source: Census 2001, Office for National Statistics; Census 2001, General Register Office for Scotland

Table 4.29

Home ownership:[1] by ethnic group,[2] April 1991 and April 2001

Great Britain

Percentages

	1991	2001
White	66	69
Indian	82	76
Pakistani	76	67
Bangladeshi	44	37
Black Caribbean	48	48
Black African	28	26
Chinese	62	62

1 Owned outright or owned with a mortgage
2 Of household reference person.

Sources: Census 2001, Office for National Statistics; Census 2001, General Register Office for Scotland; Ratcliffe P (1985)

Overcrowding

The Census occupancy rating provides a measure of under occupancy and overcrowding. It represents the ratio of actual number of rooms in the household compared with the estimated required number of rooms (based on relationships between household members and ages of household members).[20] Overcrowding was greatest among Bangladeshi (44 per cent) and Black African households (42 per cent), these households being seven times more likely than White British households (6 per cent) to be overcrowded (Figure 4.30 overleaf).

Looking at households by religion, Muslim households were most likely to be overcrowded (32 per cent) (Figure 4.31 overleaf). This proportion was substantially higher than the next most likely groups, Hindu (22 per cent) and Sikh households (19 per cent). Households headed by Christians and Jews were least likely to be overcrowded (6 and 7 per cent respectively).

The variations by religion were not entirely explained by the ethnicity of their populations. In most ethnic groups, Muslim households were more likely than other households to be overcrowded. For example, among White British households in England and Wales, about two in ten Muslim households (22 per cent) were overcrowded compared with one in ten Buddhist

Figure **4.30**

Overcrowded households:[1] by ethnic group,[2] April 2001

Great Britain

Percentages

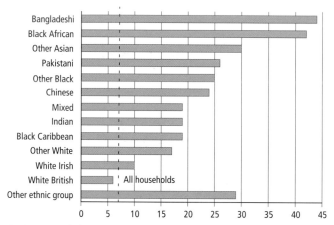

1 Accommodation is overcrowded if the Census occupancy indicator is -1 or less.
2 Of household reference person.

Source: Census 2001, Office for National Statistics; Census 2001, General Register Office for Scotland

Figure **4.31**

Overcrowded households:[1] by religion,[2] April 2001

Great Britain

Percentages

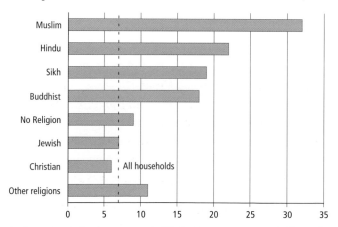

1 Accommodation is overcrowded if the Census occupancy indicator is -1 or less.
2 Of household reference person.

Source: Census 2001, Office for National Statistics; Census 2001, General Register Office for Scotland

households (10 per cent) and one in twenty Jewish and Christian households (6 per cent and 5 per cent respectively). Among people from a Mixed ethnic group, Muslim households were more than twice as likely as Christian households to be overcrowded (37 per cent compared with 16 per cent). Half (51 per cent) of Black African Muslim households in England and Wales were overcrowded compared with 42 per cent of Black African Christian households (Appendix Table A4.4).

The larger household size of Muslim families partly explains their greater vulnerability to overcrowding. However, household size alone does not explain all variation in overcrowding. While the average Pakistani household contained 4.1 people in 2001, only 26 per cent of Pakistani households were overcrowded. By comparison, Black African households were smaller than Pakistani households, with an average of 2.7 people, but were more likely to be overcrowded (42 per cent). This disparity may reflect variations in area of residence and type of accommodation.

In 2001 overcrowding was highest in London, 17 per cent of households being overcrowded compared with 7 per cent overall in Great Britain (Appendix Table A4.5). More than four in ten (45 per cent) of Great Britain's non-White population lived in London in 2001 and, for all ethnic groups, overcrowding was greatest in London. Over three-quarters (78 per cent) of Black Africans lived in London, compared with 20 per cent of Pakistanis, and this may contribute to the higher overcrowding of Black African households relative to Pakistani households.[21] The Bangladeshi population were also more likely than Pakistani counterparts to live in London; 54 per cent of Bangladeshis lived in London in 2001 and more than half of Bangladeshi households in London were overcrowded (Appendix Table A4.5). In all Government Office Regions Muslim households were more likely than other households to be overcrowded, and Muslim households in London were most likely to be overcrowded (42 per cent) (Appendix Table A4.6).

Variations in household tenure may also have implications for overcrowding. As discussed previously, Bangladeshi households relied on public sector rented accommodation to a far greater extent than Pakistani households (48 per cent compared with 16 per cent). This may increase their vulnerability to overcrowding, as providers of public sector housing offer relatively few houses with more than three bedrooms, reflecting the requirements of the general population. The Pakistani population are more likely than the Bangladeshi population to own their homes, possibly reflecting their greater settlement in the North of England and the Midlands, where house prices are generally less expensive than London. Tenure may also contribute to the high rates of overcrowding among Black African households; as discussed previously, Black African households were more likely than any other ethnic group to live in socially-rented accommodation in 2001 (50 per cent). Hence overcrowding in households, while largely related to household size, is also related to the availability of adequate housing in different parts of the country.

Non-working households

A third indicator of material or economic deprivation is the proportion of households in which no one is in employment. Households in which no adult is employed may be termed non-working households or workless households. In 2001, 36 per cent of households in Great Britain contained no working adults.[22]

A non-working household is not necessarily economically deprived. Many workless households are headed by pensioners who have retired from work. Pensioner households accounted for around six in ten White British (64 per cent) and White Irish (59 per cent) non-working households (Appendix Table A4.7). Some, but by no means all, will be relatively comfortable in economic terms. Non-working households with dependent children may be at greater risk of economic deprivation.

In 2001 almost one in five (17 per cent) households with dependent children contained no working adults (Figure 4.32). Bangladeshi, Black African, Mixed and Other Black households with dependent children were most likely to contain no

Figure **4.32**

Households with dependent children with no working adults: by ethnic group,[1] April 2001

Great Britain

Percentages

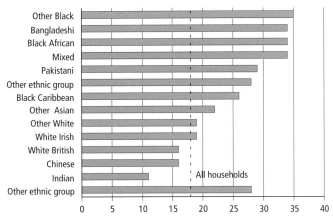

1 Of household reference person.

Source: Census 2001, Office for National Statistics; Census 2001, General Register Office for Scotland

working adults, over a third (34 to 35 per cent) in each case, followed by Pakistani (29 per cent) and Black Caribbean households (26 per cent). Among White British households with dependent children, 16 per cent contained no working adult. Indian households with dependent children were least likely to contain no working adult (11 per cent).

Across religious groups, 33 per cent of Muslim households with dependent children had no adults in employment (Figure 4.33). This proportion was significantly higher than the next main groups, Buddhist households (23 per cent) and those with no religion (20 per cent). Less than one in ten Jewish and Hindu households with dependent children (9 per cent respectively) contained no working adults.

Figure **4.33**

Households with dependent children with no working adults: by religion,[1] April 2001

Great Britain

Percentages

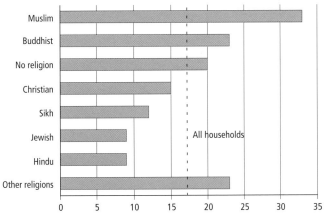

1 Of household reference person.

Source: Census 2001, Office for National Statistics; Census 2001, General Register Office for Scotland

Households headed by someone belonging to an Other religion had the same proportion of non-working households as Buddhist households with dependent children (23 per cent). The relatively high proportion of workless households with dependent children among Buddhists, Other religion households and households with no religion corresponds with a high percentage of lone parent households in these groups, discussed previously in the chapter (Figure 4.7). Households are more likely to contain no working adults if the joint burden of caring for children and working falls to one person.

High rates of lone parenthood may also contribute to workless households in the Mixed, Black African and Other Black groups, these groups all having a high proportion of lone parent households (Figure 4.6). But lone parenthood does not account for all variations; Black Caribbean households with dependent children were more likely than Black African and Mixed households to be headed by a lone parent but they were less likely to be workless.

Pakistani, Bangladeshi and Muslim households were far less likely to be lone parent households but the high proportion of workless households in these groups reflects high rates of unemployment and economic inactivity in these populations. Economic inactivity rates are particularly high for women in these groups while Black and Mixed ethnic groups have particularly high rates of unemployment.

The reasons for unemployment and economic inactivity are complex. The age structure of populations, levels of skills and qualifications and the availability of jobs in the areas where communities live are all important factors. Labour market variations by ethnic and religious group, and some of the explanations for them, are discussed in Chapter 5.

Notes and references

1. See Glossary for definition of household reference person.

2. See Glossary for definition of family households.

3. Office for National Statistics (2005) *Focus on Families Overview Report.* Available at: www.statistics.gov.uk/focuson/families

4. 1991 Census data from Peach C (1996) 'Introduction', in *Ethnicity in the 1991 Census: Volume 2: The ethnic minority populations of Great Britain,* p 22, Table 12.

5. See Glossary for definition of dependent child.

6. The Office for National Statistics has published analysis of the Other Black groups. See Gardener D and Connolly H (2005) *Who are the 'Other' ethnic groups?* Available at: www.statistics.gov. uk/cci/article.asp?id=1291

7. Office for National Statistics (2005) *Focus on Ethnicity & Identity Overview Report.* Data available in Download Data/Population www.statistics.gov.uk/focuson/ethnicity

8. Berrington A (1996) 'Marriage patterns and inter-ethnic unions', in Coleman D and Salt J (eds.) *Ethnicity in the 1991 Census: Volume 1: Demographic Characteristics of the ethnic minority populations,* p191.

9. Office for National Statistics (2005) *Focus on Families Overview Report.* Available at: www.statistics.gov.uk/focuson/families.

10 Haskey J (1989) Families and households of the ethnic minority and White populations of Great Britain. *Population Trends* **57**, 8–19.

11. Haskey J (1988) The ethnic minority populations of Great Britain: their size and characteristics. *Population Trends* **54**, 29–31.

12. 1991 Census data from Murphy M (1996) 'Household and family structure among ethnic minority groups', in Coleman D and Salt J (eds.) *Ethnicity in the 1991 Census: Volume 1: Demographic Characteristics of the ethnic minority populations,* p 218, Table 8.3.

13. Office for National Statistics (2006) Focus on Ethnicity & Identity Overview Report. Available at: www.statistics.gov.uk/cci/nugget. asp?id=456

14. Smallwood S and Jefferies J (2003) Family building intentions in England and Wales: trends, outcomes and interpretations. *Population Trends* **112**, 15–28.

15. Murphy (1996) 'Household and family structure among ethnic minority groups', in Coleman D and Salt J (eds.) *Ethnicity in the 1991 Census: Volume 1: Demographic Characteristics of the ethnic minority populations,* p 233.

16. The Poverty and Social Exclusion Survey measured poverty in relation to a list of 'socially perceived necessities'. These were items that 50 per cent or more of the general population in Great Britain considered no household or family should be without. Households that lacked two or more of these items were below the poverty threshold. For more information follow link: www. bris.ac.uk/poverty/pse/welcome.htm.

17. House Price Index (HPI) published in July 2004 by the Office of the Deputy Prime Minister.

18. 1991 Census data from Ratcliffe, P (1985) *'Race', ethnicity and housing differentials in Britain', in Karn V(ed.) Ethnicity in the 1991 Census: Volume 4: Employment, education and housing among the ethnic minority populations of Britain,* p 134, Table 7.1.

19. 1991 Census data from Ratcliffe, P (1985) 'Race', ethnicity and housing differentials in Britain in Karn V (ed.) Ethnicity in the 1991 Census: Volume 4: Employment, education and housing among the ethnic minority populations of Britain, p134, Table 7.1.

20. See Glossary for definition of Census 2001 measure of overcrowding.

21. Office for National Statistics (2004) 'Geographic Distribution', in *Focus on Ethnicity & Identity Overview Report Distribution.* Available at: www.statistics.gov.uk/cci/nugget.asp?id=457

22. Focus on Ethnicity & Religion Report (2006) Office for National Statistics. Data is available as Download data.

Appendix Table **A4.1**

Household type: by main ethno-religious groups,[1] April 2001

England and Wales

	One person households			One family and no others[2]				
	Pensioner	Other	**All one person households**	Pensioner only[3]	Married couple families[4]	Cohabiting couple families[4]	Lone parent families[4]	**All one family households**
White British Christian	17	13	**30**	11	38	7	9	**65**
White British Buddhist	6	40	**45**	1	24	11	10	**46**
White British Jewish	21	17	**37**	13	34	4	5	**57**
White British Muslim	6	19	**25**	3	41	4	16	**64**
White British No Religion	5	24	**29**	3	33	16	11	**63**
White Irish Christian	18	18	**36**	9	31	6	10	**56**
White Irish No Religion	6	34	**40**	2	24	14	8	**48**
Other White Christian	11	17	**28**	7	38	8	8	**60**
Other White Jewish	11	18	**29**	7	42	6	5	**60**
Other White Muslim	3	17	**20**	2	50	4	10	**66**
Other White No Religion	4	26	**30**	2	29	15	7	**52**
Mixed Christian	7	22	**29**	3	27	10	20	**59**
Mixed Muslim	2	21	**23**	1	41	5	13	**60**
Mixed No Religion	2	31	**33**	1	17	16	19	**53**
Indian Christian	8	19	**27**	5	43	4	10	**61**
Indian Hindu	3	10	**14**	3	55	2	7	**68**
Indian Muslim	3	10	**13**	2	57	2	8	**70**
Indian Sikh	3	9	**12**	3	52	2	9	**66**
Pakistani Muslim	2	9	**10**	1	52	2	11	**66**
Bangladeshi Muslim	1	6	**7**	0	56	2	11	**69**
Other Asian Christian	8	16	**24**	4	42	4	11	**61**
Other Asian Hindu	2	9	**11**	2	50	2	6	**61**
Other Asian Muslim	2	15	**18**	1	51	3	10	**65**
Black Caribbean Christian	10	25	**36**	3	21	7	24	**55**
Black Caribbean No Religion	6	41	**46**	1	13	10	21	**45**
Black African Christian	3	26	**29**	1	26	6	19	**52**
Black African Muslim	2	25	**27**	0	22	4	24	**51**
Other Black Christian	5	27	**32**	1	18	7	29	**56**
Chinese Christian	7	26	**32**	3	39	4	8	**54**
Chinese Buddhist	5	20	**25**	3	41	3	11	**58**
Chinese No Religion	3	23	**26**	2	43	5	8	**57**
Other ethnic group Christian	4	16	**20**	1	42	5	12	**61**
Other ethnic group Buddhist	3	22	**25**	1	42	4	14	**61**
Other ethnic group Muslim	2	19	**21**	1	49	3	9	**62**
All households[8]	**14**	**16**	**30**	**9**	**37**	**8**	**10**	**63**

1 Of household reference person.
2 A family comprises a group of people consisting of a married or cohabiting couple with or without child(ren), or a lone parent with child(ren). It also includes a married or cohabiting couple with their grandchild(ren) or a lone grandparent with his or her grandchild(ren) where there are no children in the intervening generation in the household.
3 One family consisting only of related people of pensionable age (males aged 65 and over and females aged 60 and over).
4 One family in which at least one person is below pensionable age with or without dependent children. Cohabiting couple families also include same sex couples.
5 Households with more than one family and/or unrelated people.
6 Households in which all members are students.
7 Household consisting only of people of pensionable age (males aged 65 and over and females aged 60 and over). These can be any relationship except spouse, partner or parent and child.
8 Includes households not shown in table due to small numbers.

Source: Census 2001, Office for National Statistics

Percentages

		Other households[5]				
All student[6]	All pensioner[7]	With dependent children	Other	Total other households	All households (=100%) (Numbers)	
0	0	2	3	5	14,833,624	White British Christian
1	0	2	7	9	30,014	White British Buddhist
0	1	2	4	6	98,606	White British Jewish
0	0	6	4	11	17,242	White British Muslim
1	0	2	5	8	2,886,000	White British No Religion
0	1	2	5	7	303,710	White Irish Christian
1	0	2	9	12	23,652	White Irish No Religion
1	0	2	8	12	353,252	Other White Christian
1	0	3	6	11	13,985	Other White Jewish
1	0	6	7	14	42,135	Other White Muslim
2	0	2	14	18	90,555	Other White No Religion
1	0	5	6	12	78,299	Mixed Christian
1	0	8	8	17	14,468	Mixed Muslim
2	0	4	9	15	33,346	Mixed No Religion
1	0	4	7	12	20,917	Indian Christian
1	0	10	7	18	144,635	Indian Hindu
1	0	11	6	17	36,106	Indian Muslim
1	0	13	7	21	84,700	Indian Sikh
1	0	16	6	23	158,137	Pakistani Muslim
0	0	18	5	24	57,242	Bangladeshi Muslim
0	0	6	8	15	12,397	Other Asian Christian
1	0	14	13	28	20,307	Other Asian Hindu
1	0	9	7	17	29,217	Other Asian Muslim
0	0	5	4	9	202,846	Black Caribbean Christian
0	0	4	4	9	33,507	Black Caribbean No Religion
2	0	9	9	19	125,033	Black African Christian
1	0	12	8	22	32,723	Black African Muslim
0	0	7	4	12	19,909	Other Black Christian
3	0	3	7	13	18,315	Chinese Christian
4	0	6	7	17	12,756	Chinese Buddhist
5	0	5	8	17	38,400	Chinese No Religion
1	0	6	12	19	23,190	Other ethnic group Christian
3	0	5	7	14	11,067	Other ethnic group Buddhist
3	0	6	9	17	19,613	Other ethnic group Muslim
0	**0**	**2**	**4**	**7**	**21,660,475**	**All households[8]**

Appendix Table **A4.2**

Households with dependent children: by number of dependent children and main ethno-religious groups,[1] April 2001

England and Wales

Percentages

	One dependent child	Two dependent children	Two or more dependent children	Three or more dependent children	Total with dependent children	All households (Numbers)
White British Christian	11	11	16	5	27	14,833,624
White British Buddhist	12	9	12	3	24	30,014
White British Jewish	9	9	14	5	23	98,606
White British Muslim	18	17	30	13	48	17,242
White British No Religion	16	14	21	6	36	2,886,000
White Irish Christian	9	7	11	4	21	303,710
White Irish No Religion	11	9	13	4	24	23,652
Other White Christian	12	11	16	5	28	353,252
Other White Jewish	12	12	22	10	34	13,985
Other White Muslim	20	20	32	12	53	42,135
Other White No Religion	12	10	13	4	26	90,555
Mixed Christian	19	15	22	8	41	78,299
Mixed Muslim	18	18	35	16	53	14,468
Mixed No Religion	19	14	20	6	39	33,346
Indian Christian	15	15	21	6	36	20,917
Indian Hindu	20	21	28	7	49	144,635
Indian Muslim	18	20	42	21	60	36,106
Indian Sikh	20	22	36	13	56	84,700
Pakistani Muslim	18	20	50	30	68	158,137
Bangladeshi Muslim	18	22	58	37	77	57,242
Other Asian Christian	17	15	21	6	39	12,397
Other Asian Hindu	21	23	31	8	53	20,307
Other Asian Muslim	18	19	39	20	57	29,217
Black Caribbean Christian	19	13	19	6	38	202,846
Black Caribbean No Religion	18	11	17	6	35	33,507
Black African Christian	19	16	29	13	48	125,033
Black African Muslim	17	15	37	22	54	32,723
Other Black Christian	23	16	26	9	49	19,909
Chinese Christian	14	13	17	4	32	18,315
Chinese Buddhist	16	14	22	8	38	12,756
Chinese No Religion	18	15	22	7	40	38,400
Other ethnic group Christian	20	16	22	6	43	23,190
Other ethnic group Buddhist	19	17	23	6	42	11,067
Other ethnic group Muslim	17	17	34	17	51	19,613
All households[2]	**12**	**12**	**17**	**5**	**29**	**21,660,475**

1 Of household reference person.
2 Includes households not shown in table due to small numbers.

Source: Census 2001, Office for National Statistics

Appendix Table **A4.3**

Average household size: by main ethno-religious groups,[1] April 2001

England and Wales

	Average household size	All households (=100%) (Numbers)
White British Christian	2.3	14,833,624
White British Buddhist	2.0	30,014
White British Jewish	2.2	98,606
White British Muslim	2.8	17,242
White British No Religion	2.4	2,886,000
White Irish Christian	2.2	303,710
White Irish No Religion	2.1	23,652
Other White Christian	2.4	353,252
Other White Jewish	2.6	13,985
Other White Muslim	3.0	42,135
Other White No Religion	2.3	90,555
Mixed Christian	2.5	78,299
Mixed Muslim	3.1	14,468
Mixed No Religion	2.3	33,346
Indian Christian	2.6	20,917
Indian Hindu	3.2	144,635
Indian Muslim	3.7	36,106
Indian Sikh	3.6	84,700
Pakistani Muslim	4.2	158,137
Bangladeshi Muslim	4.6	57,242
Other Asian Christian	2.7	12,397
Other Asian Hindu	3.4	20,307
Other Asian Muslim	3.4	29,217
Black Caribbean Christian	2.3	202,846
Black Caribbean No Religion	2.1	33,507
Black African Christian	2.7	125,033
Black African Muslim	3.1	32,723
Other Black Christian	2.5	19,909
Chinese Christian	2.4	18,315
Chinese Buddhist	2.8	12,756
Chinese No Religion	2.7	38,400
Other ethnic group Christian	2.8	23,190
Other ethnic group Buddhist	2.6	11,067
Other ethnic group Muslim	3.2	19,613
All households[2]	**2.4**	**21,660,475**

1 Of household reference person.
2 Includes households not shown in table due to small numbers.
Source: Census 2001, Office for National Statistics

Appendix Table A4.4

Overcrowded households: by government office region (GOR) and main ethno-religious groups,[1] April 2001

England and Wales

Percentages

	North East	North West	Yorkshire and the Humber	East Midlands	West Midlands	East	London	South East	South West	Wales/ Cymru	England and Wales
White British Christian	5	4	4	3	4	4	10	5	4	4	5
White British Buddhist	6	8	7	6	7	7	18	9	9	7	10
White British Jewish	4	4	6	5	4	3	7	5	5	3	6
White British Muslim	12	16	17	14	18	15	28	17	13	13	22
White British No Religion	6	6	7	5	6	6	14	8	7	6	8
White Irish Christian	6	7	7	6	7	7	15	7	7	6	10
White Irish No Religion	6	8	8	6	9	8	18	10	11	9	12
Other White Christian	9	8	9	7	8	8	24	9	8	7	14
Other White Jewish	4	7	9	8	5	7	13	8	9	5	11
Other White Muslim	23	26	28	30	26	25	39	25	22	23	35
Other White No Religion	11	11	12	9	11	9	26	12	11	8	18
Mixed Christian	9	10	10	8	12	10	27	11	10	9	16
Mixed Muslim	32	27	31	24	24	24	47	27	29	24	37
Mixed No Religion	11	11	13	10	12	12	25	12	12	10	16
Indian Christian	16	10	6	10	13	11	20	12	16	10	16
Indian Hindu	11	14	17	16	15	17	24	17	15	15	20
Indian Muslim	19	18	26	22	17	15	27	17	16	19	22
Indian Sikh	14	15	15	13	14	13	23	15	13	14	17
Pakistani Muslim	20	25	26	18	22	27	33	29	19	16	26
Bangladeshi Muslim	31	38	30	31	30	35	54	37	37	28	45
Other Asian Christian	9	12	13	10	11	13	32	16	12	10	25
Other Asian Hindu	14	19	21	22	21	21	46	25	22	17	39
Other Asian Muslim	26	28	29	26	28	24	38	24	19	20	31
Black Caribbean Christian	6	10	10	10	12	11	23	13	10	8	18
Black Caribbean No Religion	5	13	12	12	15	16	25	20	16	14	21
Black African Christian	18	23	25	22	24	27	46	32	24	18	42
Black African Muslim	22	32	38	40	36	31	55	42	41	29	51
Other Black Christian	12	13	15	13	15	13	34	17	11	13	26
Chinese Christian	17	15	20	17	17	13	24	15	16	11	19
Chinese Buddhist	26	24	24	21	23	24	32	24	23	19	27
Chinese No Religion	21	23	26	23	24	22	29	24	23	22	25
Other ethnic group Christian	21	19	26	15	24	19	39	22	19	20	31
Other ethnic Buddhist	13	19	27	16	16	18	29	17	11	12	24
Other ethnic group Muslim	31	27	31	27	28	25	44	26	23	25	36
All households[2]	**5**	**5**	**6**	**4**	**6**	**5**	**17**	**6**	**5**	**4**	**7**

1 Of household reference person.
2 Includes households not shown in table due to small numbers.

Source: Census 2001, Office for National Statistics

Appendix Table A4.5

Overcrowded households: by government office region (GOR) and ethnic group,[1] April 2001

Great Britain   Percentages

	North East	North West	Yorkshire and the Humber	East Midlands	West Midlands	East	London	South East	South West	Wales	Scotland	England and Wales	All households in Great Britain
White British	5	5	5	4	4	5	11	5	5	4	11	5	6
White Irish	6	7	7	6	7	7	16	8	7	6	14	10	10
Other White	10	9	11	8	10	9	26	11	10	8	15	17	17
Mixed	12	12	14	11	13	12	29	13	12	11	22	19	19
Indian	13	16	18	16	14	15	23	15	14	14	22	19	19
Pakistani	20	24	26	18	22	26	32	28	16	16	31	26	26
Bangladeshi	29	37	30	30	30	34	53	35	32	27	31	44	44
Other Asian	21	24	25	20	22	18	38	21	16	16	30	30	30
Black Caribbean	7	11	11	10	13	12	23	14	11	9	18	19	19
Black African	19	24	28	27	26	27	46	33	28	22	30	42	42
Other Black	15	14	15	13	17	13	33	17	12	14	24	25	25
Chinese	20	21	24	21	22	20	28	21	21	19	24	24	24
Other ethnic group	24	22	28	19	23	19	36	21	18	19	28	29	29
All households	**5**	**5**	**6**	**4**	**6**	**5**	**17**	**6**	**5**	**4**	**12**	**7**	**7**

1 Of household reference person.

Source: Census 2001, Office for National Statistics; Census 2001, General Register Office for Scotland

Appendix Table A4.6

Overcrowded households: by government office region (GOR) and religion,[1] April 2001

Great Britain   Percentages

	North East	North West	Yorkshire and the Humber	East Midlands	West Midlands	East	London	South East	South West	Wales	Scotland	England and Wales	All households in Great Britain
Christian	5	5	4	4	4	4	15	5	4	4	11	6	6
Buddhist	11	13	13	11	13	13	27	14	11	9	18	18	18
Hindu	11	14	18	17	15	17	28	18	15	15	21	22	22
Jewish	5	4	7	6	5	4	9	6	6	4	24	7	7
Muslim	24	25	27	23	24	26	42	28	24	21	9	32	32
Sikh	14	15	16	13	14	13	24	16	13	15	33	17	19
Other religion	6	6	8	6	8	7	19	10	9	7	17	10	11
No religion	6	6	7	6	7	7	17	8	7	6	12	8	9
All households[2]	**5**	**5**	**6**	**4**	**6**	**5**	**17**	**6**	**5**	**4**	**12**	**7**	**7**

1 Of household reference person.
2 Includes religion not stated.

Source: Census 2001, Office for National Statistics; Census 2001, General Register Office for Scotland

Appendix Table A4.7

Workless households: by age[1] and ethnic group,[2] April 2001

Great Britain   Percentages

	Pensioner households	Non-pensioner households	All workless households (=100%) (Numbers)
White British	64	36	7,905,454
White Irish	59	41	159,950
Other White	45	55	170,144
Mixed	20	80	52,100
Indian	33	67	62,353
Pakistani	11	89	58,739
Bangladeshi	6	94	21,388
Other Asian	20	80	22,910
Black Caribbean	33	67	95,653
Black African	9	91	61,274
Other Black	15	85	11,889
Chinese	23	77	22,565
Other ethnic group	11	89	23,842
All households	**61**	**39**	**8,668,261**

1 Pensioner households contain only men aged 65 and over and women aged 60 and over.
2 Of household reference person.

Source: Census 2001, Office for National Statistics; Census 2001, General Register Office for Scotland

Appendix Table A4.8

Workless households: by age[1] and religion[2], April 2001

Great Britain   Percentages

	Pensioner households	Non-pensioner households	All workless households (=100%) (Numbers)
Christian	67	33	6,814,708
Buddhist	20	80	19,488
Hindu	34	66	30,564
Jewish	73	27	44,139
Muslim	9	91	152,621
Sikh	29	71	19,101
Other religion	31	69	27,979
No religion	29	71	889,166
All households[3]	**61**	**39**	**8,668,261**

1 Pensioner households contain only men aged 65 and over and women aged 60 and over.
2 Of household reference person.
3 Includes religion not stated.

Source: Census 2001, Office for National Statistics; Census 2001, General Register Office for Scotland

Employment and labour market participation

Ben Bradford and Frances Forsyth

Chapter 5

Introduction

This chapter illustrates the position of people from different ethnic and religious groups in the labour market and describes changes between 1991 and 2001. Firstly, it examines differences in employment, unemployment and economic inactivity rates by ethnic and religious group, and the main reasons for being outside the labour market (see Box 1 for definitions of labour market terminology). It then looks at economic activity rates more closely, discussing labour market activity among different ethnic and religious groups. Unemployment, a key measure of labour market disadvantage, is also examined in more depth, and attention is drawn to those groups with disproportionately high rates of unemployment. Ethnic and religious differences in areas such as occupational status, self-employment and part-time working are also compared.

Great Britain's different ethnic and religious populations vary in age structure, educational profile and the proportion born in the UK. After describing economic activity status for the whole population of working age, key influences on labour market position such as sex, age, country of birth and educational attainment are also considered. (See Box 2 for the definition of the working age population.)

The analysis in this chapter adds to the existing literature on employment and ethnicity in two main ways:

- It reports on ethnicity and religion in combination. This was made possible by the availability of religion data, first collected by the Census in 2001. This indicates that many ethnic and religious minorities tended to do less well in the labour market than the majority White British and Christian population, although some ethnic and religious groups were exceptions to this pattern.

- It supports the findings of earlier studies that have shown that members of ethnic and religious minority groups were more likely to be outside the labour market, and those within it had greater risk of unemployment, even when they were born in the UK and had equivalent age and educational characteristics to the White British or Christian populations.[2–7] (The Office for National Statistics proposes to conduct further research into the labour market position

Box 1

Labour market terminology

Economic activity

People are defined as economically active, or in the labour force, if they are aged 16 and over and are either employed or unemployed. Economic activity is therefore a measure of participation in the labour market and gives an indication of the potential size of the workforce.

Employment

Individuals who are in employment include employees, those who are self-employed, participants in government employment and training programmes, and people doing unpaid work for a family business.

Unemployment

The term unemployment refers to being without work but actively seeking it. This definition was developed by the International Labour Organisation (ILO), which regards people as unemployed only if they are not in employment and are actively seeking and available for work.[1] The unemployment rate is generally calculated as a proportion of economically active people, not of the entire population. The unemployment rates quoted in this chapter are calculated on this basis unless otherwise stated.

Economic inactivity

People are economically *inactive* if they are aged 16 or over and are neither employed nor unemployed. For example, people who are retired or who cannot work because of ill health are considered to be economically inactive.

Box 2

Note on the data reported

This chapter reports on the working-age population only (men aged 16–64 and women aged 16–59) unless otherwise stated.[8] Figures for men and women are presented separately throughout because employment status and the factors associated with it vary between the two sexes.[9] The labour market and employment information in this chapter is drawn from the 1991 and 2001 Censuses. The Office for National Statistics' Annual Local Area Labour Force Survey (ALALFS), which became part of the Annual Population Survey (APS) in 2004, provides reliable overall unemployment and economic activity rates which are updated regularly. However, Census coverage of small ethnic and religious groups enables more detailed analysis of sub-groups, for example by age, sex, country of birth and educational qualifications. The analysis of ethnic and religious groups in this chapter is therefore based on Census data in preference to the ALALFS or APS.

of different ethno-religious groups using statistical techniques such as regression analysis.)

Economic activity status

Employment rates varied greatly by ethnic and religious group in 2001. Many ethnic minority groups had low employment rates and high unemployment and economic inactivity rates. The White British group had the highest employment rates, coupled with the lowest unemployment rates and low economic inactivity rates. Employment rates were particularly low in the Bangladeshi, Pakistani and Black African groups and among men from the Other Black group. Bangladeshi and Pakistani women had markedly lower employment rates than those of other ethnic groups.

Of the different religious groups, Muslims had the lowest employment rates, particularly among women, a pattern that was consistent among Muslims of different ethnic groups. However, there was some variation among Muslims by ethnic group: Indian Muslim men had higher employment rates than Muslim men of other ethnic groups, while White British Muslim women had the highest female employment rate among Muslims. In contrast, Pakistani and Bangladeshi Muslim women had the lowest employment rates of any Muslims.

Economic inactivity

Ethnic and religious differences in economic inactivity rates in 2001 were larger among women than men. Bangladeshi and Pakistani women had the highest female economic inactivity rates, more than double those of other ethnic groups, while Black Caribbean women had the lowest, followed by White Irish and White British women.

Male economic inactivity was highest in the Chinese group, in part related to a high proportion of full-time students in this group. White British men had the lowest economic inactivity rates of any ethnic group, followed by Other White, White Irish and Indian men. Of the different religious groups, Muslims stood out as having the highest economic inactivity rates, followed by Buddhists. Studying full-time was the most common reason for economic inactivity among men from most ethnic minority groups, while permanent sickness or disability were more common reasons among White British and White Irish men. These differences can largely be attributed to the young age profiles of most ethnic minority groups.

Unemployment

In 2001 unemployment rates in many ethnic minority groups were more than double those of the White British group – almost four times higher in the case of the Other Black ethnic group. Male unemployment rates were also high in the Black

African, Black Caribbean, Bangladeshi, Pakistani and Mixed ethnic groups. Among women, Pakistanis and Bangladeshis had some of the highest female unemployment rates, along with those from the Other Black, Black African and Mixed ethnic groups. In contrast, White Irish and White British women had the lowest female unemployment rates of any ethnic group.

Unemployment was higher among Muslims than among other religious groups. Some variation was evident by ethnic group; Black African Muslims of both sexes had the highest unemployment rates of any Muslims, almost three times the rate of Indian Muslims, who had the lowest. However Indian Muslims had higher unemployment rates than Indian Sikhs, Hindus and Christians. Muslims of other ethnic groups also tended to have higher unemployment rates than non-Muslims from the same ethnic group; for example, Black African Muslims' unemployment rates were double those of Black African Christians.

Change in economic activity status by ethnic group, 1991–2001

Between 1991 and 2001 male and female unemployment rates fell, while economic inactivity rates rose among men but fell among women. This was reflected by a drop in male employment rates, but a rise in levels of female employment, by 2001. In some ethnic groups male employment rose, particularly among Black Africans and also among Pakistanis and Bangladeshis. Female employment rates rose over the decade in almost all ethnic groups, with the biggest increases occurring in the Bangladeshi, Indian and Pakistani groups. Despite these increases, the employment rates of Black African men, and of Bangladeshis and Pakistanis of both sexes, remained the lowest of any ethnic groups in 2001.

The lower unemployment rates in 2001 reflected an overall reduction in unemployment from a peak in the early 1990s. There was a particularly large percentage point fall in unemployment among Bangladeshis and Pakistanis of both sexes and Black African women, but as unemployment rates fell within all ethnic groups between 1991 and 2001, large differences in unemployment rates by ethnic group remained in 2001.

Economic activity rates and other factors

Economic activity rates vary by age and country of birth, with young people and the overseas-born tending to have lower economic activity rates. Ethnic and religious differences in economic activity rates in 2001 were less pronounced among 25- to 39-year-olds than among other age groups. The UK-born in this age range were less affected than those born overseas by ethnic and religious variation in economic activity rates. However, ethnic and religious differences were still present, especially among women.

Higher levels of qualifications are associated with higher rates of economic activity. Among women in 2001 this pattern was particularly evident, with female economic activity rates much higher among those with a degree or equivalent than those with lower or no qualifications. Degree-qualified Muslim women of all ethnic groups had substantially higher economic activity rates than those with no qualifications. Nevertheless, economic activity rates still varied by ethnic and religious group among those with similar levels of qualification.

The presence of dependent children in the household was associated with lower economic activity rates among women from most ethnic groups. Bangladeshi and Pakistani women with dependent children had lower economic activity rates than those of any other ethnic group, while women from the White British, Black Caribbean and Indian groups had the highest economic activity rates among those living with dependent children. Bangladeshi and Pakistani women living in households with no dependent children had economic activity rates more than twice as high as their counterparts with dependent children.

Unemployment rates and other factors

Variations in unemployment rates by ethnic group were present in all age groups and among the UK-born. Unemployment was high among UK-born people aged 16–24 from many ethnic minority groups, particularly those from the Black Caribbean, Black African, Other Black, Bangladeshi and Pakistani groups. Within most ethnic groups, men aged 25–39 who were born in the UK were as likely to be unemployed as those of similar age born overseas. Among women the UK-born tended to have lower unemployment rates than the overseas-born in the 25–39 age group, particularly within the South Asian and Black groups. Despite this, unemployment rates were high among UK-born women of many ethnic minority groups.

Lack of qualifications appeared to cause greater disadvantage to people from most ethnic minority groups than to the White British group. Of those with no qualifications, male unemployment rates were highest in the Black African, Mixed White and Black Caribbean and Other Black groups, while female unemployment rates were highest among Bangladeshis and Black Africans with no qualifications. Unemployment rates were especially high among young people aged 16–24 with no qualifications, rising above 50 per cent among young Black Caribbean, Black African and Other Black men and women.

Unemployment rates were higher among degree-qualified people from ethnic minority groups than degree-qualified White British people, and higher among degree-qualified Muslims and Buddhists than those of other religions. Men from the Black African, Other Black and Pakistani groups had particularly high unemployment rates among the degree-qualified, as did Bangladeshi, Pakistani and Black African women.

Occupational class

Among those who were employed, many ethnic and religious minorities were better represented in the managerial and professional occupations than White British people. A high proportion of employed Other White, White Irish and Indian men and White Irish, Other White and Black Caribbean women worked in managerial and professional occupations. The proportion employed in managerial and professional occupations was lowest among Pakistanis and Bangladeshis of both sexes and Black Caribbean and Other Black men.

Although members of most religious minorities were generally less well represented in managerial and professional occupations than the Christian majority, some groups were better represented, for example Hindu and Jewish men. Muslims in employment had the lowest proportion of workers in managerial and professional occupations.

Economic activity status

The population can be divided into three economic activity status categories: the employed, who are in work; the unemployed, who are not in work but actively seeking it; and the economically inactive, who are neither working nor seeking work. This section describes the economic activity status of the working-age population in 2001 within each of the different ethnic and religious groups, looking at employment rates, unemployment rates, economic inactivity and reasons for economic inactivity. (See Box 1 for definitions of labour market terminology and Box 3 for details of how unemployment is calculated in this section.)

Economic activity status in 2001

Ethnic minority groups typically had lower employment rates and higher unemployment and economic inactivity rates than the White British group, a pattern that also held among many of the non-Christian religions. In 2001, the working-age male employment rate was highest in the White British group, 78 per cent (Figure 5.1). The Indian, Other White and White Irish groups also had relatively high employment rates, over 70 per cent. Male employment rates were lower in the other ethnic minority groups, with the lowest rates in the Bangladeshi and Other Black groups (55 per cent and 57 per cent).

Figure **5.1**

Male economic activity status:[1] by ethnic group, April 2001

England and Wales

Percentages

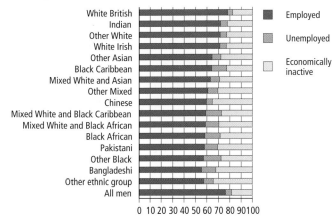

1 *Working-age population (16–64).*

Source: Census 2001, Office for National Statistics

Box 3

Calculating unemployment

Figures 5.1–5.6 show unemployment as a proportion of the total working-age population, in order to show how the entire working age population is distributed among the three types of economic activity status (employed, unemployed and economically inactive). This allows employment, unemployment and economic inactivity to be directly compared. This varies from the standard method used elsewhere in this chapter, which calculates unemployment rates as a proportion of the *economically active* population.

Those who were not employed were predominantly economically inactive rather than unemployed. For example, among Bangladeshi men of working age 32 per cent were economically inactive, more than double the proportion who were unemployed (13 per cent). Among White British men of working age the proportion who were economically inactive was more than three times the proportion who were unemployed (17 per cent compared with 5 per cent). Male economic inactivity was particularly high among Chinese, Bangladeshi, Pakistani and Black African men (between 29 per cent and 35 per cent), groups that contained a large proportion of students (Figure 5.7 on page 119). Variation in unemployment rates is discussed in more detail later in the chapter.

Female employment rates were high within the White British group (69 per cent), and the White Irish, Black Caribbean and Other White groups also had relatively high rates (over 60 per cent) (Figure 5.2). In contrast Pakistani and Bangladeshi women had low employment rates, just 25 per cent and 21 per cent. In most other ethnic groups, more than half the women of working age were employed. Of those who were not employed, a higher proportion overall were economically inactive than unemployed (30 per cent compared with 3 per cent).

Female economic inactivity rates were highest among Bangladeshi and Pakistani women (73 per cent and 70 per cent), more than twice the rates of Black Caribbean, White British and White Irish women, the groups with the lowest inactivity rates (27 per cent, 28 per cent and 30 per cent). Rates were around 40 per cent in most other ethnic groups. Reasons for economic inactivity included looking after the home or family and studying, and are shown in Table 5.7 on page 119.

Of the different religious groups, Christians had the highest male employment rates (77 per cent), while rates were also relatively high in the Jewish, Hindu and Sikh groups and among those with no religion (over 70 per cent) (Figure 5.3 overleaf). Male employment was lowest among Muslims (56 per cent), and also relatively low among Buddhists (66 per cent).

Muslims had the highest male economic inactivity rates (33 per cent) as well as the highest proportion of the working-age

Figure **5.2**

Female economic activity status:[1] by ethnic group, April 2001

England and Wales

Percentages

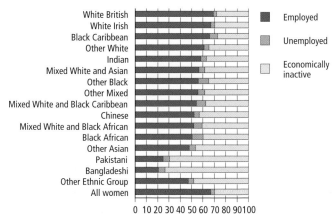

1 *Working-age population (16–59).*

Source: Census 2001, Office for National Statistics

Figure **5.3**

Male economic activity status:[1] by religion, April 2001

England and Wales

Percentages

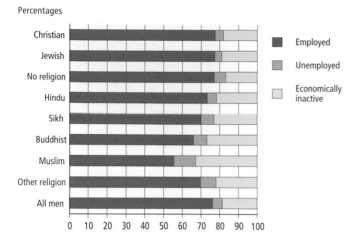

1 Working-age population (16–64).

Source: Census 2001, Office for National Statistics

Figure **5.4**

Female economic activity status:[1] by religion, April 2001

England and Wales

Percentages

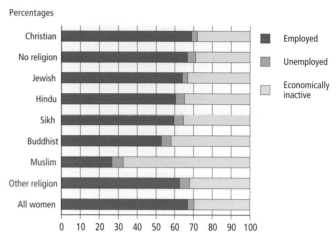

1 Working-age population (16–59).

Source: Census 2001, Office for National Statistics

population who were unemployed (12 per cent). Rates of economic inactivity and unemployment were considerably lower in other religious groups. Men with no religion had the lowest economic inactivity rate (17 per cent), and rates of less than 20 per cent also occurred in the Christian and Jewish groups. Jewish men also had the lowest unemployment rate (4 per cent), followed by Christian and Hindu men (5 per cent).

Female employment rates in most religious groups were 60 per cent or over, with Christians having the highest rate (69 per cent) (Figure 5.4). Muslim women were the exception, with an employment rate of 27 per cent. Buddhist women also had lower employment rates than those of other religions, 53 per cent. Economic inactivity rates were highest among Muslim women, 67 per cent, compared with between 28 and 42 per cent in the other religious groups.

Changes in economic activity status, 1991–2001

This section examines the change between 1991 and 2001 in the levels of employment, economic inactivity and unemployment in each ethnic group (Box 4 explains which ethnic groups may be compared between 1991 and 2001). Unemployment is shown as a proportion of the total working-age population (described in Box 3).

Employment levels in Great Britain were higher in 2001 than in 1991.[11] This rise was the result of an increase in female employment, as overall male employment rates were the same in both 1991 and 2001 (76 per cent). Despite this, male employment rates rose in some ethnic groups over the decade.

Box 4

Comparing ethnic groups between 1991 and 2001

Only seven ethnic groups may be compared using 1991 and 2001 Census data because the 1991 question on ethnic group contained fewer ethnic group categories.[10] See Chapter 1 for more details.

The biggest change occurred in the Black African group, where the male employment rate rose from 49 per cent in 1991 to 58 per cent in 2001, while male unemployment in this group fell (Figure 5.5). Employment rates also increased among Pakistani and Bangladeshi men, by 4 percentage points in each group, as a large fall in unemployment outweighed the increases in male economic inactivity in both groups. Employment rates also rose slightly among Indian men (from 71 per cent to 72 per cent).

In contrast male employment rates fell in the other ethnic groups that are comparable between 1991 and 2001. The biggest fall occurred in the Chinese group (from 65 per cent in 1991 to 60 per cent in 2001) as a result of a large increase in economic inactivity, in part reflecting the large proportion of Chinese men in higher education in 2001 (see 'Reasons for economic inactivity' later in the chapter). Among Black Caribbean men employment fell by 1 percentage point, as increases in economic inactivity rates slightly outweighed the reduction in unemployment. Employment among White men was almost unchanged across the decade.

Figure **5.5**

Male economic activity status:[1] by ethnic group, April 1991 and April 2001

Great Britain

Percentages

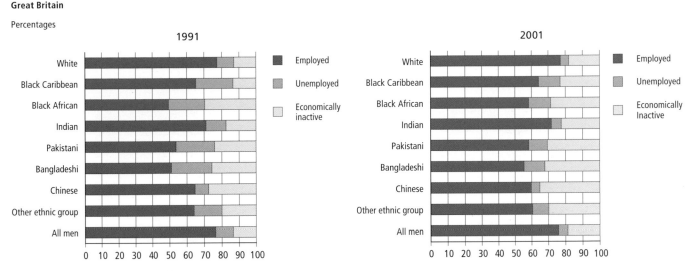

1   *Working-age population (16–64).*

Source: Census 1991 and 2001, Office for National Statistics and Census 1991 and 2001, General Register Office for Scotland

Female employment rates rose over the decade in almost all ethnic groups, with the biggest changes occurring in the Bangladeshi, Indian and Pakistani groups, an increase of between 5 and 6 percentage points in each group (Figure 5.6). Despite these relatively large increases, the employment rates of Bangladeshi and Pakistani women remained the lowest of any ethnic group in 2001. Chinese women were the only exception to the overall trend; their employment rate was the same in both 1991 and 2001.

In many ethnic groups the increase in female employment rates between 1991 and 2001 corresponded with a fall in both unemployment and economic inactivity. However, in some groups, female employment rates increased while economic inactivity rose or stayed the same; for example among Black Caribbean, Black African and Chinese women. The increased employment rates in these groups corresponded with a large fall in unemployment, particularly among Black African women.

Figure **5.6**

Female economic activity status:[1] by ethnic group, April 1991 and April 2001

Great Britain

Percentages

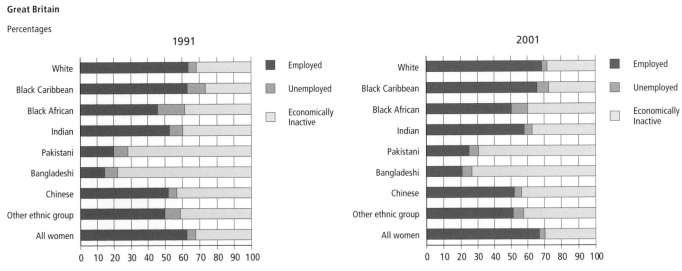

1   *Working-age population (16–59).*

Source: Census 1991 and 2001, Office for National Statistics and Census 1991 and 2001, General Register Office for Scotland

Reasons for economic inactivity

Some ethnic and religious groups, notably Muslims, had particularly low economic activity rates. Economic inactivity is not necessarily an indicator of disadvantage as people may be outside the labour market for a variety of reasons, both positive and negative. People may choose to stay outside the labour market if they are studying full time, looking after children or other family members, or able to retire early. However, economic inactivity can result from constraint, such as being unable to seek or take up employment because of illness or injury. Economic inactivity may also be 'discouraged unemployment', where, for example, someone who has been unsuccessfully seeking work for some time becomes discouraged and ceases to do so.[12] The Census provides some information on people's reasons for economic inactivity (Box 5).

Among men, long-term sickness or disability and being a student were the most common reasons for economic inactivity. For women, looking after the home or family was the most common, followed by being a student. In general

Box 5

Measuring reasons for economic inactivity in the Census

The 2001 Census included a question asking people who were not in employment whether they were retired, a student, looking after home or family, or permanently sick or disabled.

economically inactive men from ethnic minority groups were more likely to be students than men from the majority White British group (Table 5.7). At least half of economically inactive men from the Chinese, Black African, Indian and Other White groups were students, compared with a quarter of White British men. Notable exceptions to this pattern were economically inactive Black Caribbean men, with a similar proportion of students to the White British group, and White Irish men, who had the lowest proportion of students among the economically inactive.

Different rates of studying and sickness/disability among the various ethnic and religious groups in England and Wales can in part be attributed to their different age profiles, in particular the older age structure of the White British and White Irish populations compared with other ethnic groups (Chapter 2). Economically inactive White Irish and White British men had the highest levels of long term sickness or disability (46 per

cent and 37 per cent), much higher than Chinese and Black African men (4 per cent and 10 per cent). The differences in age profiles were also reflected in the proportions of men who were economically inactive because they were retired. Around one in six economically inactive White British and White Irish men were retired, compared with one in ten or less economically inactive men from all other ethnic groups.

More than half of the economically inactive women from the Pakistani and Bangladeshi groups were looking after the home and family, while just under half of their White British counterparts were doing the same. This compared with around one third of economically inactive Chinese, Black African and Black Caribbean women. Studying was more common among economically inactive women from some groups than others. Over half of economically inactive Chinese women were students, as were over two-fifths of Black African women, a higher proportion than their White British, White Irish, Pakistani, Bangladeshi and Black Caribbean counterparts (less than one-fifth were students in each case). Economically inactive women from the White Irish, White British and Black Caribbean groups had the highest levels of long-term sickness or disability relative to other ethnic groups, again related to the older age structure of these ethnic groups.

Among the different religious groups, a lower proportion of economically inactive Christians were students than those with another religion or no religion (Table 5.8 on page 120). This reflects the older age profile of Christians compared with the other religious groups (Chapter 2).

Economically inactive Muslim women were the most likely to be looking after the home or family; more than half did so, compared with around a third of economically inactive Sikh women, who were the least likely to be doing so.

Employment rates in 2001 by ethno-religious group

This section identifies differences in employment rates by ethno-religious group (Box 6), adding to previous research into the labour market characteristics of ethno-religious groups which concentrated solely on South Asians.[13, 14] Considerable religious diversity exists within several ethnic groups, most notably the Indian, Black African, and Other White groups, while the Muslim religious group is particularly ethnically diverse.

The tendency for Muslims to have much lower employment rates than those of other religions was apparent among Muslims of different ethnic groups. For example, 35 per cent of Indian Muslim women of working age were employed,

Table **5.7**

Reason for economic inactivity:[1] by ethnic group and sex, April 2001

England and Wales　　　　　　　　　　　　　　　　　　　　　　　　　　　　　　　　Percentages

	Reitred	Student	Looking after home/family	Permanently sick/disabled	Other	All economically inactive (=100%) (=numbers)
Men						
White British	18	25	6	37	15	2,493,128
White Irish	15	15	5	46	18	50,146
Other White	7	50	6	15	22	107,283
Mixed White and Black Caribbean	3	46	5	21	26	12,134
Mixed White and Black African	2	52	5	18	23	5,859
Mixed White and Asian	4	58	4	15	19	13,346
Other Mixed	4	57	5	16	19	11,681
Indian	8	51	4	21	16	80,498
Pakistani	4	45	8	21	22	66,886
Bangladeshi	5	43	10	18	24	25,920
Other Asian	5	46	6	15	27	26,957
Black Caribbean	10	28	6	28	29	39,702
Black African	3	60	5	10	22	43,506
Other Black	3	44	5	20	28	7,058
Chinese	7	77	3	4	8	29,114
Other ethnic group	3	62	5	10	20	25,157
All men	**16**	**29**	**6**	**34**	**16**	**3,038,375**
Women						
White British	5	17	48	18	11	3,712,425
White Irish	5	15	42	23	14	58,970
Other White	3	31	44	7	15	182,075
Mixed White and Black Caribbean	1	32	40	11	16	18,737
Mixed White and Black African	1	34	38	10	17	8,556
Mixed White and Asian	1	41	34	9	14	17,277
Other Mixed	1	41	35	9	14	16,371
Indian	2	29	41	13	15	130,491
Pakistani	1	18	55	7	20	145,702
Bangladeshi	1	16	57	5	21	58,857
Other Asian	2	28	42	9	19	33,778
Black Caribbean	3	27	33	18	18	54,437
Black African	1	42	32	7	18	66,675
Other Black	1	34	33	12	19	10,557
Chinese	4	53	31	3	9	38,215
Other ethnic group	1	34	46	4	15	45,902
All women	**5**	**19**	**47**	**16**	**12**	**4,599,025**

1　Among those of working age (men aged 16–64, women aged 16–59).

Source: Census 2001, Office for National Statistics

Table 5.8

Reason for economic inactivity:[1] by religion and sex, April 2001

England and Wales

Percentages

	Reitred	Student	Looking after home/family	Permanently sick/disabled	Other	All economically inactive (=100%) (=numbers)
Men						
No religion	11	38	7	26	18	529,954
Christian	19	24	5	38	14	1,977,105
Buddhist	7	50	6	20	17	15,897
Hindu	8	51	4	18	18	43,529
Jewish	12	49	3	21	14	14,463
Muslim	4	45	8	18	25	163,274
Sikh	6	47	5	23	19	26,110
Other religion	10	28	7	38	18	12,856
Religion not stated	13	31	5	31	19	255,187
All men	16	29	6	34	16	**3,038,375**
Women						
No religion	2	26	47	11	13	663,195
Christian	6	17	48	19	11	3,145,486
Buddhist	3	33	42	9	14	24,265
Hindu	3	32	39	12	15	65,610
Jewish	4	29	45	11	12	24,375
Muslim	1	20	53	7	20	305,058
Sikh	2	30	35	16	17	38,758
Other religion	4	21	39	25	11	19,420
Religion not stated	4	22	42	17	15	312,858
All women	5	19	47	16	12	**4,599,025**

1 Among those of working age (men aged 16–64, women aged 16–59).

Source: Census 2001, Office for National Statistics

Box 6

Ethno-religious groups

The analysis by ethno-religious group in this chapter is based on those groups with a reasonably large presence in England and Wales, defined as any whose population was greater than 30,000 people in 2001 (Chapter 2). The majority of analysis in this chapter uses data from the 2001 Census in England and Wales, rather than Great Britain or the UK, because the Northern Irish and Scottish Census questions on ethnic group and religion differed slightly from those asked in England and Wales, and are therefore not directly comparable (see Chapter 1, Measurement and Classification).

compared with 60 per cent of Indian Sikh and 62 per cent of Indian Hindu women (Figure 5.9). Similarly, 65 per cent of Indian Muslim men of working age were employed, compared with 71 per cent of Sikhs and 74 per cent of Hindus.

Although Indian Muslim men had the lowest employment rates of Indians of any religion in England and Wales, they had had the highest employment rates of Muslims from any ethnic group, 65 per cent (Figure 5.10). Employment rates among Muslim men from other ethnic groups were often considerably lower, with the lowest rate among Black African Muslims (45 per cent). Among Muslim women the pattern was different; those from the White British and Indian groups had the highest employment rates (41 per cent and 35 per cent). Those from

Figure **5.9**

Employment rates[1] among Indians: by selected religion and sex, April 2001

England and Wales

Percentages

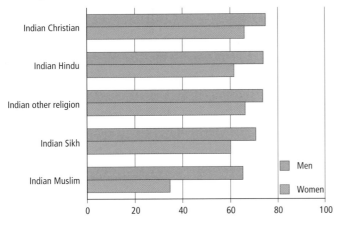

1 *Proportion of working-age population (men aged 16–64, women aged 16–59) in employment.*

Source: Census 2001, Office for National Statistics

Figure **5.10**

Employment rates among Muslims:[1] by selected ethnic group and sex, April 2001

England and Wales

Percentages

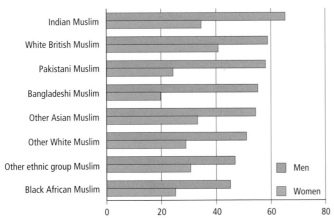

1 *Proportion of working-age population (men aged 16–64, women aged 16–59) in employment.*

Source: Census 2001, Office for National Statistics

the Bangladeshi group had the lowest employment rate (20 per cent), while around a quarter of Pakistani and Black African Muslim women were employed (24 per cent and 25 per cent).

Differences in employment rates between Muslim and non-Muslim people from the same ethnic group were particularly marked among the Other White, Black African and White British groups (Appendix Table A5.1). Among the Other White

group, for example, around half of Muslim men of working age were employed (51 per cent), compared with three-quarters (75 per cent) of those from the Christian and Jewish groups and those with no religion. For women the difference was even greater; 29 per cent of Muslim women from the Other White group were employed, compared with 68 per cent of women with no religion, 63 per cent of Christian women and 58 per cent of Jewish women. Similarly, 45 per cent of Black African Muslim men were employed, compared with 62 per cent of their Christian counterparts. For Black African women the rates were 25 per cent and 56 per cent respectively.

Looking at Muslims from the White British group, although employment rates were higher than those of Muslims from most ethnic minority groups, White British Muslims still had considerably lower employment rates than White British people from other religious groups. White British Muslim men had an employment rate of 59 per cent, compared with higher rates among Buddhists (71 per cent), Christians, Jews and those with no religion (78 per cent in each group). Similarly, White British Muslim women had a lower employment rate (41 per cent) than Buddhists, Jews, Christians and those with no religion (between 66 per cent and 70 per cent).

Unemployment rates in 2001

Unemployment is an important indicator of social inequality and can lead to problems such as poverty, ill health and homelessness. People who are defined as unemployed are unlikely to be so by choice, as they are available and actively looking for work. This section focuses on the unemployment rates of different ethnic and religious groups where the rate is based on the economically active population (Box 1).

In 2001, unemployment rates in England and Wales were lowest among people from the White British group (6 per cent among men and 4 per cent among women), followed by the White Irish, Other White, Indian and Chinese groups, whose rates were slightly higher (Figure 5.11 overleaf). Male unemployment rates were highest in the Other Black group (21 per cent), and also high (above 18 per cent) in the Mixed White and Black Caribbean, Bangladeshi and Black African groups. Female unemployment rates were highest among Bangladeshi and Pakistani women (22 per cent and 18 per cent), and were also high (above 12 per cent) among women from the Black African, Other Black, Mixed White and Black Caribbean and Mixed White and Black African groups. In contrast to the general pattern Bangladeshi and Pakistani women had higher unemployment rates than their male counterparts. In other ethnic groups, unemployment rates were higher for men than

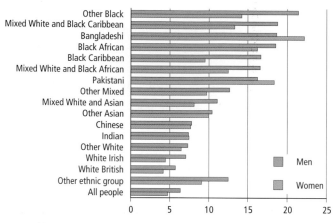

Figure 5.11

Unemployment rates: by ethnic group and sex,[1] April 2001

England and Wales

1 Working-age population (men aged 16–64, women aged 16–59).

Source: Census 2001, Office for National Statistics

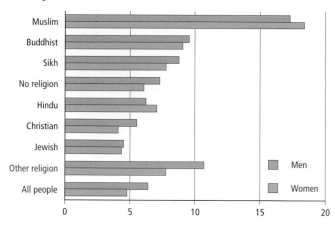

Figure 5.12

Unemployment rates: by religion and sex,[1] April 2001

England and Wales

Percentages

1 Working-age population (men aged 16–64, women aged 16–59).

Source: Census 2001, Office for National Statistics

women, particularly in the Black Caribbean group, at 17 per cent among men compared with 10 per cent among women.

Of the different religious groups, unemployment rates among Muslims were more than double those in other groups (Figure 5.12). The unemployment rate among Muslim men was 17 per cent. Buddhist and Sikh men had the next highest unemployment rates (10 per cent and 9 per cent) while Jewish and Christian men had the lowest (5 per cent and 6 per cent). Among women, the unemployment rate among Muslims was 18 per cent, while the Jewish and Christian groups again had the lowest rates (4 per cent in each group).

Unemployment rates in 2001 by ethno-religious group

This section describes unemployment rates among people of different ethno-religious groups where the rate is based on the economically active population (Box 1). The evidence from the 2001 Census confirms earlier research findings that suggested Muslims tended to have higher rates of unemployment than non-Muslims from the same ethnic group.[13, 14] It also shows that unemployment rates varied among Muslims of different ethnic groups.

Looking first at Muslims by ethnic group, Black African Muslims in England and Wales had the highest unemployment rates (28 per cent among men and 31 per cent among women), while Indian Muslims had the lowest (11 per cent among men and 12 per cent among women) (Figure 5.13). Muslim women had higher unemployment rates than Muslim men in the

Bangladeshi, Pakistani, Black African and Indian groups, while in the other ethnic groups Muslim men had higher rates of unemployment than Muslim women. Women from the Bangladeshi, Pakistani and Black African groups had low levels of participation in the labour market; their high unemployment rates suggest that even when active in the labour market they experienced difficulties finding employment.

Although Indian Muslim unemployment rates were lower than those of Muslims from other ethnic groups, they were higher than those of Indians of other religions. Indian Muslim unemployment rates were almost double those of Indian Hindus (11 per cent compared with 6 per cent among men, and 12 per cent compared with 7 per cent among women) (Figure 5.14). After Muslims, Sikhs had the next highest unemployment rates among Indians, 9 per cent among men and 8 per cent among women.

The pattern of higher unemployment rates among Muslims than people of different religions was also present in other ethnic groups (Appendix Table A5.2). White British and Other White Muslims both had unemployment rates around three times higher than those of Christians and Jews of the same ethnic groups; for example 19 per cent for Other White Muslim men compared with 6 per cent for their Christian counterparts. Among Black Africans, unemployment rates for Muslims were around twice those of Black African Christians. Male unemployment rates in the Black African group were 28 per cent for Muslims and 16 per cent for Christians, while the female unemployment rates were 31 per cent and 14 per cent respectively.

Figure **5.13**

Unemployment rates amoung Muslims:[1] by selected ethnic group and sex, April 2001

England and Wales

Percentages

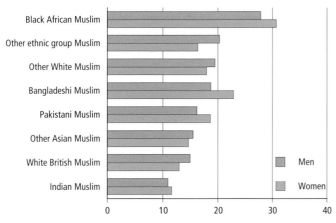

1 *Working-age population (men aged 16–64, women aged 16–59).*

Source: Census 2001, Office for National Statistics

Figure **5.14**

Unemployment rates among Indians:[1] by selected religion and sex, April 2001

England and Wales

Percentages

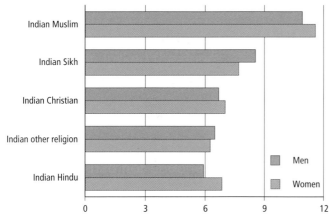

1 *Working-age population (men aged 16–64, women aged 16–59).*

Source: Census 2001, Office for National Statistics

Changes in unemployment rates, 1991–2001

Great Britain's most recent peak in unemployment occurred in 1993,[11] after which unemployment fell and reached a relatively stable level from 2001 onwards. This trend is reflected by the unemployment rates recorded in the two Censuses, which were lower in 2001 than in 1991 for both men and women. Unemployment rates quoted in this section are based on the economically active population rather than the whole working-age population (Box 1).

The overall male unemployment rate fell from 12 per cent in 1991 to 7 per cent in 2001, and this trend occurred among men from all ethnic groups (Figure 5.15). The Bangladeshi and Pakistani groups experienced the largest percentage point reduction in male unemployment rates: from 31 per cent to 19 per cent among Bangladeshis, and from 29 per cent to 16 per cent among Pakistanis. In general, the higher the unemployment rate in any particular ethnic group in 1991, the greater the percentage point reduction by 2001. White and Chinese men had the lowest unemployment rates in 1991, 11 per cent in each group; and the smallest percentage point reductions by 2001, to 6 per cent and 8 per cent respectively.

It has been suggested that unemployment in some ethnic minority groups is hypercyclical;[2] that is, ethnic minority groups are more severely affected by changes in the economic cycle than the majority White British population, suffering a greater rise in unemployment rates during economic downturns, which then fall at a faster rate as the economy improves. Ethnic minority groups with the highest unemployment rates in 1991 experienced the largest percentage point reductions by 2001, which appears to support the theory that ethnic minority unemployment is hypercyclical. However, unemployment rates fell by almost half among White men, a reduction that was *proportionally* greater than or equal to that of other ethic group. For some ethnic groups change was proportionally lower; for example, male unemployment among Black Caribbeans fell by around a third.

Figure **5.15**

Male unemployment rates:[1] by ethnic group, April 1991 and April 2001

Great Britain

Percentages

1 *Working-age population (aged 16–64).*

Source: Census 1991 and 2001, Office for National Statistics; Census 1991 and 2001, General Register Office for Scotland

Female unemployment fell from 7 per cent in 1991 to 5 per cent in 2001 (Figure 5.16). Female unemployment did not reach as high a level as male unemployment during the economic downturn of the 1990s, and this is reflected in the unemployment rates recorded by the 1991 Census. However women from some ethnic groups had high unemployment rates in both 1991 and 2001. While the reduction in unemployment among Bangladeshi, Pakistani and Black African women was almost as large as that of their male counterparts between 1991 and 2001, their unemployment rates remained high relative to White and Chinese women. The female unemployment rate among Bangladeshis fell from 35 per cent in 1991 to 22 per cent in 2001, among Pakistanis from 30 per cent to 18 per cent, and among Black Africans from 26 per cent to 16 per cent.

Similar to the trends in male unemployment, the ethnic groups with the highest female unemployment rates in 1991 experienced the greatest percentage point reduction over the decade, while those with lower unemployment rates experienced smaller reductions. Like men, women from White and Chinese ethnic groups had the lowest unemployment rates in 1991, 7 per cent and 8 per cent, and the smallest reductions in unemployment by 2001.

Relationship between economic activity rates and other factors

Economic activity rates varied substantially by ethnic and religious group. Different ethnic and religious groups vary,

Figure **5.16**

Female unemployment rates:[1] by ethnic group, April 1991 and April 2001

Great Britain

Percentages

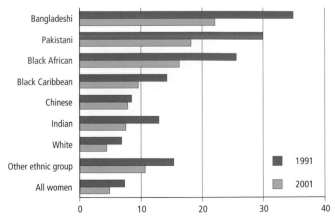

1 Working-age population (aged 16–59).

Source: Census 1991 and 2001, Office for National Statistics; Census 1991 and 2001, General Register Office for Scotland

however, in age profile, the proportion that are overseas-born, levels of educational attainment and likelihood of having children in the household, all of which can affect economic activity rates. This section describes the extent to which economic activity rates vary by ethnic and religious group when each of these four factors is taken into account.

Economic activity rates by age

Economic activity rates vary by age. Many people aged below 25 are not in the labour force as they are still in full-time education; conversely, among those aged over 50, factors such as age-related ill-health and the transition to retirement affect the proportion who are active in the labour market. This section shows ethnic and religious variation in economic activity rates among different age groups. The primary focus is the 25–39 age group, which excludes most full-time students and early retirees. In 2001 this age group included a reasonably high proportion of people from ethnic minorities who were born in the UK rather than overseas; this is important because some of the differences in economic activity rates by ethnic and religious group result from both the different age structures of different populations and the higher proportions of foreign-born people in the older age groups. Analysing this age range minimises such effects to give a clearer picture of the remaining differences by ethnic and religious group, and variation in economic activity by ethnic group was still present. This indicates that the difference in labour market participation by ethnic group is not simply a function of their different characteristics.

Men aged 25–39 in England and Wales had higher economic activity rates than other age groups overall, but rates varied considerably by ethnic group. White British and Indian men in this age range had the highest economic activity rates (92 per cent) (Table 5.17), while economic activity rates were lower (around 80 per cent) among men from the Black African, Mixed White and Black African, Other Black and Chinese groups.

Among young men aged 16–24, economic activity rates were lowest among Chinese and Black Africans (30 per cent and 44 per cent) and highest among White British men (72 per cent). Economic activity rates among young people are particularly affected by the proportion of full-time students, which varies by ethnic group (see 'Reasons for economic activity' earlier in the chapter). Among older men aged 40–64, Bangladeshi and Pakistani men had the lowest economic activity rates, 58 and 66 per cent, compared with 75 per cent or above for most other groups.

Table 5.17

Male economic activity: by ethnic group and age, April 2001

England and Wales   Percentages

	Age groups			
	16–24	25–39	40–64	All of working age
White British	72	92	80	83
White Irish	62	90	72	77
Other White	49	85	81	77
Mixed White and Black Caribbean	63	82	75	73
Mixed White and Black African	54	78	76	70
Mixed White and Asian	51	84	77	71
Other Mixed	51	81	76	70
Indian	51	92	80	78
Pakistani	53	85	66	69
Bangladeshi	54	84	58	68
Other Asian	47	79	78	72
Black Caribbean	60	85	76	77
Black African	44	78	81	71
Other Black	56	81	77	72
Chinese	30	81	82	65
Other ethnic group	35	71	79	66
All men	**68**	**91**	**80**	**82**

Source: Census 2001, Office for National Statistics

Economic activity rates varied substantially by ethnic group among women of working age in all three age bands. As for men, women aged 25–39 had higher economic activity rates than women of any other age group; three-quarters (74 per cent) were economically active (Table 5.18 overleaf). Within the 25–39 age group, over three-quarters of White Irish, Black Caribbean and White British women were economically active, compared with just a quarter of Bangladeshi and around a third of Pakistani women, who had the lowest rates.

Like young men, women aged 16–24 tended to have lower economic activity rates than those aged 25 and over. This pattern occurred in almost all ethnic groups, notably the Chinese group, where 32 per cent of young women were economically active, compared with 67 per cent of those aged 25–39. This reflected the high proportion of students within the Chinese group. However, among Bangladeshi and Pakistani women the pattern was reversed; while 16- to 24-year-olds had low economic activity rates when compared with other ethnic groups (38 and 36 per cent), they were higher than those of

Bangladeshi and Pakistani women in the older age groups.

In the 25–39 age group Muslim and Buddhist men each had economic activity rates of 80 per cent, while Christian, Jewish, Hindu and Sikh men, and those with no religion, all had rates of 90 per cent or above (Table 5.19 overleaf). There was more variation in male economic activity by religion in the 16–24 age group, reflecting to some extent the different proportions of students in different groups. Less than half of young Buddhist, Hindu, Muslim and Jewish men were economically active, compared with seven out of ten young Christian men. In the 40–64 age group, Muslim men had the lowest economic activity rate (67 per cent), while Jewish men had the highest (86 per cent).

In most religious groups, patterns of economic activity among women were broadly similar to those among men. Muslim and Buddhist women had low economic activity rates relative to women of other religions, and young women typically had lower rates than older women (Table 5.20 overleaf). Non-Christian women tended to have particularly low rates of

Table **5.18**

Female economic activity: by ethnic group and age, April 2001

England and Wales

Percentages

	Age groups			All of working age
	16–24	25–39	40–59	
White British	65	75	72	72
White Irish	58	77	68	70
Other White	52	70	66	65
MixedWhite and Black Caribbean	56	66	67	62
Mixed White and Black African	52	61	64	59
Mixed White and Asian	49	69	66	62
Other Mixed	50	67	67	62
Indian	48	71	64	63
Pakistani	36	32	21	30
Bangladeshi	38	24	13	27
Other Asian	38	55	61	53
Black Caribbean	57	77	75	73
Black African	43	63	69	60
Other Black	54	69	70	65
Chinese	32	67	66	57
Other ethnic group	34	52	62	52
All women	**62**	**74**	**71**	**70**

Source: Census 2001, Office for National Statistics

Table **5.19**

Male economic activity: by religion and age, April 2001

England and Wales

Percentages

	Age groups			All of working age
	16–24	25–39	40–64	
No religion	69	91	82	83
Christian	71	92	80	82
Buddhist	42	80	79	73
Hindu	50	91	82	78
Jewish	44	92	86	81
Muslim	49	80	67	67
Sikh	54	90	78	77
Other religion	60	85	78	78
Religion not stated	65	88	78	79
All men	**68**	**91**	**80**	**82**

Source: Census 2001, Office for National Statistics

Table **5.20**

Female economic activity: by religion and age, April 2001

England and Wales   Percentages

	Age groups			All of working age
	16–24	25–39	40–59	
No religion	62	74	75	71
Christian	65	76	72	72
Buddhist	36	58	66	58
Hindu	47	73	68	65
Jewish	46	73	70	67
Muslim	36	33	28	33
Sikh	51	74	64	65
Other religion	58	71	69	68
Religion not stated	59	72	70	68
All women	**62**	**74**	**71**	**70**

Source: Census 2001, Office for National Statistics

economic activity in the 16–24 age group but markedly higher rates in the 25–39 age group. Muslim women were an exception to this pattern; while their economic activity rates were particularly low in all age groups, they were higher in the youngest age group (36 per cent) than the older age groups.

Although the lower overall economic activity rates among people in non-Christian groups can be explained in part by the larger proportions of young people in these groups, variation existed in all age ranges, with Muslims and Buddhists tending to have low economic activity regardless of age.

Economic activity rates of the UK-born and overseas-born

This section examines the differences in the economic activity rates of people from different ethnic and religious groups after taking country of birth into account. Economic activity rates are typically lower among those born outside the UK than among the UK-born. This is partially related to the proportion of overseas students; 10 per cent of the foreign-born population of working age were full-time students in 2001.[15] However, people born outside the UK may also face barriers in the UK labour market; for example, those without English as their first language or holding non-UK qualifications may find it harder to seek and obtain work than native English speakers with UK qualifications and/or work experience,[2] while their UK-born descendents are unlikely to face the same difficulties.[16–18] These factors affect some ethnic minority groups more than others,

because of differences in the proportion of each group born in the UK and abroad.[19] The 2001 Census showed that 34 per cent of Black Africans and 55 per cent of Pakistanis were born in the UK, compared with 79 per cent of people in the Mixed and Other Black groups.[20]

Male economic activity in England and Wales was lower among the overseas-born than the UK-born in 2001, 76 per cent compared with 82 per cent (Appendix Table A5.3). In the 25 to 39 age range the difference was slightly greater, 85 per cent compared with 92 per cent (Table 5.21 overleaf). Among the UK-born, White British and Indian men had the highest economic activity rates in this age group (92 per cent), while men from the Other Black, Bangladeshi and some Mixed groups had the lowest (between 81 per cent and 83 per cent). Variation in economic activity rates was greater among the overseas-born (ranging from 71 per cent to 93 per cent), than it was among the UK-born (ranging from 81 per cent to 92 per cent).

As discussed earlier, economic activity rates among young men aged 16–24 are particularly influenced by the proportion of full-time students. In this age group variation in economic activity rates by ethnic group was just as pronounced among UK-born men as those born overseas (Appendix Table A5.3). Young UK-born men's economic activity rates ranged from 72 per cent in the White British group to below 50 per cent in the Black African, Chinese, and all three South Asian ethnic groups.

Table **5.21**

Economic activity among people aged 25–39: by ethic group, sex and whether UK-born or not, April 2001

England and Wales

Percentages

	Men			Women	
	UK-born	Overseas-born		UK-born	Overseas-born
White British	92	93		75	77
White Irish	90	90		78	76
Other White	88	85		72	70
Mixed White and Black Caribbean	83	78		66	69
Mixed White and Black African	82	75		69	54
Mixed White and Asian	88	75		73	57
Other Mixed	86	76		72	62
Indian	92	91		78	67
Pakistani	86	85		47	23
Bangladeshi	83	84		49	20
Other Asian	87	78		71	51
Black Caribbean	87	79		78	70
Black African	87	75		78	59
Other Black	81	81		71	60
Chinese	91	78		84	63
Other ethnic group	83	71		71	51
All people	**92**	**85**		**75**	**62**

Source: Census 2001, Office for National Statistics

Young UK-born Indian, Pakistani and Bangladeshi men had *lower* economic activity rates than their overseas born counterparts, whose rates were above 50 per cent.

Overall, the difference in economic activity rates between overseas-born and UK-born women, 60 per cent compared with 72 per cent, was larger than that found among men (Appendix Table A5.4). Table 5.21 shows that in the 25–39 age range there was considerable variation between ethnic groups in UK-born women's economic activity rates; the Chinese group had the highest economic activity rate (84 per cent) and the Pakistani and Bangladeshi groups the lowest (47 per cent and 49 per cent). Economic activity rates varied by ethnic group to a greater extent among overseas-born women in this age range, ranging from 20 per cent and 23 per cent among Bangladeshi and Pakistani women to 77 per cent among overseas-born White British women.

Variation by ethnic group among UK-born women's economic activity was lowest among young women aged 16–24, with rates ranging from 65 per cent in the White British group to 40 per cent in the Pakistani group (Appendix Table A5.4).

In the 25–39 age group, UK-born women from ethnic minority groups had substantially higher economic activity rates than those born overseas, particularly among South Asian, Chinese and Black African women. The economic activity rates of UK-born Pakistani and Bangladeshi women were 23 and 29 percentage points higher, respectively, than those of their overseas-born counterparts. Among Chinese women this difference was 21 percentage points, and among Black African women it was 19 percentage points. These observations suggest that overseas-born women from ethnic minority groups may face different barriers and incentives toward participation in the labour market to their UK-born counterparts.

In the 25–39 age group, UK-born men of different religious groups tended to have similar economic activity rates, above 90 per cent, with slightly lower rates among Muslims and Buddhists (84 per cent and 85 per cent) (Table 5.22). Economic activity rates varied by religion to a greater extent among overseas-born men, from 76 per cent and 78 per cent among Buddhists and Muslims to 91 per cent among Hindus.

Table 5.22

Male economic activity: by religion, age and whether UK-born or not, April 2001

England and Wales　　　　　　　　　　　　　　　　　　　　　　　　　　　　　　　　　　　　　　　Percentages

	16–24		25–39		40–64		All men of working age	
	UK-born	Overseas-born	UK-born	Overseas-born	UK-born	Overseas-born	UK-born	Overseas-born
No religion	70	49	92	87	82	83	84	78
Christian	72	53	92	87	80	79	82	78
Buddhist	53	32	84	76	78	81	76	70
Hindu	47	58	92	91	78	82	65	83
Jewish	46	34	93	86	86	87	81	80
Muslim	48	50	85	78	70	67	62	69
Sikh	54	59	91	89	76	78	73	80
Other religion	62	50	85	86	77	82	78	80
Religion not stated	67	46	89	82	78	76	80	73
All men	**70**	**51**	**92**	**85**	**80**	**77**	**82**	**76**

Source: Census 2001, Office for National Statistics

In the 16–24 age group UK-born men from the major non-Christian religions had substantially lower economic activity rates than their Christian counterparts, around 50 per cent or less, compared with 72 per cent, reflecting the high proportions of students in these non-Christian groups.

In the 25–39 age group UK-born women's economic activity rates were similar in many religious groups, around 75 per cent (Table 5.23), with the exception of Muslims, who had the lowest rates (48 per cent), and Hindus and Sikhs, who had the highest (84 per cent and 79 per cent). Variation in economic activity by religion was greater among overseas-born women; Muslims had the lowest economic activity rates (28 per cent) and those with no religion the highest (73 per cent).

There was less variation by religion among UK-born women in the 16–24 age group, with activity rates ranging from 66 per cent among Christians to 42 per cent among Muslims.

Table 5.23

Female economic activity: by religion, age and whether UK-born or not, April 2001

England and Wales　　　　　　　　　　　　　　　　　　　　　　　　　　　　　　　　　　　　　　　Percentages

	16–24		25–39		40–59		All women of working age	
	UK-born	Overseas-born	UK-born	Overseas-born	UK-born	Overseas-born	UK-born	Overseas-born
No religion	63	51	74	73	75	72	71	68
Christian	66	53	76	72	72	70	72	68
Buddhist	48	30	74	51	74	62	70	52
Hindu	47	46	84	69	69	68	62	66
Jewish	47	37	75	65	72	66	68	61
Muslim	42	29	48	28	49	26	45	28
Sikh	52	44	79	67	64	64	66	64
Other religion	60	49	71	71	68	70	68	68
Religion not stated	61	44	74	63	70	64	70	60
All women	**64**	**46**	**75**	**62**	**72**	**63**	**72**	**60**

Source: Census 2001, Office for National Statistics

Economic activity rates by level of educational attainment

Possessing skills that are desirable to employers confers advantage in the labour market. The best measure of these skills available in Census data is level of educational qualification. In general, people with a degree or equivalent level of qualification have higher economic activity rates than people with other qualifications, who in turn have higher economic activity rates than people with no qualifications. In 2001, female economic activity rates in particular were much higher among those with a degree or equivalent, 83 per cent, compared with 54 per cent among those with no qualifications or where the level of qualification was unknown. Among men, economic activity rates were 89 per cent among those with a degree or equivalent, compared with 72 per cent among those with no qualifications or where the level of qualification was unknown.[21]

The White British population of working age had one of the lowest rates of qualification to degree or equivalent level (Figure 5.24). One-fifth (19 per cent) of White British men of working age in England and Wales had a degree or equivalent in 2001, with the Mixed White and Black Caribbean, Bangladeshi and Black Caribbean ethnic groups also showing low proportions with a degree. In contrast, over two-fifths of men of working age from the Black African group held a degree, as did nearly two-fifths of Chinese men. Similarly, among women of working age those from the White British, Mixed White and Black Caribbean, Pakistani and Bangladeshi groups were the least likely to have a degree or equivalent (less than 20 per cent in each case). In contrast 39 per cent of Chinese women held a degree or equivalent.

Having no qualifications was more common among some ethnic minority groups than the White British group. Around a quarter of White British men of working age had no qualifications, compared with a third of Pakistani and White Irish men and two fifths of Bangladeshi men (Appendix Table A5.5). Among women, those from the Bangladeshi and Pakistani groups were the most likely to have no educational qualifications (48 per cent and 43 per cent), while Black Caribbean, Black African and Other Black women were the least likely (between 14 and 15 per cent). Nearly a quarter (23 per cent) of White British women had no qualifications.

Levels of educational qualification varied by age. Few people aged under 21 had obtained a degree level qualification (in England and Wales these typically take three years or more to obtain and people rarely begin studying at this level before age 18), and the proportion with a degree level qualification was also lower among people aged over 40 because higher

Figure 5.24

Working-age people[1] with a degree or equivalent: by ethnic group and sex, April 2001

England and Wales

Percentages

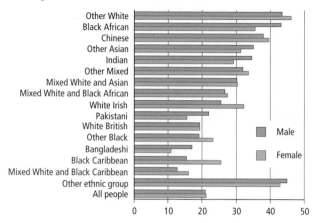

1 Men aged 16–64, women aged 16–59.
Source: Census 2001, Office for National Statistics

education participation was lower prior to the 1980s, especially among women.[22] The 25–39 age group was less affected by these age-related differences in qualification rates and is the main focus of the following analysis, which examines economic activity rates among men and women from different ethnic groups who held similar levels of qualification.

Looking first at degree-qualified men in England and Wales aged 25–39, variations in economic activity rates by ethnic group remained once qualifications were taken into account (Table 5.25). White British, White Irish and Indian men had the highest economic activity rates (between 94 and 96 per cent). Degree-qualified Chinese men and those from the Mixed White and Black African group had the lowest rates of economic activity (77 per cent and 80 per cent).

In contrast, among men aged 25–39 with no qualifications, Chinese, Indian, Bangladeshi and Pakistani men had the highest economic activity rates (between 79 per cent and 86 per cent), higher than the rate for their White British counterparts (77 per cent). Men from the Black African group with no qualifications had the lowest rate (56 per cent), and men from the Black and Mixed groups generally had lower economic activity rates than White British men with no qualifications (66 per cent or less compared with 77 per cent).

A degree level qualification appeared to make most difference to the economic activity rates of Black African and Black Caribbean men. Among Black African men with degrees the economic activity rate was 84 per cent, compared with 56 per cent among those with no qualifications; among Black

Table **5.25**

Economic activity among men aged 25–39: by ethnic group and highest qualification, April 2001

England and Wales   Percentages

	Degree or equivalent	Other qualifications[1]	No qualifications	All
White British	96	94	77	92
White Irish	94	91	71	90
Other White	88	87	70	85
Mixed White and Black Caribbean	90	87	64	82
Mixed White and Black African	80	82	62	78
Mixed White and Asian	89	86	61	84
Other Mixed	84	84	62	81
Indian	94	92	82	92
Pakistani	90	87	79	85
Bangladeshi	88	87	81	84
Other Asian	83	81	67	79
Black Caribbean	92	88	66	85
Black African	84	76	56	78
Other Black	87	83	65	81
Chinese	77	86	86	81
Other ethnic group	72	75	63	71
All men	**94**	**93**	**76**	**91**

1 Includes 'A' levels, GCSEs and vocational qualifications.

Source: Census 2001, Office for National Statistics

Caribbean men the rates were 92 per cent and 66 per cent respectively. Economic activity among Bangladeshi, Pakistani and Indian men did not vary to such an extent by level of qualification. Chinese men in this age range had lower economic activity rates if they had a degree than if they had no qualifications; this may be because a considerable number of Chinese men in this age range were studying for post-graduate qualifications.

Women's economic activity rates varied greatly by ethnic group for both those with no qualifications and those qualified to degree level. Among women in the 25–39 age range with degree-level qualifications, White British and White Irish women had the highest economic activity rates, 88 per cent (Table 5.26 overleaf). In contrast degree qualified Pakistani and Bangladeshi women had economic activity rates of 60 per cent and 62 per cent. Among those with no qualifications, Chinese women had the highest economic activity rates (54 per cent) followed by White British, Indian and Black Caribbean women. In contrast, 8 per cent of Bangladeshi women and 11 per cent of Pakistani women in this age range with no qualifications were economically active.

Educational qualifications appeared to have the greatest effect on the economic activity rates of Pakistani, Bangladeshi and Black African women, with those holding a degree much more likely to be in the labour market than their counterparts with no qualifications. Degree-qualified Pakistani and Bangladeshi women in the 25–39 age range had economic activity rates above 60 per cent, and while these rates were low compared with degree-qualified women from other ethnic groups, they were around six times higher than the rates of their counterparts with no qualifications. The difference in economic activity rates between Black African women of this age with degrees and those with no qualifications was also greater than 50 percentage points. In contrast, among Chinese women in this age group with degrees, economic activity rates were only 16 percentage points higher than among their counterparts with no qualifications.

Muslim women's economic activity rates were higher among the degree-qualified than those with no qualifications. In the 25–39 age range, 58 per cent of Muslim women with degrees were economically active compared with just 12 per cent of

Table **5.26**

Economic activity among women aged 25–39: by ethnic group and highest qualification, April 2001

England and Wales

Percentages

	Degree or equivalent	Other qualifications[1]	No qualifications	All
White British	88	76	47	75
White Irish	88	75	39	77
Other White	76	68	37	70
Mixed White and Black Caribbean	83	69	38	66
Mixed White and Black African	73	62	30	61
Mixed White and Asian	81	68	32	69
Other Mixed	76	66	34	67
Indian	79	74	47	71
Pakistani	60	40	11	32
Bangladeshi	62	34	8	24
Other Asian	68	54	26	55
Black Caribbean	86	76	47	77
Black African	78	60	26	63
Other Black	80	69	42	69
Chinese	70	67	54	67
Other ethnic group	58	53	36	52
All women	**85**	**75**	**44**	**74**

1 Includes 'A' levels, GCSEs and vocational qualifications.

Source: Census 2001, Office for National Statistics

those with no qualifications. There was some variation by ethnicity within the Muslim group. For example, among Muslim women with no qualifications, 23 per cent from the White British group were economically active, compared with 8 per cent from the Bangladeshi group (Figure 5.27). Degree-qualified Indian Muslim and White British Muslim women had high economic activity rates, 70 per cent and 68 per cent, while degree-qualified Pakistani, Bangladeshi and Black African Muslim women had lower economic activity rates, around 60 per cent. Muslim women from the Other Asian and Other ethnic groups had the lowest economic activity rates among Muslim women with degrees, 52 per cent and 46 per cent.

Muslim men from the main South Asian ethnic groups had the highest economic activity rates of any Muslims, whatever their level of qualification (Figure 5.28). For example, 93 per cent of Indian Muslim men aged 25–39 with degrees were economically active, compared with 74 per cent of Muslim men

Figure **5.27**

Economic activity rates among Muslim women aged 25–39: by selected ethnic group and highest qualification,[1] April 2001

England and Wales

Percentages

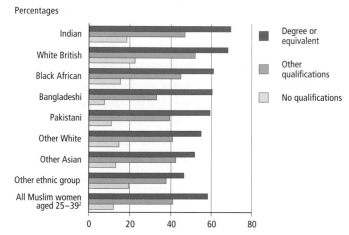

1 Includes 'A' levels, GCSEs and vocational qualifications.
2 Includes Muslims from ethnic groups not shown elsewhere.

Source: Census 2001, Office for National Statistics

Figure 5.28

Economic activity rates among Muslim men aged 25–39: by selected ethnic group and highest qualification,[1] April 2001

England and Wales

Percentages

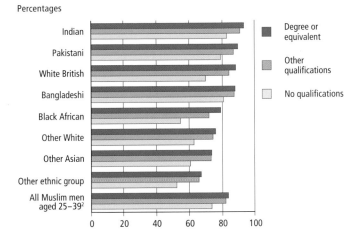

1 'Other' qualifications includes 'A' levels, GCSEs and vocational qualifications.
2 Includes Muslims from ethnic groups not elsewhere shown.

Source: Census 2001, Office for National Statistics

from the Other Asian group, 76 per cent from the Other White group, and 79 per cent from the Black African group.

Among Muslim men aged 25–39 with no qualifications, those from the Indian and Bangladeshi ethnic groups had the highest economic activity rates (83 per cent and 81 per cent), and those from the Black African and Other ethnic groups had the lowest (55 per cent and 52 per cent).

Economic activity rates by presence of dependent children

Parenthood is a factor associated with lower economic activity among women, in some ethnic groups more than others.[16, 23] This section looks at economic activity rates among people living in households with dependent children, especially young children. The analysis focuses on women aged between 25 and 39, an age group that excludes most students, includes a reasonably high proportion of people from ethnic minorities who were born in the UK, and minimises the proportion of women who may have a non-maternal relationship to the dependent children in the household. (Parental relationships are not currently available from the Census data, therefore women living in households with dependent children may be

the mothers of those children but young women may, for example, be the elder sisters, while older women may be grandmothers.) It also compares economic activity rates of men of this age living with dependent children and those without.

The 2001 Census showed the well-established pattern that women living in households with dependent children had lower economic activity rates than those living with no dependent children, 64 per cent compared with 89 per cent among women aged 25–39 (Table 5.29 overleaf). In general, the higher the age of the youngest dependent child in the household, the higher the economic activity rate, ranging from 57 per cent for those living with a child aged under five, to 77 per cent among those where the youngest child was aged 12 and over.

Rates of economic activity among women living with dependent children varied greatly by ethnic group. A fifth of Bangladeshi women and a quarter of Pakistani women aged 25–39 with dependent children were economically active. In contrast, over two-thirds of Black Caribbean, White British and Indian women in this age group with dependent children were economically active.

The higher economic activity rates among women aged 25–39 in households with no dependent children was particularly notable in the Bangladeshi and Pakistani groups. Their economic activity rates, 56 per cent and 62 per cent, were each 37 percentage points higher than their counterparts living with dependent children. In contrast, the economic activity rates of Black Caribbean, Chinese, and Other Black women from households with no dependent children were between 15 and 17 percentage points higher than those of their counterparts with dependent children.

Economic activity rates among men aged between 25 and 39 were slightly higher for those living with dependent children than those without: 93 per cent compared with 91 per cent. This pattern did not vary greatly by ethnic group, except for Bangladeshi and Mixed White and Black African men; in contrast to the general pattern, economic activity rates were slightly lower among men from these groups living with dependent children than those without (84 per cent compared with 86 per cent among Bangladeshi men).

Women aged 25–39 with dependent children in their household who belonged to the Muslim and Buddhist religious groups had the lowest economic activity rates, 26 per cent and

Table **5.29**

Economic activity among people aged 25–39: by ethnic group, sex and dependent child in household, April 2001

England and Wales

Percentages

	Women					Men	
	Youngest dependent child aged 0–4	Youngest dependent child aged 5–11	Youngest dependent child aged 12 and over	Any dependent children	No dependent children	Any dependent children	No dependent children
White British	60	73	78	67	91	94	92
White Irish	59	68	73	63	90	93	90
Other White	47	59	66	52	84	87	86
Mixed White and Black Caribbean	50	63	70	58	82	88	83
Mixed White and Black African	45	60	65	52	77	80	81
Mixed White and Asian	50	61	70	56	84	87	85
Other Mixed	48	61	68	54	82	83	82
Indian	56	73	77	64	85	93	91
Pakistani	21	29	42	25	62	86	84
Bangladeshi	17	21	32	19	56	84	86
Other Asian	39	55	64	46	72	82	78
Black Caribbean	65	75	80	71	86	90	86
Black African	53	65	65	57	75	82	78
Other Black	56	67	74	63	79	87	81
Chinese	54	65	76	60	77	90	81
Other ethnic group	32	46	58	38	66	77	70
All people	**57**	**71**	**77**	**64**	**89**	**93**	**91**

Source: Census 2001, Office for National Statistics

47 per cent respectively (Table 5.30). In contrast 70 per cent of Sikh women and 68 per cent of Christian women living in a household with dependent children were economically active, the highest figures for any religious group.

Across all religious groups women aged 25–39 living with dependent children had lower rates of economic activity than those living in households without dependent children. The difference was greatest among Muslim women and smallest among Hindu and Sikh women. Among Muslim women 61 per cent living in a household without dependent children were economically active, compared with 26 per cent of their counterparts living with dependent children. For Jewish women and those with no religion, economic activity was also substantially higher among those living in households with no dependent children (88 per cent compared with 59 per cent in the case of Jewish women). In contrast, the economic activity rates for Sikh women were 86 per cent and 70 per cent respectively.

Men aged 25–39 from all religious groups had slightly higher economic activity rates if there was a dependent child in their household. Among those living with dependent children, Muslim and Buddhist men had the lowest economic activity rates (83 per cent and 87 per cent), while Christian men had the highest (94 per cent).

Relationship between unemployment rates and other factors

Unemployment rates vary substantially by ethnic and religious group. Different ethnic and religious groups also vary from each other in age profile, the proportion of people that were born overseas, and educational attainment, all of which can affect unemployment. As with the previous section on economic activity, this section looks at the extent to which unemployment rates vary once these other characteristics are taken into account, to show whether differences by ethnic and

Table **5.30**

Economic activity among people aged 25–39: by religion, sex and dependent child in household, April 2001

England and Wales   Percentages

	Women					Men	
	Youngest dependent child aged 0–4	Youngest dependent child aged 5–11	Youngest dependent child aged 12 and over	Any dependent children	No dependent children	Any dependent children	No dependent children
No religion	55	67	75	61	90	92	92
Christian	61	74	79	68	90	94	91
Buddhist	40	53	69	47	70	87	81
Hindu	58	76	81	67	84	93	90
Jewish	54	69	74	59	88	94	92
Muslim	22	32	42	26	61	83	78
Sikh	63	76	80	70	86	92	90
Other religion	50	64	69	58	84	87	86
Religion not stated	54	68	74	62	87	91	89
All people	**57**	**71**	**77**	**64**	**89**	**93**	**91**

Source: Census 2001, Office for National Statistics

religious group are present even among people who are similar in other respects. This section uses the standard unemployment rate which is based on the economically active population (Box 1).

High rates of unemployment can be related to lack of skills or work experience, which are more prevalent in younger age groups. If high rates of unemployment exist among specific ethnic or religious groups even when they have similar qualifications, age and other relevant characteristics, it suggests that other factors may be disproportionately affecting these groups. Such factors can include characteristics that are not measured by the Census, for example work experience and relevant skills (including fluency in English), but may also include factors such as discrimination by employers.[5] The Race Relations Act 1976 made it illegal to discriminate against applicants for jobs or workers on the grounds of race, colour, nationality, or ethnic group.

Unemployment rates by age

This section examines patterns of unemployment among people of different ethnic and religious groups by age, comparing those aged 25–39 with older and younger age groups and looking specifically at young people's unemployment. The 25–39 age group included a reasonably high proportion of people from ethnic minorities who were born in the UK and also excludes most full-time students. Some

of the differences in unemployment by ethnic and religious group result from the different age profiles of different populations and the higher proportions of foreign-born people in the older age groups (Chapter 2). Analysing age groups separately minimises such effects to give a clearer picture of the remaining differences by ethnic and religious group.

The 2001 Census data show the well-established pattern of higher unemployment rates among young people aged 16–24 than among those in older age groups (Table 5.31 overleaf). White British people had the lowest unemployment rates within all age groups, suggesting that the high overall unemployment rates among most ethnic minority groups were not simply a result of their younger age profiles, but that other factors contributed. For example, 5 per cent of White British men aged 25–39 were unemployed, compared with 13 per cent of Pakistani men and 18 per cent of Black African men.

Unemployment rates among young people were highest for Bangladeshis, Pakistanis and the three Black ethnic groups. Unemployment rates in these groups were particularly high at age 16 and 17 (above 40 per cent for men and above 35 per cent for women), more than twice the rates of their White British counterparts (19 per cent and 15 per cent). The same ethnic groups were also affected by high unemployment in the 18–24 age group (above 20 per cent among both men and women, compared with 11 per cent and 8 per cent in the White British group).

Table 5.31

Unemployment rates: by ethnic group, age and sex, April 2001

England and Wales

Percentages

	Men					Women				
	16–17	18–24	25–39	40–64	All men of working age	16–17	18–24	25–39	40–59	All women of working age
White British	18	11	5	4	6	15	8	4	3	4
White Irish	23	13	6	7	7	19	9	4	4	4
Other White	26	14	7	6	7	19	10	6	5	7
Mixed White and Black Caribbean	36	27	14	11	19	28	18	10	7	13
Mixed White and Black African	31	25	15	12	17	27	17	11	9	13
Mixed White and Asian	27	18	9	8	11	18	13	7	6	8
Other Mixed	26	19	11	9	13	23	14	9	6	10
Indian	29	16	6	6	7	27	13	6	5	7
Pakistani	45	26	13	12	16	39	23	15	13	18
Bangladeshi	48	24	15	18	19	45	23	18	17	22
Other Asian	33	18	10	8	10	29	17	10	7	10
Black Caribbean	44	34	15	13	17	35	20	9	6	10
Black African	49	32	18	13	18	40	25	16	11	16
Other Black	44	34	19	13	21	36	23	12	8	14
Chinese	21	19	6	6	8	19	15	7	5	8
Other ethnic group	35	25	13	8	13	27	17	9	7	9
All people	**20**	**12**	**6**	**5**	**6**	**16**	**9**	**5**	**3**	**5**

Source: Census 2001, Office for National Statistics

Table 5.32

Unemployment rates: by religion, age and sex, April 2001

England and Wales

Percentages

	Men					Women				
	16–17	18–24	25–39	40–64	All men of working age	16–17	18–24	25–39	40–59	All women of working age
No religion	23	13	6	5	7	19	10	5	4	6
Christian	18	11	5	4	5	14	7	4	3	4
Buddhist	21	21	9	8	10	27	17	10	7	9
Hindu	27	14	5	5	6	25	12	6	5	7
Jewish	19	11	4	3	5	12	9	4	3	4
Muslim	45	26	15	13	17	40	23	16	13	18
Sikh	33	19	7	6	9	29	14	6	5	8
Other religion	29	20	11	8	11	22	14	8	5	8
Religion not stated	22	14	7	6	8	17	10	5	4	6
All people	**20**	**12**	**6**	**5**	**6**	**16**	**9**	**5**	**3**	**5**

Source: Census 2001, Office for National Statistics

In the 25–39 age group male unemployment was highest in the Other Black and Black African ethnic groups (20 per cent and 18 per cent), while female unemployment was highest among Bangladeshis and Black Africans (18 and 16 per cent). These rates were around four times those of White British men and women (5 per cent and 4 per cent). In this age range the White Irish, Other White, Indian and Chinese ethnic groups had unemployment rates only slightly higher than the White British.

Muslims of both sexes had the highest unemployment rates of the different religious groups in each age range, followed in most cases by Buddhists. Christians and Jews had the lowest unemployment rates. Among young Muslims, male unemployment rates reached 45 per cent among 16- to 17-year-olds and 26 per cent among 18- to 24-year olds, with similar rates for females (Table 5.32). Unemployment rates were also high among Muslims in the 25–39 age group (15 per cent among men and 16 per cent among women). Although young Hindus had relatively high unemployment rates (for example 27 per cent among 16- to 17-year-old men), Hindus in the 25–39 age group had broadly similar unemployment rates to their Christian and Jewish counterparts (5 per cent among men and 6 per cent among women).

Unemployment rates of the UK-born and overseas-born

People born outside the UK may face difficulties obtaining work if they do not have English as a first language, UK qualifications or work experience. These factors affect some ethnic minority groups more than others (see 'Economic activity rates of the UK-born and overseas born' earlier in the chapter). This section compares the unemployment rates for the UK-born and overseas-born among ethnic minority groups and shows that unemployment was high even among the UK born. It concentrates primarily on the 16–24 and 25–39 age groups, as the population aged 40 and over contained proportionally fewer UK-born members of ethnic minorities (see Chapter 2, Population).

Before taking age into account, unemployment was higher among men born overseas than those born in the UK, 9 per cent compared with 6 per cent in England and Wales in April 2001 (Table 5.33). However, within many ethnic groups young UK-born men aged 16–24 had higher unemployment rates than those born overseas, for example 31 per cent compared with 21 per cent among Pakistanis. Young UK-born Other Black and Black Caribbean men had the highest unemployment rates

Table 5.33

Male unemployment rates: by ethnic group, age and whether UK-born or not, April 2001

England and Wales   Percentages

	16–24		25–39		40–64		All men of working age	
	UK-born	Overseas-born	UK-born	Overseas-born	UK-born	Overseas-born	UK-born	Overseas-born
White British	12	12	5	5	4	5	6	6
White Irish	15	13	6	5	7	7	7	7
Other White	17	14	8	7	6	6	9	7
Mixed White and Black Caribbean	29	16	14	10	10	12	19	12
Mixed White and Black African	27	23	14	15	13	11	18	15
Mixed White and Asian	19	21	8	12	7	9	11	11
Other Mixed	20	18	10	12	9	9	14	12
Indian	19	14	7	5	8	6	11	6
Pakistani	31	21	13	13	14	12	22	13
Bangladeshi	30	24	14	15	18	18	24	17
Other Asian	21	18	10	10	9	8	14	10
Black Caribbean	36	33	14	17	12	13	18	14
Black African	29	36	15	19	14	13	18	19
Other Black	37	25	21	15	15	11	24	14
Chinese	14	23	5	6	6	6	9	8
Other ethnic group	23	27	9	13	9	8	15	12
All men	13	18	5	9	4	7	6	9

Source: Census 2001, Office for National Statistics

(37 per cent and 36 per cent), around three times higher than young UK-born White British men (12 per cent). Young UK-born Pakistani, Bangladeshi and Black African men also had high unemployment rates (around 30 per cent). However, unemployment rates among young UK-born Chinese and White Irish men were only slightly higher than those of their White British counterparts.

There were also differences in unemployment rates by ethnic group among UK-born men in the 25–39 age group. UK-born male unemployment rates were highest in the Other Black group (21 per cent), four times higher than in the White British group (5 per cent). Unemployment was also high among UK-born Black African, Black Caribbean, Bangladeshi and Pakistani men, and those from two of the Mixed groups (more than twice as high as the rate for UK-born White British men of this age). In contrast, UK-born men from the Chinese, White Irish and Indian ethnic groups had unemployment rates closer to that of their White British counterparts in this age group (below 7 per cent).

In the 25–39 age group, overseas-born men tended to have similar unemployment rates to UK-born men of the same ethnic group, with the exception of Black Africans, whose unemployment rate was higher among the overseas-born (20 per cent compared with 15 per cent of the UK-born), and Indians, whose rate was lower among the overseas-born (5 per cent compared with 6 per cent). This suggests that within most ethnic groups, men born in the UK were no more likely to avoid unemployment than the overseas-born.

Before taking age into account, overseas-born women tended to have higher unemployment rates than UK-born women, the same pattern as for men; 8 per cent compared with 5 per cent in 2001 (Table 5.34). However, high rates of unemployment for women from ethnic minorities were present even among the UK-born. Unemployment rates among young UK-born women aged 16–24 were highest in the Bangladeshi, Pakistani, Black Caribbean and Other Black ethnic groups (above 22 per cent), and were around three times that of their White British counterparts (9 per cent). In common with young UK-born

Table 5.34

Female unemployment rates: by ethnic group, age and whether UK-born or not, April 2001

England and Wales   Percentages

	16–24		25–39		40–59		All women of working age	
	UK-born	Overseas-born	UK-born	Overseas-born	UK-born	Overseas-born	UK-born	Overseas-born
White British	9	9	4	4	3	4	4	4
White Irish	11	10	4	4	4	4	5	4
Other White	13	10	6	6	4	5	7	6
Mixed White and Black Caribbean	21	18	11	9	7	9	14	10
Mixed White and Black African	19	17	10	12	8	10	12	13
Mixed White and Asian	13	15	6	9	5	6	8	8
Other Mixed	15	17	8	9	7	6	10	9
Indian	14	18	5	7	6	5	9	7
Pakistani	23	30	12	18	13	13	18	18
Bangladeshi	26	26	12	20	9	18	22	22
Other Asian	16	21	7	12	7	7	11	10
Black Caribbean	22	24	8	10	7	6	11	8
Black African	19	30	11	18	12	11	13	17
Other Black	26	23	12	13	8	8	15	12
Chinese	10	21	7	7	6	5	8	8
Other ethnic group	17	19	8	9	7	7	12	9
All women	9	15	4	8	3	6	4	8

Source: Census, April 2001, Office for National Statistics

men, the lowest unemployment rates among young UK-born women from ethnic minorities were found in the Chinese and White Irish groups (10 and 11 per cent).

Similar patterns were present in the 25–39 age group. While overall unemployment rates were lower than for those aged 16–24, UK-born Bangladeshi, Other Black, Pakistani and Black African women had rates above 11 per cent, compared with 4 per cent for White British women in this age group. UK-born women in this age group from the White Irish and Indian groups had similar unemployment rates to the White British (4 per cent and 5 per cent).

Unlike men, UK-born women in the 25–39 age group tended to have lower unemployment rates than overseas-born women of the same ethnic group. This pattern was most pronounced in the Asian ethnic groups and among Black Caribbeans and Black Africans. For example the unemployment rate was 20 per cent among overseas-born Bangladeshi women aged 25–39, compared with 12 per cent among their UK-born counterparts. This suggests that ethnic minority women born in the UK had

some advantage over the overseas-born in avoiding unemployment, although their unemployment rates remained higher than those of White British women.

Unemployment rates by level of educational attainment

Educational qualifications typically confer an advantage in avoiding unemployment. The 2001 Census data showed the well-established pattern of highest unemployment rates among people with no qualifications (11 per cent for men and 7 per cent for women), and lowest rates among those with a degree or equivalent (4 per cent for men and 3 per cent for women). Research has suggested that a degree or equivalent qualification conferred less advantage to people from ethnic minorities in avoiding unemployment.[5, 18] This is also apparent in the 2001 Census results, where degree-qualified people from most ethnic minorities had higher unemployment rates than White British people with the same level of qualification (Table 5.35). For example, 13 per cent of Black African male graduates were unemployed, compared with 3 per cent of

Table 5.35

Unemployment rates among those with degree-level qualifications: by ethnic group, sex and age, April 2001

England and Wales   Percentages

	Men				Women			
	16–24[1]	25–39	40–64	All men of working age	16–24[1]	25–39	40–59	All women of working age
White British	6	3	3	3	4	2	2	2
White Irish	6	3	4	4	4	2	2	2
Other White	11	4	4	5	9	5	4	5
Mixed White and Black Caribbean	13	8	8	9	9	6	5	6
Mixed White and Black African	14	10	8	10	11	8	8	8
Mixed White and Asian	12	5	6	6	8	4	4	5
Other Mixed	12	8	7	8	8	6	5	6
Indian	11	3	3	4	10	6	4	6
Pakistani	19	8	9	10	16	9	9	11
Bangladeshi	15	9	8	10	14	11	8	11
Other Asian	13	8	6	7	11	8	5	7
Black Caribbean	18	8	9	9	11	6	4	5
Black African	21	13	11	13	17	11	8	10
Other Black	19	13	9	12	13	9	6	8
Chinese	16	5	4	6	13	6	4	6
Other ethnic group	15	8	6	7	13	7	5	7
All people	**7**	**3**	**3**	**4**	**5**	**3**	**2**	**3**

1 The age range 16–24 has been used in order to allow comparisons with the age ranges in the rest of this chapter, although most people holding degrees were aged 21 and over. People without degrees are excluded from the table.

Source: Census 2001, Office for National Statistics

White British male graduates. The following analysis, covering England and Wales, looks at unemployment by age because of the different rates of degree-level qualifications in younger and older age groups (see 'Economic activity rates by level of educational attainment' earlier in the chapter), and the higher proportion of young people in many ethnic minority groups.

Looking first at those with degree level qualifications, in all age ranges and among both men and women, unemployment rates among people from most ethnic minority groups were at least twice as high as those of White British people, with the Pakistani and Black African groups the most strongly affected. Among young degree qualified men (aged 16–24) unemployment rates were highest in the Black African, Other Black and Pakistani groups, 19 per cent or more, compared with 6 per cent among their White British counterparts. Unemployment rates among degree-qualified young men from all ethnic minority groups except the White Irish were two to three time higher than those of young White British men.

In the 25–39 age group, those from the Other Black and Black African groups had the highest unemployment rates among degree-qualified men (13 per cent in each group), while White British, White Irish and Indian groups had the lowest (3 per cent in each case). In most other ethnic groups, unemployment rates of degree-qualified men of this age were at least twice as high as those of their White British counterparts.

Degree-qualified women had lower unemployment rates than degree-qualified men, but, like men, graduate women from ethnic minority groups had higher unemployment rates than White British and White Irish women. Young degree-qualified women from the Pakistani and Black African groups had the highest unemployment rates (over 16 per cent), while young White British and White Irish women had the lowest (4 per cent in each case). In the 25–39 age group, degree-qualified women from the Black African and Bangladeshi groups had the highest unemployment rates, 11 per cent in each case, while White British and White Irish women in this age group had the lowest (2 per cent each). Unemployment rates among degree-qualified women of most other ethnic groups were more than twice as high as those of White British and White Irish women.

In 2001, 23 per cent of the population of working age had no educational qualifications.[24] While the proportion of people with no qualifications is decreasing,[25] they still form a substantial part of the population, and experience higher unemployment rates than those with qualifications. In addition, lack of qualifications appeared to cause greater employment disadvantage to people from most ethnic minority groups than it did to White British people. While White British people with

no qualifications had higher unemployment rates than those with qualifications (10 per cent among men and 7 per cent among women), these were low compared with people with no qualifications from most other ethnic groups (Table 5.36).

Men in the Black African, Mixed White and Black Caribbean and Other Black ethnic groups had the highest unemployment rates of those with no qualifications (over 30 per cent). Unemployment rates among men with no qualifications from most other ethnic groups were around twice as high as among White British men with no qualifications. The exceptions were Chinese men, who had the lowest unemployment rate for men with no qualifications (8 per cent); Indian men with no qualifications, whose unemployment rate (10 per cent) was close to that of similar White British men; and White Irish and Other White men, whose unemployment rates were only slightly higher.

Unemployment rates were especially high among young men aged 16–24 with no qualifications, 29 per cent overall and exceeding 50 per cent in some ethnic minority groups. Young men from the Black Caribbean, Black African and Other Black ethnic groups had the highest unemployment rates among those with no qualifications (almost 60 per cent), followed by those from the Mixed White and Black Caribbean and Mixed White and Black African groups. Unemployment among young men with no qualifications from the White British and South Asian groups was considerably lower (around 30 per cent), while young Chinese men had the lowest unemployment rate of those with no qualifications (15 per cent).

Among women with no qualifications, Bangladeshis and Black Africans had the highest unemployment rates (above 30 per cent) and the White British and White Irish had the lowest (7 per cent). Among many other ethnic groups, unemployment rates for women with no qualifications were at least double those of White British and White Irish women with no qualifications.

Like men, young women aged 16–24 with no qualifications had high unemployment rates (26 per cent overall). Young Black Caribbean, Black African and Other Black women had the highest unemployment rates among those with no qualifications, over 50 per cent in each case, followed by young Pakistani and Bangladeshi women and those from the Mixed White and Black Caribbean group, over 40 per cent. Unemployment among young women with no qualifications was lowest in the Other White and Chinese ethnic groups (around 18 per cent) and around 25 per cent in the Indian and White British groups.

Table **5.36**

Unemployment rates among those with no qualifications: by ethnic group, sex and age, April 2001

England and Wales   Percentages

	Men				Women			
	16–24	25–39	40–64	All men of working age	16–24	25–39	40–59	All women of working age
White British	29	14	6	10	25	11	4	7
White Irish	38	16	10	11	35	15	5	7
Other White	24	17	9	14	18	13	7	10
Mixed White and Black Caribbean	52	28	16	34	43	22	13	26
Mixed White and Black African	50	25	16	27	38	26	11	22
Mixed White and Asian	41	23	13	24	35	20	9	18
Other Mixed	43	28	14	26	35	22	9	19
Indian	28	10	8	10	23	10	8	9
Pakistani	32	17	15	19	42	30	20	29
Bangladeshi	32	20	24	23	44	37	35	39
Other Asian	30	19	13	18	37	20	10	16
Black Caribbean	59	29	16	23	51	20	8	15
Black African	58	40	19	36	57	39	20	32
Other Black	59	30	17	31	50	25	11	24
Chinese	15	8	8	8	18	7	7	8
Other ethnic group	45	26	15	23	26	14	10	13
All people	**29**	**14**	**7**	**11**	**26**	**12**	**4**	**7**

Source: Census 2001, Office for National Statistics

Table **5.37**

Unemployment rates among those with degree-level qualifications: by religion, sex and age, April 2001

England and Wales   Percentages

	Men				Women			
	16–24[1]	25–39	40–64	All men of working age	16–24	25–39	40–59	All women of working age
No religion	7	3	3	4	5	3	2	3
Christian	6	3	3	3	4	2	2	2
Buddhist	18	6	5	6	15	7	4	6
Hindu	9	3	3	4	10	6	4	6
Jewish	7	3	2	3	6	3	3	3
Muslim	18	10	9	11	16	11	8	11
Sikh	13	4	3	5	10	5	3	5
Other religion	11	7	6	7	10	6	5	6
Religion not stated	8	4	4	5	6	4	3	4
All people	**7**	**3**	**3**	**4**	**5**	**3**	**2**	**3**

1 The age range 16–24 has used in order to allow comparisons with the age ranges in the rest of this chapter, although most people holding degrees were aged 21 and over. People without degrees are excluded from the table.

Source: Census, April 2001, Office for National Statistics

The effect of educational qualifications on unemployment rates also varied across the different religious groups. Among working age men with degrees or equivalent, Muslims had the highest unemployment rate (11 per cent), while Christians and Jews had the lowest (3 per cent in each case) (Table 5.37 on previous page). Similar rates occurred among working age women, 11 per cent among Muslims and 2 per cent among Christians. Among degree-qualified young people aged 16–24, Muslims and Buddhists had particularly high unemployment rates (around 18 per cent among men and around 15 per cent among women), around three times the rate of their Christian and Jewish counterparts and those with no religion.

Among those with no qualifications, there was substantial variation by religion in the 25–39 age group (Table 5.38). Hindus in this age group with no qualifications had unemployment rates of 8 per cent among men and 9 per cent among women, the lowest of any religious group, while Muslims had the highest, 21 per cent among men and 31 per cent among women.

Considering ethno-religious groups, Muslims had higher rates of unemployment than those of other religions; this was the case within most ethnic groups and among both the degree-qualified and people with no qualifications. In the 25–39 age group, degree-qualified Black African Muslim men had higher unemployment rates than similarly qualified Black African Christian men (20 per cent compared with 12 per cent). Among men in this age group with no qualifications, the unemployment rate for Other White Muslims was more than

twice as high as that of Other White Christians (27 per cent compared with 11 per cent). Unemployment rates were also higher among Black African Muslim men with no qualifications than among their Christian counterparts (45 per cent compared with 35 per cent). Indian Muslim men were an exception to this pattern; among those with the same level of educational qualification unemployment rates were similar to Indian Sikh men and slightly higher than Indian Hindu men (Appendix Table A5.6).

Among women aged 25–39 Muslims also tended to have higher unemployment rates than women of other religions from the same ethnic group and with the same level of qualification. The unemployment rates of Black African Muslim women with no qualifications were around twice as high as those of their Christian counterparts (58 per cent compared with 30 per cent), and in the Other White group three times as high for Muslims as for Christians (31 per cent compared with 10 per cent). Indian Muslim women with no qualifications also had higher unemployment rates than Indian women from other religions (16 per cent, compared with 8 per cent of Hindus and 11 per cent of Sikhs). The difference in unemployment rates between degree-qualified Indian Muslim women of this age and Indian women from other religions was relatively small (7 per cent compared with 6 per cent among Hindus and 5 per cent among Sikhs). In other ethnic groups degree-qualified Muslim women had higher unemployment rates than those of other religions, for example in the Other White group (13 per cent compared with 5 per cent among Christians) (Appendix Table A5.6).

Table **5.38**

Unemployment rates among those with no qualifications: by religion, sex and age, April 2001

England and Wales

Percentages

	Men				Women			
	16–24	25–39	40–64	All men of working age	16–24	25–39	40–59	All women of working age
No religion	32	16	9	15	30	14	6	13
Christian	28	13	6	9	23	11	4	6
Buddhist	25	15	13	14	23	15	12	13
Hindu	23	8	7	8	23	9	7	8
Jewish	31	10	5	8	18	13	5	6
Muslim	35	21	18	22	43	31	21	30
Sikh	32	12	8	11	24	11	7	9
Other religion	45	26	11	18	32	20	6	10
Religion not stated	33	16	8	13	27	13	5	9
All people	29	14	7	11	26	12	4	7

Source: Census, April 2001, Office for National Statistics

Employment status

Employment is important for the income it provides and for opportunities for personal and professional development, all of which influence people's quality of life. This section analyses how occupation and employment status varies by ethnic and religious group, focusing on socio-economic class, rates of self-employment and part-time working.

Occupational position by ethnic and religious group

This section illustrates how the occupational position of employed people varied by ethnic and religious group in 2001, based on the National Statistics Socio-economic Classification (NS-SEC) (Chapter 2 Appendix). NS-SEC measures the structure of socio-economic positions in society.[26] In this chapter the NS-SEC classes are divided into three groups: managerial and professional occupations; intermediate, lower supervisory and technical occupations and small employers; and semi-routine and routine occupations. The NS-SEC classification also includes categories for full-time students and those who are long-term unemployed or have never worked; these groups are excluded from the following analysis, which focuses only on people in employment.

In general people in occupations associated with the managerial and professional social classes, for example company directors or doctors and teachers, have greater earning potential, job security and career opportunities than those in occupations associated with the routine and semi-routine classes, for example catering or retail workers.[26] Low representation within the managerial and professional classes among those who are employed can indicate disadvantage in the labour market. This analysis shows that several ethnic and religious minority groups were well represented in managerial and professional occupations, although others were more heavily concentrated in routine and semi-routine occupations.

Among employed men in England and Wales, the group with the highest proportion of managers and professionals in 2001 was the Other White group (57 per cent) (Figure 5.39). Men from several other ethnic groups, including Mixed White and Asian, White Irish, Indian and Black African also had a higher rate of managers and professionals than White British men (between 42 and 53 per cent, compared with 41 per cent). Men from some ethnic groups were much less likely to work in managerial and professional occupations, most notably Pakistanis and Bangladeshis (29 per cent and 23 per cent). Pakistani and Bangladeshi men were the most likely to work in routine and semi-routine occupations (34 per cent and 43 per cent).

Figure **5.39**

Working-age men[1] in employment: by ethnic group and NS-SEC,[2] April 2001

England and Wales

Percentages

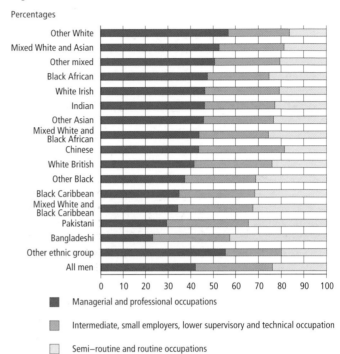

1 Aged 16–64. Excludes full-time students.
2 National Statistics Socio-economic Classification.
Source: Census 2001, Office for National Statistics

Similar patterns occurred among employed women, although the differences by ethnic group were smaller (Figure 5.40 overleaf). Nearly two-fifths (38 per cent) of White British women in employment worked in managerial and professional occupations, along with half or more of women from the Other White, White Irish and Mixed White and Asian groups (52 per cent, 51 per cent and 50 per cent), and over two-fifths of Black Caribbean and Chinese women (44 per cent and 43 per cent). Among employed women from the South Asian ethnic groups, smaller proportions worked in managerial and professional occupations – 32 per cent of Bangladeshis, 34 per cent of Pakistanis and 37 per cent of Indians.

Higher proportions of men than women work in managerial and professional occupations (42 per cent compared with 38 per cent in 2001) and lower proportions work in routine and semi-routine occupations (24 per cent compared with 29 per cent in 2001). There were exceptions to this general pattern. Among Black Caribbeans, 44 per cent of employed women worked in managerial and professional occupations, compared with 35 per cent of men. Employed Bangladeshi and Pakistani women were also more likely than their male counterparts to work in managerial and professional occupations (32 per cent

143

Figure **5.40**

Working-age women[1] in employment: by ethnic group and NS-SEC,[2] April 2001

England and Wales

Percentages

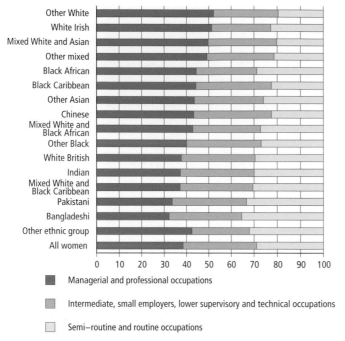

- ■ Managerial and professional occupations
- ▨ Intermediate, small employers, lower supervisory and technical occupations
- ▢ Semi–routine and routine occupations

1 Aged 16–59. Excludes full-time students.
2 National Statistics Socio-economic Classification.

Source: Census 2001, Office for National Statistics

compared with 23 per cent and 34 per cent compared with 29 per cent). However the proportion of women from these groups who were employed was relatively low (see 'Economic activity status' earlier in this chapter).

Among religious groups Jewish men were the most likely to work in managerial and professional occupations (68 per cent) and the least likely to work in semi-routine and routine occupations (6 per cent). Muslim and Sikh men had the lowest proportions in managerial and professional occupations (32 per cent and 35 per cent) and the highest in semi-routine and routine occupations (33 per cent of Muslims and 29 per cent of Sikhs) (Appendix Table A5.7).

The tendency for men to be more likely than women to work in managerial and professional occupations was greatest in the Jewish and Hindu groups (68 per cent of Jewish men compared with 57 per cent of Jewish women and 50 per cent of Hindu men compared with 38 per cent of Hindu women). Sex differences in socio-economic class were lower among Sikhs, Muslims and Christians. Muslims were the only group in which, of those who were employed, the proportion of men in

managerial and professional occupations was lower than the proportion of women, 32 per cent compared with 35 per cent (Appendix Table A5.7).

Socio-economic class also varied by religion within specific ethnic groups. Among employed White British men, some minority religions tended to have higher proportions of people working in managerial and professional occupations than their Christian counterparts; for example 68 per cent of Jews and 55 per cent of Buddhists were in these occupations, compared with 40 per cent of Christians and 39 per cent of Muslims. In other ethnic groups Christians tended to be better represented in managerial and professional occupations. For example, 58 per cent of Indian Christians were in managerial and professional occupations, compared with 51 per cent of Hindus, 37 per cent of Muslims and 35 per cent of Sikhs. Similarly, 61 per cent of Chinese Christians were in managerial and professional occupations, compared with 32 per cent of Chinese Buddhists. Similar patterns were also observed among women (Appendix Table A5.8).

Self-employment

The employed population includes those who work for an employer (that is, employees) and those who are self-employed. This section examines the self-employed as a proportion of those in employment to highlight the variation between ethnic and religious groups.

Research has suggested that people from ethnic minority groups may become self-employed to escape from prejudice among employers.[27] However if this is the case the effect is not consistent across different ethnic groups, which indicates that other factors, such as skills and the nature of local labour markets, may also contribute to higher levels of self-employment among some ethnic minority groups. Men from the Chinese and Pakistani groups had high self-employment rates (29 per cent and 26 per cent) (Figure 5.41). However men from the three Black groups had lower self-employment rates than White British men; for example, 12 per cent in the Black African group and 10 per cent in the Other Black group were self-employed, compared with 17 per cent in the White British group.

Self-employment rates among women from ethnic minority groups were generally similar to or lower than those of White British women (7 per cent), with the exception of Chinese and Other White women (18 per cent and 11 per cent respectively). Black Caribbean women had the lowest rate of self-employment (3 per cent).

Figure 5.41

Self-employment:[1] by ethnic group and sex, April 2001

England and Wales

Percentages

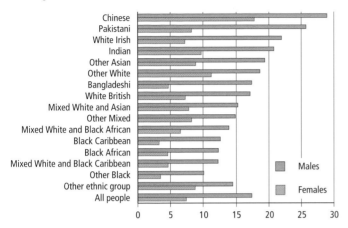

1 Among those of working age (men aged 16–64, women aged 16–59) in employment.

Source: Census 2001, Office for National Statistics

Part-time working

Although many people choose to work part time, others may take a part-time job if they find it difficult to obtain full-time employment. Among part-time workers in 2003, 16 per cent of men and 6 per cent of women stated that they were working part time because they could not find a full-time job.[28] Other research has suggested that a significant proportion of men who worked part time would prefer to do a full-time job, and that part-time working can be an indicator of lower socio-economic status among men.[29]

Many women have caring responsibilities that are incompatible with full-time work. Women therefore tend to have much higher rates of part-time working than men. In 2001, 39 per cent of employed women in England and Wales worked 30 hours a week or less in their main job, compared with just 7 per cent of men.

Employed men from ethnic minority groups were much more likely to work part time in their main job than those from the White British group (Table 5.42). Nearly two-fifths (38 per cent)

Table 5.42

Proportion of men in employment[1] working 30 hours or less a week in their main job: by ethnic group and NS-SEC[2], April 2001

England and Wales   Percentages

	Managerial and professional	Intermediate[3]	Routine and semi-routine	All
White British	5	7	9	6
White Irish	5	7	8	6
Other White	6	10	17	9
Mixed White and Black Caribbean	7	9	13	10
Mixed White and Black African	8	11	17	11
Mixed White and Asian	6	11	21	10
Other Mixed	7	11	20	11
Indian	4	9	15	8
Pakistani	9	19	27	19
Bangladeshi	16	29	56	38
Other Asian	7	12	22	12
Black Caribbean	7	8	12	9
Black African	8	13	17	12
Other Black	9	9	17	12
Chinese	5	8	25	10
Other ethnic group	7	13	24	12
All men	5	7	10	7

1 Of working age (16–64). Excludes full-time students in employment.
2 National Statistics Socio-economic Classification.
3 Includes lower supervisory, small employers and own account workers, and technical craft and process operator occupations.

Source: Census 2001, Office for National Statistics

of Bangladeshi men worked 30 hours a week or less, followed by Pakistani men, with just under one-fifth (19 per cent) working part-time. Men from the semi-routine and routine occupational groups were most likely to work part time (10 per cent), and men from ethnic minority groups in these occupations had the highest rates of part-time working. More than half (56 per cent) of Bangladeshi men employed in routine and semi-routine occupations worked part time, as did around a quarter of Chinese, Pakistani, and Other Asian men. Less than one-tenth (9 per cent) of White British men employed in these occupations worked part time.

Among men in managerial and professional occupations, Bangladeshis again had the highest rate of part-time working (16 per cent), almost twice that of Pakistani men (9 per cent) and four times that of White British, White Irish, Indian, and Chinese men (4 to 5 per cent).

Male part-time working rates were higher among Muslim men than those of other religions, at over one-fifth (21 per cent)

(Appendix Table A5.10). This pattern held within most ethnic groups: among employed Indian men, the proportion of Indian Muslims working part time was over three times greater, at 21 per cent, than those of Indian Hindu, Sikh and Christian men, of whom 6 to 7 per cent worked part time (Table 5.43). Similarly, 15 per cent of Muslims from the White British group and 19 per cent from the Other White group worked part time, compared with 6 per cent and 7 per cent of White British and Other White Christians. A smaller differential in part-time working was found in the Black African group (15 per cent of Muslims and 11 per cent of Christians).

Part-time working was more common among employed White British women than in most other ethnic groups. A lower proportion of women were economically active in most ethnic minority groups, and those who were employed were more likely to be in full-time jobs than their White British counterparts. For example, a quarter (25 per cent) of Black Caribbean and Black African women worked part time in 2001, compared with over two-fifths (41 per cent) of White British

Table 5.43

Weekly hours worked by men of working age[1] in their main job: by selected ethno-religious group, April 2001

England and Wales

Percentages

	Hours of work					Total (=100%) (numbers)
	1–15	16–30	All 30 or less	31–48	48 and over	
White British Christian	2	5	6	68	25	7,813,003
White British Buddhist	4	11	14	64	22	18,683
White British Jewish	2	7	9	56	34	48,297
White British Muslim	4	11	15	61	24	9,240
White British no religion	2	5	7	70	24	2,202,393
Other White Christian	2	5	7	61	32	195,431
Other White Jewish	3	9	12	49	39	8,025
Other White Muslim	4	15	19	56	25	23,660
Other White no religion	2	6	9	63	29	64,134
Indian Christian	2	4	6	72	22	12,775
Indian Hindu	2	4	6	67	26	115,657
Indian Muslim	2	18	21	63	16	26,389
Indian Sikh	2	5	7	69	24	69,377
Pakistani Muslim	3	16	19	64	17	110,560
Bangladeshi Muslim	4	35	39	50	11	38,509
Black African Christian	3	7	11	73	17	58,002
Black African Muslim	5	10	15	68	18	12,145
All men[2]	2	5	7	68	25	12,196,504

1 Aged 16–64. Excludes full-time students in employment.
2 Includes other groups not elsewhere shown.

Source: Census 2001, Office for National Statistics

Table **5.44**

Proportion of women in employment[1] working 30 hours or less a week in their main job: by ethnic group and NS-SEC[2], April 2001

England and Wales

Percentages

	Managerial and professional	Intermediate[3]	Routine and semi-routine	All
White British	24	39	63	41
White Irish	21	34	59	33
Other White	20	31	50	29
Mixed White and Black Caribbean	18	28	53	32
Mixed White and Black African	17	27	50	29
Mixed White and Asian	19	31	54	29
Other Mixed	19	29	50	28
Indian	18	29	43	29
Pakistani	24	35	55	38
Bangladeshi	25	31	57	38
Other Asian	19	31	51	31
Black Caribbean	16	23	48	25
Black African	14	24	44	25
Other Black	17	26	50	29
Chinese	16	23	48	26
Other ethnic group	16	29	44	29
All women	**23**	**38**	**62**	**39**

1 Of working age (16–59). Excludes full-time students in employment.
2 National Statistics Socio-economic Classification.
3 Includes lower supervisory, small employers and own account workers, and technical craft and process operator occupations.

Source: Census 2001, Office for National Statistics

women (Table 5.44). Pakistani and Bangladeshi women were the exceptions, with overall rates of part-time working similar to those of White British women (38 per cent among Pakistani and Bangladeshi women and 41 per cent among White British women).

As with men, part-time working was most common among women employed in the routine and semi-routine occupations (62 per cent overall). However, relatively high rates of part-time working among White British women were evident in all three socio-economic groupings, with 24 per cent of women in managerial and professional occupations and 39 per cent in intermediate occupations working part time.

White British women had higher employment rates than women from most other ethnic groups, which meant that their high rates of part-time working translated into a large proportion of all White British women of working age in part-time work. Looking at the whole working-age population excluding students, three in ten (29 per cent) of all White

British women worked part time in 2001, compared with less than two in ten women from most other ethnic groups. Bangladeshi and Pakistani women's rates of part-time working were similar to those of the White British as a percentage of employed women, although their lower employment rates meant that just one in ten of all Bangladeshi and Pakistani women aged 16–59 worked part time (9 per cent and 11 per cent). A slightly higher proportion of working-age Indian, Black Caribbean and Black African women worked part time (19 per cent, 19 per cent and 16 per cent, respectively) (Appendix Table A5.9).

Looking at religious groups, Sikhs and Hindus had the lowest rates of part-time working among employed women (28 per cent and 29 per cent), whereas Christian, Jewish and Muslim women had the highest (between 38 per cent and 41 per cent) (Appendix Table A5.10). Rates of part-time working among Muslim women were consistently high (38 per cent or above) in the Indian, Pakistani, Bangladeshi, White British and Other White ethnic groups, and Muslim women often had the

Table **5.45**

Weekly hours worked by women of working age[1] in their main job: by selected ethno-religious group, April 2001

England and Wales

Percentages

	Hours of work					Total (=100%) (numbers)
	1–15	16–30	All 30 or less	31–48	48 and over	
White British Christian	12	30	42	51	7	6,883,853
White British Buddhist	11	27	38	52	10	10,813
White British Jewish	14	27	41	48	10	38,112
White British Muslim	11	28	39	53	8	6,791
White British no religion	9	24	33	59	8	1,314,794
Other White Christian	9	21	30	58	12	199,620
Other White Jewish	13	24	38	47	15	6,303
Other White Muslim	11	27	38	52	10	9,597
Other White no religion	7	17	24	63	14	58,021
Indian Christian	7	19	26	66	8	11,786
Indian Hindu	7	22	29	61	10	93,986
Indian Muslim	13	29	42	52	6	13,380
Indian Sikh	6	21	27	64	8	56,942
Pakistani Muslim	12	26	38	56	6	42,268
Bangladeshi Muslim	11	27	39	57	4	12,504
Black African Christian	6	18	24	71	5	60,922
Black African Muslim	10	23	33	62	5	6,394
All women[2]	11	28	39	53	7	**9,905,665**

1 Aged 16–59. Excludes full-time students in employment.
2 Includes other groups not elsewhere shown.

Source: Census 2001, Office for National Statistics

highest rates of part-time working within specific ethnic groups (Table 5.45). For example, Indian Muslims had the highest rate of part-time working among Indian women, 42 per cent, compared with Indian Christian women who had the lowest rate, 26 per cent. In the Other White group Muslim and Jewish women had the highest part-time working rates (38 per cent in each case) while Christian women and women with no religion had lower rates (30 per cent and 24 per cent). The White British group was an exception to this pattern, with part-time working being less common among White British Muslim women than among their Christian counterparts (39 per cent compared with 42 per cent).

Notes and references

1. Office for National Statistics (2005) *How exactly is unemployment measured?*
    Available at: www.statistics.gov.uk/downloads/theme_labour/unemployment.pdf

2. Berthoud R (2000) Ethnic employment penalties in Britain. *Journal of Ethnic and Migration Studies* **26 (3)**, 389–416.

3. Blackaby D H, Leslie D G, Murphy P D and O'Leary N C (2002) White/ethnic minority earnings and unemployment differentials in Britain: evidence from the LFS. *Oxford Economic Papers* **54**, 270–297.

4. Carmichael F and Woods R (2000) Ethnic penalties in unemployment and occupational attainment: evidence for Britain. *International Review of Applied Economics* **14 (1)**, 71–98.

5. Heath A and Cheung S Y (2006) *Ethnic penalties in the labour market: employers and discrimination*. Department for Work and Pensions/TSO.

6. Heath A and McMahon D (1997) 'Education and occupational attainments: the impact of ethnic origins' pp 91–113 and Owen D (1997) 'Labour force participation rates, self-employment and unemployment', pp 29–66 in Karn V (ed.) *Ethnicity in the 1991 Census, Volume 4: Employment, education and housing among the ethnic minority populations of Britain*, TSO: London.

7. Simpson L, Purdam K, Tajar A, Fieldhouse E, Gavalas V, Tranmer M, Pritchard J and Dorling D (2006) *Ethnic minority populations and the labour market: an analysis of the 1991 and 2001 Census*, Department for Work and Pensions/TSO.

8. National Statistics on unemployment may also be based on the population aged 16 and older (that is, including those above retirement age), but as the retirement age population contains a low proportion of people from ethnic minority groups the analysis here is restricted to those of working age.

9. For details of employment, economic activity and unemployment of the total population see Labour Market, in Babb P, Butcher H, Church J and Zealey L (eds.) (2006) *Social Trends 36*, Palgrave MacMillan: Basingstoke.

10. Bosveld K, Connolly H and Rendall M (2006) *A guide to comparing 1991 and 2001 ethnic group data*. Available at: www.statistics.gov. uk/CCI/article.asp?ID=1471

11. Babb P, Butcher H, Church J and Zealey L (2006) *Social Trends 36*, Palgrave MacMillan: Basingstoke, Figure 4.1 p 50.

12. Machin A (2004) Comparisons between unemployment and the claimant count. *Labour Market Trends* **112 (2)**, 59–62.

13. Brown M S (2000) Religion and economic activity in the South Asian population. *Ethnic and Racial Studies* **23 (6)**, 1035–1061.

14. Lindley J (2002) Race or religion? The impact of religion on the employment and earnings of Britain's ethnic communities. *Journal of Ethnic and Migration Studies* **28 (3)**, 427–442.

15. Rendall M and Salt J (2005) 'The foreign-born population', in Chappell R (ed.) *Focus on People and Migration*, Palgrave MacMillan: Basingstoke.

16. Dale A, Shaheen N, Fieldhouse E and Kalra V (2002) Labour Market Prospects for Pakistani and Bangladeshi Women. *Work, Employment and Society* **16(1)**, 5–25.

17. Dustmann C and Fabbri F (2003) Language proficiency and labour market performance of immigrants in the UK. *The Economic Journal* **113**, 695–717.

18. Heath A F and Yu S (2005) 'The puzzle of ethnic minority disadvantage', in Heath A F, Ermisch J and Gallie D (eds.) *Understanding Social Change: Proceedings of the British Academy*, Oxford University Press: Oxford, pp.187–224.

19. For a summary of the different in migration and settlement patterns of the UK's main ethnic groups during the 20th century see Connolly H and White A (2006) 'The different experiences of the UK's ethnic and religious populations', in Babb P et al, *Social Trends 36*, Palgrave Macmillan: Basingstoke.

20. Office for National Statistics (2006) *Focus on ethnicity and identity overview*. Available at www.statistics.gov.uk/cci/nugget.asp?id=459

21. Office for National Statistics (2003) *Census 2001: National Report for England and Wales; Table S032*, TSO: London.

22. Haezewindt P (2004) 'Education, Training and Skills', in Babb P, Martin J and Haezewindt P (eds.) *Focus on Social Inequalities,* TSO: London.

23. Lindley J, Dale A and Dex S (2004) Ethnic differences in women's demographic, family characteristics and economic activity profiles, 1992 to 2002. *Labour Market Trends* **112 (4)**, 153–165.

24. Office for National Statistics (2003) *Census 2001: National Report for England and Wales; Table S105,* TSO: London.

25. Department for Education and Skills (2006) *The level of highest qualification held by young people and adults: England 2005*. SFR 05/2006.

26. Office for National Statistics (2005) *The National Statistics Socio-economic Classification: User Manual*. Available at: www.statistics. gov.uk/StatBase/Product.asp?vlnk=14066

27. Heath A and McMahon D (1999) *Ethnic differences in the labour market: the role of education and social class origins*. Centre for Research into Elections and Social Trends: Working paper no.69.

28. Shaw M (2004) 'Work', in Babb P, Martin J and Haezewindt P (eds.) *Focus on Social Inequalities*, TSO: London.

29. Francesconi M and Gosling A (2005) *Career paths of part-time workers*. Equal Opportunities Commission Working Paper Series No.19.

Appendix Table **A5.1**

Employment rates:[1] by selected ethno-religious group and sex, April 2001

England and Wales   Percentages

	Men	Women
White British Christian	78	70
White British Buddhist	71	66
White British Jewish	78	66
White British Muslim	59	41
White British No religion	78	68
White Irish Christian	72	67
White Irish No religion	73	71
Other White Christian	75	63
Other White Jewish	75	58
Other White Muslim	51	29
Other White No religion	75	68
Mixed Christian	64	58
Mixed Muslim	48	32
Mixed No religion	64	57
Indian Christian	75	66
Indian Hindu	74	62
Indian Muslim	65	35
Indian Sikh	71	60
Pakistani Muslim	58	24
Bangladeshi Muslim	55	20
Other Asian Christian	71	60
Other Asian Hindu	73	53
Other Asian Muslim	54	33
Black Caribbean Christian	66	67
Black Caribbean No religion	62	60
Black African Christian	62	56
Black African Muslim	45	25
Chinese Christian	62	57
Chinese Buddhist	58	51
Chinese No religion	60	51
Other ethnic group Christian	68	63
Other ethnic group Buddhist	61	38
Other ethnic group Muslim	47	31
All people[2]	**76**	**67**

1 Proportion of working age population (men aged 16–64, women
   aged 16–59) in employment.
2 Includes other groups not elsewhere shown.

Source: Census 2001, Office for National Statistics

Appendix Table **A5.2**

Unemployment rates:[1] by selected ethno-religious group and sex, 2001

England and Wales   Percentages

	Men	Women
White British Christian	5	4
White British Buddhist	10	8
White British Jewish	4	4
White British Muslim	15	13
White British No Religion	7	6
White Irish Christian	7	4
White Irish No Religion	9	6
Other White Christian	6	6
Other White Jewish	5	6
Other White Muslim	19	18
Other White No Religion	7	6
Mixed Christian	13	10
Mixed Muslim	20	17
Mixed No Religion	15	11
Indian Christian	7	7
Indian Hindu	6	7
Indian Muslim	11	12
Indian Sikh	9	8
Pakistani Muslim	16	19
Bangladeshi Muslim	19	23
Other Asian Christian	8	8
Other Asian Hindu	7	9
Other Asian Muslim	15	15
Black Caribbean Christian	15	9
Black Caribbean No Religion	21	14
Black African Christian	16	14
Black African Muslim	28	31
Chinese Christian	6	6
Chinese Buddhist	10	9
Chinese No Religion	7	8
Other ethnic group Christian	8	6
Other ethnic group Buddhist	9	12
Other ethinic group Muslim	20	16
All people[2]	**6**	**5**

1 Working age population (men aged 16–64, women aged 16–59).
2 Includes other groups not elsewhere shown.

Source: Census 2001, Office for National Statistics

Appendix Table **A5.3**

Male economic activity: by ethnic group, age, and whether UK-born or not, April 2001

England and Wales

Percentages

	16–24		25–39		40–64		All men of working age	
	UK-born	Overseas-born	UK-born	Overseas-born	UK-born	Overseas-born	UK-born	Overseas-born
White British	72	64	92	93	80	83	83	84
White Irish	61	63	90	90	78	70	81	74
Other White	57	48	88	85	79	82	78	77
Mixed White and Black Caribbean	63	56	83	78	77	70	73	70
Mixed White and Black African	55	53	82	75	77	74	71	70
Mixed White and Asian	54	38	88	75	80	75	73	68
Other Mixed	54	44	86	76	75	76	70	69
Indian	50	56	92	91	79	80	69	82
Pakistani	48	63	86	85	63	66	62	73
Bangladeshi	46	61	83	84	61	58	56	71
Other Asian	45	48	87	78	71	78	63	74
Black Caribbean	61	54	87	79	84	74	80	73
Black African	47	42	87	75	77	81	73	71
Other Black	56	55	81	81	78	76	72	75
Chinese	41	24	91	78	78	82	63	65
Other ethnic group	45	32	83	71	73	79	59	66
All men	**70**	**51**	**92**	**85**	**80**	**77**	**82**	**76**

Source: Census 2001, Office for National Statistics

Appendix Table **A5.4**

Female economic activity: by ethnic group, age, and whether UK-born or not, April 2001

England and Wales

Percentages

	16–24		25–39		40–59		All women of working age	
	UK-born	Overseas-born	UK-born	Overseas-born	UK-born	Overseas-born	UK-born	Overseas-born
White British	72	64	92	93	80	83	83	84
White British	65	61	75	77	72	73	72	72
White Irish	56	60	78	76	72	67	73	69
Other White	53	52	72	70	71	65	67	65
Mixed White and Black Caribbean	56	52	66	69	68	66	62	65
Mixed White and Black African	54	49	69	54	68	61	64	55
Mixed White and Asian	52	39	73	57	69	63	64	56
Other Mixed	52	44	72	62	68	66	63	60
Indian	49	44	78	67	67	64	62	63
Pakistani	41	26	47	23	39	20	43	23
Bangladeshi	42	34	49	20	36	12	44	22
Other Asian	42	34	71	51	62	61	55	53
Black Caribbean	58	49	78	70	79	74	74	71
Black African	49	40	78	59	70	69	68	58
Other Black	55	47	71	60	73	69	66	62
Chinese	47	25	84	63	71	66	63	55
Other ethnic group	46	31	71	51	63	62	55	52
All women	**64**	**46**	**75**	**62**	**72**	**63**	**72**	**60**

Source: Census 2001, Office for National Statistics

Appendix Table **A5.5**

Working-age population:[1] by ethnic group, sex, and highest qualification, April 2001

England and Wales

Percentages

	Men				Women			
	Degree or equivalent	Other qualifications[2]	No qualifications	Total (=100%) (numbers)	Degree or equivalent	Other qualifications[2]	No qualifications	Total (=100%) (numbers)
British	19	57	24	14,363,102	19	58	23	13,309,867
Irish	26	42	32	215,555	32	43	25	198,062
Other White	43	40	17	470,310	46	41	13	523,045
Mixed White and Black Caribbean	13	61	26	44,335	16	62	22	49,906
Mixed White and Black African	27	55	19	19,808	27	55	18	21,036
Mixed White and Asian	30	53	16	46,108	30	54	16	45,070
Other Mixed	32	52	16	38,318	34	52	14	42,601
Indian	35	44	21	360,042	29	45	26	352,547
Pakistani	22	43	35	218,086	16	41	43	209,342
Bangladeshi	17	41	42	80,810	11	41	48	80,177
Other Asian	35	48	17	96,349	31	50	19	72,573
Black Caribbean	15	58	26	173,088	26	60	15	200,163
Black African	43	47	10	152,345	36	50	15	167,415
Other Black	19	61	20	25,621	23	63	14	30,252
Chinese	38	39	23	82,534	39	38	23	88,149
Other ethnic group	45	35	20	73,171	43	33	24	95,497
All people	**21**	**55**	**24**	**16,459,582**	**21**	**56**	**23**	**15,485,702**

1 Men aged 16–64, women aged 16–59.
2 Includes 'A' levels, GCSEs and vocational qualifications.

Source: Census 2001, Office for National Statistics

Appendix Table A5.6

Unemployment among 25- to 39-year-olds: by selected ethno-religious group, sex and highest qualification, April 2001

England and Wales

Percentages

	Men				Women			
	Degree or equivalent	Other qualifications[2]	No qualifications	All	Degree or equivalent	Other qualifications[2]	No qualifications	All
White British Christian	2	4	13	4	2	4	10	4
White British Buddhist	7	12	24	11	6	12	26	9
White British Jewish	3	4	9	4	3	4	11	4
White British Muslim	9	13	20	13	7	11	22	11
White British no religion	3	6	16	6	3	5	14	5
White Irish Christian	2	5	14	5	2	4	14	4
White Irish no religion	5	9	23	7	4	7	27	6
Other White Christian	3	6	11	5	5	6	10	6
Other White Jewish	4	7	10	5	5	8	21	6
Other White Muslim	13	18	27	19	13	16	31	17
Other White no religion	4	8	16	6	5	7	12	6
Mixed Christian	6	10	24	10	5	9	19	8
Mixed Muslim	14	20	28	19	11	16	31	15
Mixed no religion	5	11	28	11	5	9	22	8
Indian Christian	4	7	11	6	7	7	12	7
Indian Hindu	3	5	8	4	6	5	8	6
Indian Muslim	4	9	12	8	7	10	16	10
Indian Sikh	4	7	11	7	5	6	11	6
Pakistani Muslim	8	13	17	13	10	14	30	15
Bangladeshi Muslim	9	13	20	15	11	17	37	19
Other Asian Christian	6	8	17	8	6	11	16	9
Other Asian Hindu	5	7	10	7	7	10	15	9
Other Asian Muslim	12	16	25	16	12	14	31	14
Black Caribbean Christian	7	12	27	13	5	8	19	8
Black Caribbean no religion	11	18	32	19	8	12	22	12
Black African Christian	12	20	35	16	10	18	30	14
Black African Muslim	20	27	45	27	17	30	58	30
Chinese Christian	4	8	9	5	5	8	6	6
Chinese Buddhist	6	8	9	7	6	7	11	8
Chinese no religion	5	6	6	5	7	8	6	7
Other ethnic group Christian	5	9	15	7	4	9	11	6
Other ethnic group Buddhist	3	8	17	7	9	10	16	12
Other ethnic group Muslim	15	24	41	23	14	15	18	15
All people aged 25–39[1]	**3**	**5**	**14**	**6**	**3**	**4**	**12**	**5**

1 Includes other groups not shown elsewhere.

Source: Census 2001, Office for National Statistics

Appendix Table **A5.7**

Working-age population[1] in employment: by sex, religion and NS-SEC,[2] April 2001

England and Wales   Percentages

	Managerial and professional occupations	Intermediate occupations, small employers, lower supervisory and technical occupations	Semi-routine and routine occupations	Total (=100%) (numbers)
Men				
No religion	47	32	21	2,367,702
Christian	40	35	25	8,359,477
Buddhist	53	31	17	37,374
Hindu	50	30	20	139,871
Jewish	68	26	6	58,171
Muslim	32	34	33	259,173
Sikh	35	36	29	75,391
Other Religion	53	31	17	39,861
Religion not stated	42	33	25	859,484
All men	**42**	**34**	**24**	**12,196,504**
Women				
No religion	45	30	25	1,445,111
Christian	37	33	30	7,466,379
Buddhist	47	29	24	29,003
Hindu	38	33	29	107,168
Jewish	57	31	11	45,749
Muslim	35	33	32	108,262
Sikh	31	33	36	60,825
Other Religion	49	32	20	36,363
Religion not stated	39	32	29	606,805
All women	**38**	**33**	**29**	**9,905,665**

1   Men aged 16–64, women aged 16–59. Excludes full-time students.
2   National Statistics Socio-economic Classifications.

Source: Census 2001, Office for National Statistics

Appendix Table **A5.8**

Working-age people[1] in employment: by selected ethno-religious group, sex and NS-SEC,[2] April 2001

England and Wales

Percentages

	Men				Women			
	Managerial and professional occupations	Intermediate occupations, small employers, lower supervisory and technical occupations	Semi-routine and routine occupations	All (=100%) (numbers)	Managerial and professional occupations	Intermediate occupations, small employers, lower supervisory and technical occupations	Semi-routine and routine occupations	All (=100%) (numbers)
White British Christian	40	35	25	7,813,003	36	34	30	6,883,853
White British Buddhist	55	30	15	18,683	60	26	14	10,813
White British Jewish	68	26	6	48,297	55	33	12	38,112
White British Muslim	39	37	24	9,240	36	35	29	6,791
White British no religion	47	32	21	2,202,393	44	30	25	1,314,794
White Irish Christian	44	34	22	123,530	50	26	24	112,232
White Irish no religion	62	26	12	15,941	66	21	12	8,461
Other White Christian	55	28	17	195,431	50	29	21	199,620
Other White Jewish	76	19	5	8,025	70	23	7	6,303
Other White Muslim	34	36	30	23,660	38	31	31	9,597
Other White no religion	64	23	12	64,134	59	26	15	58,021
Mixed Christian	43	31	26	42,439	42	32	26	46,172
Mixed Muslim	41	33	26	7,941	41	31	28	3,961
Mixed no religion	51	28	21	21,876	50	28	22	18,226
Indian Christian	58	25	18	12,775	51	29	20	11,786
Indian Hindu	51	30	19	115,657	37	34	29	93,986
Indian Muslim	37	30	33	26,389	33	35	32	13,380
Indian Sikh	35	36	29	69,377	31	33	36	56,942
Pakistani Muslim	29	37	35	110,560	33	34	34	42,268
Bangladeshi Muslim	22	34	44	38,509	31	32	37	12,504
Other Asian Christian	53	27	20	7,655	48	30	23	6,582
Other Asian Hindu	41	32	28	19,671	39	32	29	9,667
Other Asian Muslim	44	33	23	17,488	43	31	25	7,635
Black Caribbean Christian	35	34	31	75,383	45	33	22	98,113
Black Caribbean no religion	36	32	32	16,272	41	34	25	11,253
Black African Christian	49	27	24	58,002	45	27	28	60,922
Black African Muslim	39	29	32	12,145	35	29	36	6,394
Chinese Christian	61	27	12	9,276	55	29	16	11,285
Chinese Buddhist	32	46	22	6,507	37	37	26	6,635
Chinese no religion	40	40	20	25,102	38	37	25	19,996
Other ethnic group Christian	49	24	26	11,950	44	22	34	23,329
Other ethnic group Buddhist	63	21	17	5,654	27	32	41	6,072
Other ethnic group Muslim	50	29	21	10,971	45	26	29	4,384
All people[3]	**42**	**34**	**24**	**12,196,504**	**38**	**33**	**29**	**9,905,665**

1 Men aged 16–64, women aged 16–59. Excludes full-time students.
2 National Statistics Socio-Economic Classification
3 Includes other groups not elsewhere shown.

Source: Census 2001, Office for National Statistics

Appendix Table **A5.9**

Labour market status of working-age population:[1] by sex and ethnic group, April 2001

England and Wales   Percentages

	Economically inactive	Unemployed	Working part time in main job	Working full time in main job	All (=100%) (numbers)
Men					
White British	17	5	6	71	14,363,102
White Irish	23	5	5	66	215,555
Other White	23	6	8	64	470,310
Mixed White and Black Caribbean	27	14	9	50	44,335
Mixed White and Black African	30	12	9	49	19,808
Mixed White and Asian	29	8	9	54	46,108
Other Mixed	30	9	10	51	38,318
Indian	22	6	8	64	360,042
Pakistani	31	11	13	45	218,086
Bangladeshi	32	13	22	33	80,810
Other Asian	28	8	10	55	96,349
Black Caribbean	23	13	7	57	173,088
Black African	29	13	10	48	152,345
Other Black	28	15	9	48	25,621
Chinese	35	5	9	51	82,534
Other ethnic group	34	8	9	48	73,171
All men	**18**	**5**	**7**	**70**	**16,459,582**
Women					
White British	28	3	29	40	13,309,867
White Irish	30	3	23	44	198,062
Other White	35	4	19	42	523,045
Mixed White and Black Caribbean	38	8	20	34	49,906
Mixed White and Black African	41	7	18	34	21,036
Mixed White and Asian	38	5	20	37	45,070
Other Mixed	38	6	19	36	42,601
Indian	37	5	19	39	352,547
Pakistani	70	6	11	14	209,342
Bangladeshi	73	6	9	11	80,177
Other Asian	47	5	16	32	72,573
Black Caribbean	27	7	19	47	200,163
Black African	40	10	16	35	167,415
Other Black	35	9	19	37	30,252
Chinese	43	4	16	36	88,149
Other ethnic group	48	5	15	32	95,497
All women	**30**	**3**	**28**	**39**	**15,485,702**

1 Men aged 16–64, women aged 16–59.

Source: Census 2001, Office for National Statistics

Appendix Table **A5.10**

Weekly hours worked by working-age people[1] in their main job: by religion and sex, April 2001

England and Wales

Percentages

	Men					Women				
	1–30	31–40	41–50	50 and over	All (=100%) (numbers)	1–30	31–40	41–50	50 and over	All (=100%) (numbers)
No religion	7	50	30	13	2,367,702	32	50	14	5	1,445,111
Christian	6	49	30	15	8,359,477	41	45	10	4	7,466,379
Buddhist	13	46	25	16	37,374	33	44	14	8	29,003
Hindu	7	53	22	18	139,871	29	54	10	7	107,168
Jewish	10	37	34	19	58,171	41	38	16	6	45,749
Muslim	21	49	18	12	259,173	38	49	9	4	108,262
Sikh	7	54	23	16	75,391	28	57	10	5	60,825
Other religion	12	48	25	14	39,861	35	47	12	5	36,363
Religion not stated	8	50	28	14	859,484	37	48	11	4	606,805
All people	**7**	**49**	**30**	**14**	**12,196,504**	**39**	**46**	**11**	**4**	**9,905,665**

1 Men aged 16–64, women aged 16–59. Excludes full-time students in employment.

Source: Census 2001, Office for National Statistics

Glossary

Baby boom

Period in which there is an unusually high number of births.

Census 2001 measure of overcrowding

This provides a measure of under occupancy and overcrowding. It relates to the actual number of rooms in the household relative to the number of rooms 'required' by the members of the household (based on the relationship between them and their ages). The room requirement is calculated as follows:

- a one person household is assumed to require three rooms (two common rooms and a bedroom)

- where there are two or more residents it is assumed that they require a minimum of two common rooms plus one bedroom for:

  a. Each couple (as determined by the relationship question).
  b. Each lone parent.
  c. Any other person aged 16 and over
  d. Each pair aged 10–15 of the same sex
  e. Each pair formed from a remaining person aged 10–5 with a child aged under 10 of the same sex.
  f. Each pair of children aged under 10 remaining.
  g. Each remaining person (either aged 10 to 15 or under 10).

Dependent child

A dependent child is a person aged 0–15 in a household (whether or not in a family) or aged 16–18 in full-time education and living in a family with his or her parent(s). An 'adult' in a household is any person who is not a dependent child.

Economic activity

People are defined as economically active, or in the labour force, if they are aged 16 and over and are either in work or actively looking for work. Economic activity includes both those who are employed and those who are unemployed. Economic activity is therefore a measure of participation in the labour market and gives an indication of the potential size of the workforce.

Economic inactivity

People are economically *inactive* if they are aged 16 and over and are neither employed nor actively looking for work. These include those who want a job but have not been seeking work in the last four weeks, those who want a job and are seeking work but not available to start, and those who do not want a job. Reasons for economic inactivity include: studying; retirement; looking after the home or family; and permanently sick or disabled. Full-time students may be economically active or inactive.

Employment

Individuals who are in employment include employees, those who are self-employed, participants in government employment and training programmes, and people doing unpaid work for a family business.

Family

A family comprises a group of people consisting of a married or cohabiting couple with or without children, or a lone parent with children. It also includes a married or cohabiting couple with their grandchildren or a lone grandparent with his or her grandchildren where there are no children in the intervening generation. Cohabiting couples include same sex couples. Children in couple families need not belong to both members of the couple.

Family Reference Person

In a lone parent family, the Family Reference Person (FRP) is taken to be the lone parent. In a couple family, the FRP is chosen from the two people in the couple on the basis of their economic activity (in the following priority order: full-time job, part-time job, unemployed, retired, other). If both people have the same economic activity, the FRP is the elder of the two or, if they are the same age, the first member of the couple listed on the form.

Great Britain

Includes England, Wales and Scotland.

Household

A household comprises one person living alone, or a group of people (not necessarily related) living at the same address with common housekeeping – that is, sharing either a living room or sitting room or at least one meal a day.

Household Reference Person

The concept of Household Reference Person (HRP) is new in 2001 Census outputs. It replaces Head of Household used in the 1991 Census. For a person living alone, it follows that this person is the HRP. If the household contains only one family (with or without ungrouped individuals) the HRP is the same as the Family Reference Person (FRP). If there is more than one family in the household, the HRP is chosen from among the FRPs using the same criteria as for choosing the FRP (economic

activity, then age, then order on the form). If there is no family, the HRP is chosen from among the individuals using the same criteria. In 1991, the Head of Household was taken as the first person on the form unless that person was aged under 16 or was not usually resident in the household.

Median age

The midpoint age that separates the younger half of a population from the older half.

One family and no others households

A household comprises one family and no others if there is only one family in the household and there are no non-family people (ungrouped individuals).

Unemployment

The term unemployment refers to being without work but actively seeking it. This definition was developed by the International Labour Organisation (ILO), which regards people as unemployed only if they are not in employment *and* are actively seeking and available for work. The unemployment rate is therefore calculated as a proportion of economically active people, not of the entire population. The unemployment rates quoted in this report are based on the ILO definition unless otherwise stated.

United Kingdom

Includes England, Wales, Scotland and Northern Ireland.

Working age

People aged between 16 and state pension age (currently 65 for men and 60 for women).